The Battle of Anghiari, 29 June 1440

The Battle for Control of Tuscany in Fifteenth Century Italy

Massimo Predonzani

Translated by Rachel Tiso

Helion & Company Limited
Unit 8 Amherst Business Centre
Budbrooke Road
Warwick
CV34 5WE
England
Tel. 01926 499 619
Email: info@helion.co.uk
Website: www.helion.co.uk
X (formerly Twitter): @Helionbooks
Facebook: @HelionBooks
Visit our blog at helionbooks.wordpress.com

Published by Helion & Company 2026
Designed and typeset by Mary Woolley, Battlefield Design (www.battlefield-design.co.uk)
Cover designed by Paul Hewitt, Battlefield Design (www.battlefield-design.co.uk)

ISBN 978-1-804519-93-6

British Library Cataloguing-in-Publication Data.
A catalogue record for this book is available from the British Library.

For details of other military history titles published by Helion & Company Limited contact the above address or visit our website: http://www.helion.co.uk.

We always welcome receiving book proposals from prospective authors.

Contents

Introduction

This volume is an English-language reprint of my first book, originally published approximately 13 years ago.[1] For the present edition, the text has been revised, corrected, and updated where necessary.

The outcome of the Battle of Anghiari, fought on 29 June 1440 between the Milanese forces of Filippo Maria Visconti and the Florentine Army supported by Papal and Sforza contingents, proved decisive for the city of Florence. The victory marked a turning point, effectively freeing the 'City of the Lily' from the long-standing Milanese threat that had weighed upon it and Tuscany since the time of Gian Galeazzo Visconti, and that was characterised by war and devastation.

For a long time thereafter, Florence commemorated the victory at Anghiari of 29 June with two *palii*, including both horse and foot races. The event would also be celebrated in artistic and literary forms through paintings and poems.

Today, the battle is most commonly associated with the lost fresco executed by Leonardo da Vinci in the Salone dei Cinquecento of Palazzo Vecchio in Florence, primarily painted in 1504. This work remained unfinished, as da Vinci encountered technical difficulties while experimenting with a new technique combining oil painting and fresco. About 60 years later, Giorgio Vasari redecorated the Salone with new frescoes commissioned by Duke Cosimo I de' Medici. Whether Vasari destroyed Leonardo's painting or concealed it beneath a wall or a layer of plaster remains uncertain. Despite extensive investigations by scholars and scientific teams employing sophisticated technologies, no conclusive trace of the original fresco has yet been identified.

Nevertheless, although incomplete and partially deteriorated, Leonardo's work remained visible for several years and was widely admired and fortunately copied. In the seventeenth century, Rubens reworked a sixteenth century drawing by an anonymous artist, producing the most renowned version of Leonardo's battle.

1 Massimo Predonzani, *Anghiari 29 giugno 1440. La battaglia, l'iconografia, le compagnie di ventura, l'araldica* (Il Cerchio: Città di Castello, 2010).

Through these copies, it is still possible to gain an indirect appreciation of the Italian master's work. The composition focuses on the climax of the fight, that is, the struggle for a standard between two pairs of cavalrymen. Scholars generally identify these figures as the commanders of the opposing armies: on the Milanese side, Piccinino and his son, and on the Florentine side, Orsini and Scarampi Mezzarota. The figures are depicted in sixteenth century clothing and weapons with several elements from the military symbolism of the period. An example is the first cavalryman on the left, Francesco Piccinino, represented by Leonardo with a set of symbols (the horns of Ammon on his headdress and a ram on the chest) linked to Mars, the God of war. Horses are meanwhile depicted fighting each other with a wild impetus, notably without the harness typical of fifteenth century warfare, thereby emphasising the beauty of their musculature. Leonardo's aim, rather than providing a documentary representation of the Battle of Anghiari, was to convey the fury of war.

Aside from Leonardo's work, other pictorial representations offer accurate depictions of the historical event. These include three painted chest panels illustrating the Battle of Anghiari dating to approximately the second half of the fifteenth century, produced in Florentine workshops specialising in the decoration of wedding chests, and gifted to newlyweds for their wedding. Two of these panels are preserved in the National Gallery of Ireland in Dublin and the Archaeological Museum in Madrid, while a third – formerly part of the Bryce Collection in London – is now lost and survives only in photographs. Among these, the Dublin panel is both the best preserved and the most accurate, and it served as the starting point for the present research.

My interest in this subject originated from the study of a photographic slide of the Dublin Chest, obtained through friends who had travelled to the city. Struck by the colours of the harnesses and garments, I began an investigation, initially drawing on the resources of the Civic Library of Trieste, where I live. From the outset, it appeared that the artist of the painting had reproduced with remarkable precision the setting, events and protagonists of the battle of 29 June 1440.

This intuition led me to extend my research to other libraries and archives across Italy, including those of Florence, Milan, Venice, Arezzo, and Rome returning several times as the research deepened. After studying essays and chronicles, I engaged directly with original documents, including Latin texts – studied autodidactically – such as the record of the *Dieci di Balìa* preserved in the State Archive of Florence, as well as contemporary manuscripts such as the *Registri della compagnia di ventura di Micheletto Attendolo,* held at the Fraternita dei Laici of Arezzo.

This research brought to light several interesting, unpublished details, such as the standard with the impresa of the leopard sejant associated with the Bracceschi, clearly visible on the Dublin Chest and mentioned, therefore corroborated, by several pieces of documentary evidence of the time. I was also able to identify one of the emblems of Niccolò Piccinino, commander-in-chief of the Milanese forces, and the impresas of Guidantonio Manfredi, Lord of Faenza, as well as other emblems and their owners.

At the same time, the study revealed certain inaccuracies in modern historiography, such as the supposed presence of a Venetian cavalry contingent under Micheletto Attendolo at Anghiari. No such Venetian contingent existed, at least not under Micheletto. The records of his company demonstrate that the few Venetians present came from territories annexed by the Republic of Venice, for example a certain Captain Martino Schiavo and three Istrians – a captain and two handgunners, all from Koper.

Further investigation required the study of several texts on restoration. The chest frontal panels were painted on wooden surfaces, and certain pigments, such as blues and greens, were unstable and altered over time, often darkening to black. Consequently, the blue and silver wavy impresa of the Attendolo family is now black and silver. Variations in colour do not pose a problem for known emblems or coats of arms but may create difficulties in the case of those not yet identified.

A particular aspect of the research involved the study of the organisation and structure of the *condotta di ventura*, the mercenary company. For this purpose, I relied both on the studies by del Treppo and Mallett and on original documents, such as the contracts between the *condotta* and the *signorie*. Particular attention was also devoted to military equipment of the time, including the renowned Milanese armour and a range of offensive weapons, such as long spears, brown bills, crossbows, and hand cannons. The latter, an innovative weapon increasingly widespread in the mid-fifteenth century, were operated by specialised soldiers (handgunners) who enjoyed individual contracts within the company and higher pay than other infantrymen. Moreover, in battle they often formed independent units.

Finally, this study also devotes a chapter to the presence of 'non-combatants', that is, the myriads of auxiliaries, *saccomanni*, and simple camp followers, who played an active role in the life of the *condotta*, even after the end of a military campaign. Rarely recorded in administrative documents of the *condotte*, these individuals – often relatives of the soldiers, such as wives, children, and servants – nonetheless constituted the majority of those killed in battle. Nor should one overlook the peasants and other defenceless people who were robbed, raped, or killed. During the Milanese advance into Tuscany, the contemporary chronicler Giovanni Cavalcanti notes that such acts were committed indiscriminately by both armies.

1

Historical Context

At the beginning of the fifteenth century, five states ruled Italy: the Republics of Florence and Venice, the State of the Church, the Kingdom of Naples and the Duchy of Milan. Under the rule of the Visconti, Milan had become the most powerful Italian lordship, especially thanks to Gian Galeazzo Visconti, 1st Duke of Milan, who had power over much of Northern Italy and a good part of central Italy.

Visconti's territories included the entirety of Lombardy, the Piedmontese cities of Asti, Alba, Alessandria and Vercelli in the west, and the Canton of Ticino, Bellinzona and Locarno in the north. He had also subdued the Houses of Scaligeri and Carraresi, thereby acquiring the cities of Vicenza, Verona, Padua, Feltre and Belluno, and reducing the Gonzaga family to the status of vassals. Bologna, Parma and Reggio were also part of his dominion. To the south, he expanded his influence in Tuscany by occupying Lucca, Pisa, and Siena. He advanced as far as Umbria, annexing the cities of Perugia and Assisi.

However, on 4 September 1402, Gian Galeazzo Visconti died of plague, and with his sudden death, the duchy collapsed. Most of its lands reverted to their former rulers or passed into the hands of new powers.

The State of the Church regained Bologna, Perugia and Assisi.

In Tuscany, Siena established the government of the Ten Priors in 1404 and concluded peace with Florence.

Pisa regained its independence and, in 1405, elected Giovanni Gambacorti as Captain of the People. A year later, however, the Republic of Florence besieged and occupied the city.

Rebellions and internal conflicts soon broke out within the duchy among members of the Visconti family. Within a decade, the state was dismembered, lost its major cities, and suffered severe economic and monetary decline. The condottieri formerly in Visconti service took advantage of this critical situation. Ottobuono Terzi, a former governor, proclaimed himself lord of the Emilian cities of Parma, Piacenza and Reggio. His rule was short-lived: in 1409, he was defeated and killed by Muzio Sforza, who reconquered Parma and Reggio on behalf of Niccolò III d'Este.

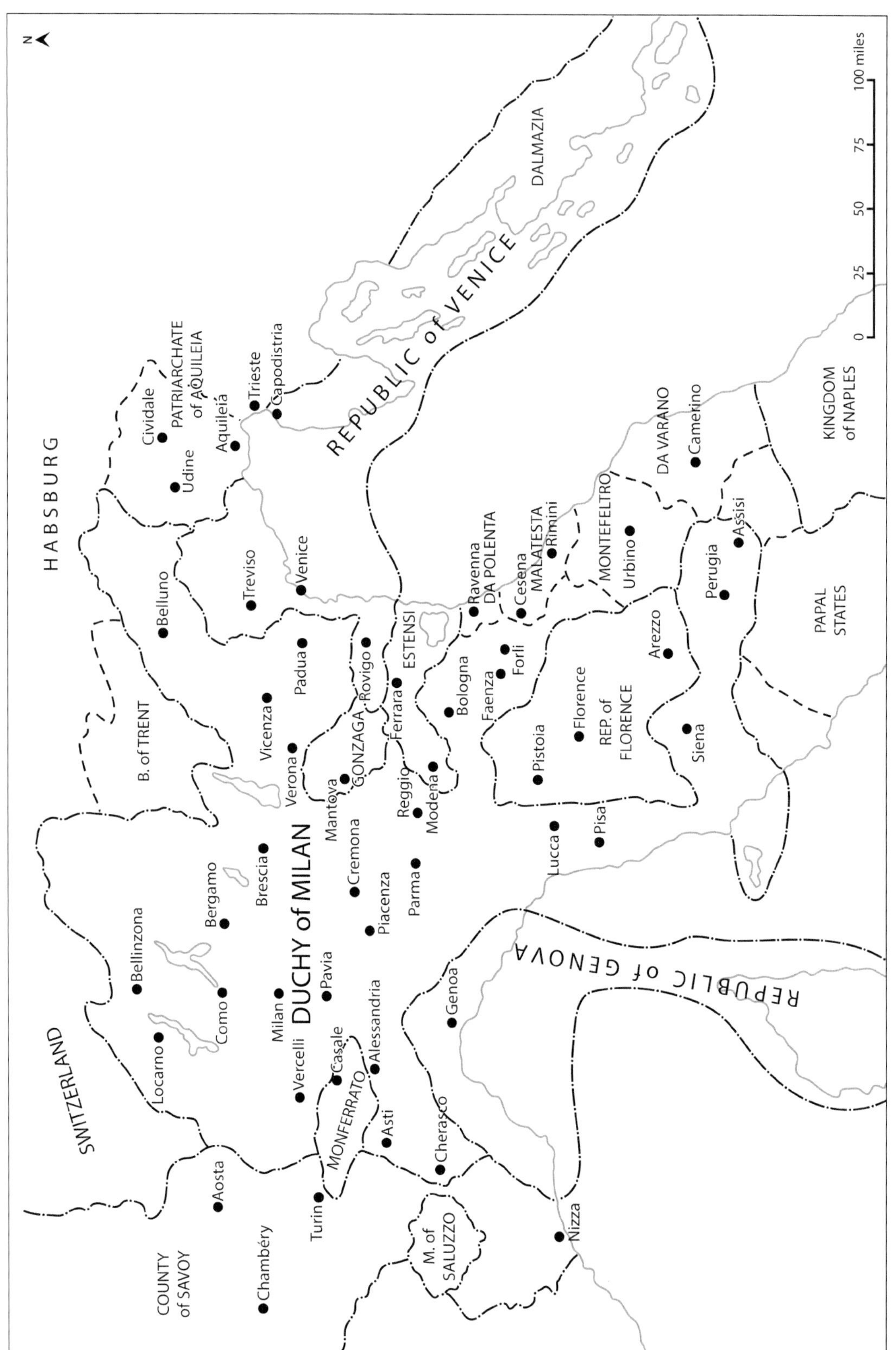

1. The Duchy of Milan at the end of the fourteenth century.

In eastern Italy, the Republic of Venice occupied Cividale, Vicenza, Feltre, Belluno and Bassano. Shortly afterwards, in 1405, it seized Verona and Padua from Francesco Novello da Carrara, who was executed in Venice the following year.

In the west, the remaining Visconti possessions also came under attack. The French, who already controlled Genoa and Asti, attempted to conquer Alessandria and Vercelli. They were repelled by the Marquess of Monferrato and Facino Cane, a captain who had served Gian Galeazzo and later his heirs. The young heirs of the duke were Giovanni Maria, who inherited the ducal title and most of the territories, and his younger brother Filippo Maria, who received the county of Pavia. Facino Cane supported their cause energetically, driven by the concealed ambition of replacing them at the head of the duchy.[1] He would probably have succeeded had he not died of illness on 17 May 1412.

The previous day, on 16 May, Giovanni Maria Visconti was murdered[2] in a palace conspiracy. As a result, Estorre and Giovanni Carlo Visconti settled in Milan as lords. They were respectively the son and grandson of Barnabò Visconti, who had died in 1385.

The legitimate heir to the duchy was Filippo Maria, then 20 years old, who had lived in Pavia since 1402. He promptly married Facino Cane's widow, Beatrice di Tenda,[3] and made use of his troops to claim the ducal crown.

On 15 June 1412, Filippo Maria reconquered Milan. The following day, he entered the city in triumph.

Estorre and Giovanni Carlo fled to Monza. Francesco da Bussone, known as Carmagnola – a captain under Filippo's service, and defeated in 1413 – besieged the city. Estorre died during the siege, while Giovanni Carlo sought refuge in Hungary.

From that moment onwards, Filippo Maria Visconti devoted himself to the reconstruction of his father's dominion. He relied heavily on the military skills of Carmagnola, whom he appointed commander of his armies.

In 1415, he captured Lodi and the county of Cremona. In 1416, he took Trezzo d'Adda, and in 1418 Piacenza.[4] In 1420, he reconquered Parma and Reggio from Niccolò d'Este. In 1421, he seized Bergamo and Brescia, previously held by Pandolfo Malatesta.

In November 1421, he captured Genoa,[5] and in 1422 he conquered Asti. In the Battle of Arbedo (1422), fought near Bellinzona, Carmagnola

1 Facino Cane had seized Alessandria, Novara, Tortona, Piacenza and Pavia, the latter at the expense of the young Filippo Maria, who had to negotiate with the captain.

2 Some historians say that Facino Cane died before Giovanni Maria Visconti, while others state that they died on the same day.

3 Beatrice was also part of the de Cani family and a relative of Facino. She was 22 years older than Filippo Maria.

4 Cremona was taken by subduing Cabrino Fondulo and Piacenza from the rebel captain, Filippo Arcelli.

5 Genoa had been independent since 1413.

defeated the Swiss forces and occupied the Canton of Ticino in the name of the Visconti.

By this point, Filippo Maria had recovered most of his father's former territories. Nevertheless, he was fully aware that the political balance of Northern Italy had changed profoundly after Gian Galeazzo's death. To the east, the Serenissima had emerged as a dominant power. After overthrowing the lordships of the Carraresi and the Scaligeri, Venice defeated the Patriarchate of Aquileia and Emperor Sigismund in 1420. It subsequently conquered Udine, Friuli and Istria and expanded its empire through the occupation of Scutari (Shkodër), Corfu and the ports of the Morea.

To the west, the House of Savoy had unified its possessions under Amadeus III, appointed duke in 1416 by Emperor Sigismund, and aimed to expand towards France, Saluzzo, Monferrato and Liguria. Visconti therefore had only two options left: to advance south towards Tuscany or south-east towards Romagna.

Filippo Maria took advantage of the succession struggles within the lordship of Forlì between the Ordelaffi and Alidosi families. He appointed Sicco da Montagna as his captain, and who occupied Forlimpopoli shortly after taking Forlì. Florence, concerned about Milan's intervention within its sphere of influence, sought allies, above all Venice. However, the Serenissima had no intention of breaking its agreements with Visconti. As a result, in March 1423, Florence took direct action.

Between 1423 and 1424, Florentine troops commanded by Pandolfo and Carlo Malatesta suffered repeated defeats at the hands of Milanese forces commanded by Montagna and Angelo della Pergola. In July 1424, at Zagonara, the commander-in-chief, Carlo Malatesta, was captured. Shortly thereafter, Visconti occupied Imola and Faenza.

The Florentines then appealed for Venetian intervention. Venice entered the conflict at the beginning of 1426, entrusting command of its forces to Carmagnola, who had left the duke's service and sided with the Republic. Under his leadership, Venetian troops occupied Brescia and, after alternating fortunes, inflicted a decisive defeat on the Milanese at Maclodio on 12 October 1427.[6]

Filippo Maria immediately sought to dismantle the anti-Visconti League, to which Amadeus of Savoy also belonged. In December 1427, Visconti married Amadeus' daughter, Marie of Savoy, thereby sealing their alliance.[7]

Shortly afterwards, on 19 April 1428, Filippo Maria signed the Peace of Ferrara with the Serenissima and the Republic of Florence. The treaty proved extremely costly for Visconti. He was forced to cede the Counties of Brescia and Bergamo and to swear not to interfere in the affairs of Tuscany and Romagna.

---

6 In May of the same year, 1427, Filippo Maria finally obtained the ducal investiture from Emperor Sigismund.

7 Marie of Savoy was the second wife of Filippo Maria since he had sentenced Beatrice di Tenda to death in 1418 for, unproven, adultery.

The peace did not last long. Florence sought revenge for its defeats at the hands of Lucca and laid siege to the city. Duke Visconti dispatched Niccolò Piccinino to its aid. After defeating the Florentine Army at the River Serchio, Piccinino freed Lucca on 2 December 1430.

In the following year, hostilities between Milan and Venice resumed with uncertain results. Fighting took place both on land and along the River Po where, in June 1431, the Venetian flotilla was defeated near Cremona. In Monferrato, whose marquess had aligned himself with Venice, Francesco Sforza – at the time a captain in Visconti service – succeeded in capturing almost all the fortresses. Meanwhile, on 5 May 1432, Francesco Carmagnola was executed for treason in Piazza San Marco.

In November of the same year, Giorgio Corner, a superintendent of the Venetian Army, was defeated and captured by Milanese forces in Valtellina. This episode led to a new peace agreement which was signed in Ferrara in April 1433.

Another conflict soon followed, which broke out on 28 August 1434, this time in Romagna.

The Venetian and Florentine forces of the League were defeated by Piccinino at Castelbolognese, near Imola, and Niccolò da Tolentino was taken prisoner.

The following year, the Battle of Ponza was fought on 5 August 1435. Filippo Maria allied himself with the Angevin faction to support Genoa against the threat of the Aragonese expansion in the Mediterranean. The Visconti-Genoese Fleet defeated the Aragonese Fleet near the island of Ponza. King Alfonso of Aragon along with his brothers – John, King of Navarre, Henry and Peter – were taken prisoner. Filippo Maria brought the King of Aragon to Milan but chose to ally himself with the captive, whom he subsequently released. This decision provoked intense resentment among the Genoese population, which soon erupted into rebellion.

In June 1436, a new war broke out. Milan now faced a coalition formed by Venice, Genoa and Florence, later joined by the States of the Church. At the time, Pope Eugene IV resided in Florence, having fled Rome in May 1434 because of the hostility of the powerful Colonna family. Although Patriarch Giovanni Vitelleschi restored papal authority in Rome in October of the same year, the pope did not return to the Vatican for almost 10 years.

In September 1437, Gianfrancesco Gonzaga, Lord of Mantua and a Venetian captain, attempted to invade Lunigiana sull'Adda. He was repelled by Niccolò Piccinino, who hastened to the area from Liguria. Gonzaga soon changed allegiance, entered Visconti service, joined his troops with Piccinino's, and assisted in the Siege of Brescia. The city, although severely tested, succeeded in resisting the Milanese assaults. The focus of the war then shifted to the Veronese region. After defeating a Venetian flotilla on Lake Garda, ducal forces captured and sacked Verona. Francesco Sforza – commander of the Venetian Army since 1439 – swiftly recaptured the city.

At this point, Filippo Maria Visconti resolved to alter his strategy and dispatched Piccinino to Romagna and Tuscany, where he remained active until the Battle of Anghiari.

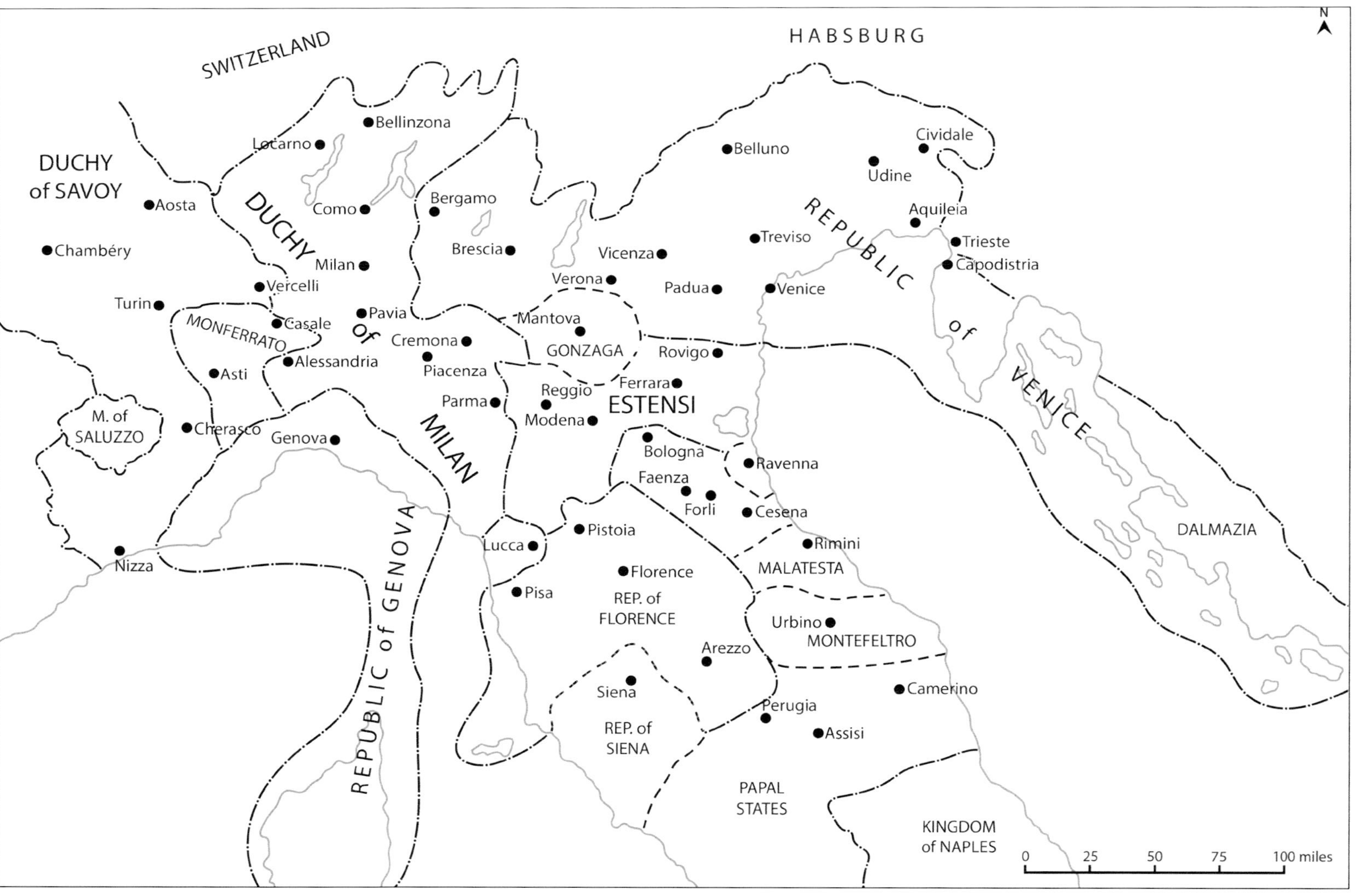

2. Northern Italy around 1440.

2

Principal Commanders at the Battle of Anghiari

Niccolò Piccinino

Niccolò Piccinino was born in Callisciana, near Perugia, around 1386 and was of humble origins. His father, Francesco, was a butcher, but his family name is unknown. Because of his short stature he was nicknamed '*Piccinino*' and, as was often the case at the time, his surname Piccinino was derived from his nickname.

Like many poor men of his time, he set out to seek his fortune and became a page in the service of a captain named Bartolomeo da Sesto. Bartolomeo recognised Niccolò's natural talent for combat, appointed him a man-at-arms, and gave him his daughter Gabriella in marriage. She would later be killed by her husband on suspicion of adultery.

3. Niccolò Piccinino. Medal made by Pisanello. (Public domain)

Poggio relates that in 1407, after returning home from an 11-month campaign, Niccolò found his wife with a new-born child a few days old. He ordered the infant to be taken away and commanded the woman to follow him. He made her ride a fierce horse and led her to a nearby place. She soon fell, was dragged by the animal, and died as a result. Other chroniclers instead report that Piccinino poisoned his wife. In any case, shortly after her death, his mother convinced him that no adultery had occurred and that the child was his. Piccinino therefore arranged proper funeral rites for his wife and kept the child, his firstborn, Francesco.

After the death of Bartolomeo da Sesto, Piccinino served under Guglielmo Lancelotti. In 1416, he entered the service of Braccio da Montone and soon distinguished himself as his most capable lieutenant. He repeatedly proved his valour in battle and on one occasion even saved his commander's life. He also assisted Braccio to become Lord of Perugia and, in gratitude, was appointed commander of 100 horsemen.

Always loyal to Braccio, he fought for him in the Marche, Umbria and the Kingdom of Naples. In 1417, Muzio Attendolo Sforza captured Piccinino at Palestrina, but after four months, he was released in a prisoner exchange.

Fortebraccio, impressed by his courage and military exploits, gave him his niece in marriage. The dowry included the Castello di Todi.

Later, Braccio sent Piccinino with 400 horsemen to the aid of Queen Giovanna II of Naples. Threatened by rebellious princes and barons, the queen was helped by Niccolò to regain control of the city.

Piccinino then moved to Abruzzo to assist Braccio against a large Papal and Angevin Army led by Muzio Sforza. On 3 January 1424, events appeared to favour Braccio when Muzio drowned in the river Pescara. Without delay, Niccolò attacked the Sforza forces, taking 400 prisoners. He then rejoined Montone, who had been besieging L'Aquila since May 1423. On 2 June 1424 however, the Angevin Army commanded by Jacopo Caldora attacked Braccio's troops beneath the walls of L'Aquila. Caldora's forces included Francesco Sforza, Bartolomeo Coglioni and Micheletto Attendolo. Braccio, on the other hand, relied on Niccolò Piccinino, Gattamelata and Niccolò da Pisa.

Piccinino was tasked with controlling the city to prevent sorties by the besieged. After hours of fierce fighting, Caldora's numerically superior army began to prevail. Seeing his men in difficulty, Piccinino abandoned his post at the city gates and rushed to their aid. However, by doing so he allowed the citizens to sally out of the city and force Braccio's troops to retreat. Braccio was mortally wounded in the fighting.

This episode weighed heavily on Piccinino's reputation. Most historians regard him as primarily responsible for the defeat and death of his commander.

After the defeat, Niccolò and Oddo, Braccio's son, gathered the surviving troops. Piccinino then entered the service of Florence in the war against Filippo Maria Visconti, Duke of Milan.

Sent to Romagna with 5,000 men, on 1 February he was surprised and defeated in the Lamone valley near Marradi. Oddo was killed and mutilated along with several of his men. Piccinino was captured together with his son Francesco, Niccolò da Tolentino and Niccolò Orsini. Guidantonio Manfredi took the prisoners to Faenza.

During his imprisonment, Piccinino did not lose heart. On the contrary, through persuasion he succeeded in winning Manfredi over to the Florentine cause and secured his own release.

After Oddo's death and the expiry of his contract with Florence, Piccinino, now the sole commander of Bracceschi forces, entered Visconti service. He remained loyal to the Duke of Milan until his death.

The outraged Florentines ordered Niccolò da Tolentino to arrest him. When this failed, they attempted to poison Piccinino's food while he was in Milan. The plot was discovered, and the cook and his accomplices were condemned to death.

In 1426, Venice entered the war against Visconti in support of Florence. Command of the Venetian Army was entrusted to the Count of Carmagnola. He took Brescia and defeated Milanese forces at the Battle of Maclodio on 12 October 1427. Visconti's army, numbering 12,000 cavalry and 6,000 infantry, was led by Carlo Malatesta with Francesco Sforza, and Piccinino as his second in command. The opposing army, under Carmagnola, Gianfrancesco Gonzaga and Niccolò da Tolentino, fielded 18,000 cavalry and 8,000 infantry. Ignoring Piccinino and Sforza's calls for caution, Malatesta fell into Carmagnola's trap. He was captured with 8,000 of his men.

Piccinino and Sforza escaped and, in the following days, slowed the Venetian advance. This allowed Visconti valuable time to raise a new army.

Piccinino then declared war on Genoa, an ally of Venice, and seized several Genoese territories and strongholds. He subsequently marched to the aid of Lucca, which was besieged by Florentine forces. On 2 December 1430, he defeated the besiegers on the river Serchio, captured 1,500 of the enemy and freed the city.

He later distinguished himself alongside Sforza near Cremona. On 21 June 1431, he defeated the Venetians at the river Oglio. During the battle, Piccinino was struck in the neck by a crossbow bolt. The wound damaged his nerves and left him permanently crippled.

In October 1431, Filippo Maria Visconti sent Piccinino to suppress the Genoese rebels led by Barnabò Adorno. Piccinino defeated them at Sestri Ponente, pursued Adorno as far as Novara, captured him, and had him executed.

He then went to Monferrato, an ally of Venice. There he devastated the countryside with systematic sackings and pillage, forcing the marquess to flee to Venice. As a reward for these successes, Duke Visconti appointed him captain general of the Milanese Army.

Meanwhile, on 5 May 1432, Carmagnola was executed in Piazza San Marco on charges of treason. Venice now found itself reliant on captains of lesser ability, including Giorgio Corner. In November 1432, Corner was defeated and captured in Valtellina, together with a large part of the Venetian Army, by Piccinino.

In April 1433, the combatants signed a new peace. This agreement allowed Sforza to attack the Papal States. Shortly thereafter, Sforza changed sides and entered the service of Pope Eugene IV. In response, Piccinino intervened, together with Niccolò della Stella, nephew of the late Braccio. The two entered Rome and succeeded in inciting the population against the pope, who was forced to flee first to Civitavecchia and then to Livorno.

Piccinino and his allies subsequently confronted Francesco Sforza, who was supported by Micheletto degli Attendolo. Owing to the mediation of ambassadors sent by Filippo Maria, open hostilities were avoided and a truce was agreed.

Piccinino entrusted Fortebraccio with the defence of the Sabina region, in central Italy. He then went to Romagna, where Bologna had rebelled against papal authority and sought Duke Filippo's support. On 28 August 1434, near Castelbolognese, Piccinino defeated the Venetian forces under Gattamelata and the Florentine troops commanded by Tolentino. Approximately 3,000 cavalry and 1,500 infantry were taken prisoner. Among the captives were the Captains Giovanpaolo Orsini, Taddeo da Este, Niccolò Guerriero, Cesare da Martinengo and Niccolò da Tolentino. Tolentino would die the following year in captivity, apparently on the orders of Duke Filippo.

Piccinino also played a leading role in the expedition against Genoa, which rebelled once again against the duke in December 1435. The uprising followed the Genoese naval victory at Ponza in August of that year. Allied with Visconti, the Genoese defeated and captured King Alfonso of Aragon. It was a memorable victory, only one Aragonese ship managed to escape. The victors seized a rich booty and took 5,000 prisoners. Among them were the king, his brothers Enrico and Pietro, his son Ferdinand, John of Aragon, King of Navarre, and numerous southern princes and nobles. When the prisoners were sent to Milan, the duke released them and instead allied himself with the Aragonese King. This decision deeply enraged the Genoese population.

With 20,000 men, Piccinino defeated the insurgents and advanced towards Genoa. He was soon recalled to Lombardy by order of the duke. The region was threatened by the Venetians, now allied with Genoa and led by Gianfrancesco Gonzaga, Lord of Mantua.

In September 1437, Piccinino defeated Gonzaga in a major engagement at Lunigiana sull'Adda. In recognition of this victory, the duke admitted him as part of the House of Visconti. He was also appointed captain general for life and granted the titles of marquess and count of several territories.

In 1438, Piccinino reconquered Bologna, which had returned to papal allegiance. He then seized the Venetian town of Casalmaggiore and laid siege to Brescia, devastating its surrounding lands.

In 1439, Venice replaced Gattamelata with Francesco Sforza as captain general. Hostilities against Milan resumed with renewed intensity. During a series of alternate fortunes, Piccinino captured Verona by surprise on the night of 17 November. Three days later, however, Sforza reconquered the city with a numerically superior army.

At the beginning of 1440, Piccinino left the command of operations in Lombardy to his captains. He then planned the famous diversionary campaign against Tuscany. This manoeuvre ended in defeat at Anghiari on 29 June.

He reorganised his forces and returned to Brescia in February 1441 to confront Sforza. Meanwhile, Visconti had begun peace negotiations. These were formalised in Cremona on 3 August 1441. According to the treaty,

Bianca, daughter of Filippo Maria, was given in marriage to Francesco Sforza. She had been promised to him since childhood and brought the city of Cremona as her dowry.

In 1442, Pope Eugene, determined to recover Sforza's possessions in the Marca, entered into secret negotiations. These involved the King Alfonso I of Naples and the Duke of Milan to the detriment of Francesco. Filippo Maria Visconti feigned Piccinino's dismissal and sent him to Romagna. There, the pope appointed him Gonfalonier of the Church. Piccinino reached Umbria, took Todi, and then travelled to the Marca to attack Sforza, who was supported by Venetian and Florentine forces. Fighting between the Bracceschi and the Sforzeschi near Macerata was halted by a truce granted by the pope in Sforza's favour.

Piccinino then seized Gualdo di Nocera and advanced on Assisi. The city was defended by Alessandro Sforza, Francesco's brother. After a two-month siege, Assisi fell on 30 November 1442 and was mercilessly sacked.

Piccinino later travelled to Terracina, where he met King Alfonso. The king received him with great honours and appointed him commander of his army. Together, they marched towards Fano, where Sforza was based. Concerned by Alfonso's territorial ambitions, Duke Filippo Maria, secretly intervened. His ambassadors persuaded the Aragonese King to withdraw his army.

Left without support, Piccinino was forced to abandon the siege of Fano. In November 1443, heavily outnumbered, he was defeated by Sforza at Monteluro.

In the spring of 1444, the Braccesco captain returned to the Marca with papal support. During the summer, however, Visconti once again summoned him to Milan.

This marked the end of his military career. Dismissed by both duke and pope, he formally took leave of his troops with a great ceremonial. He entrusted command to his son Francesco and retired to his villa at Corsico.

Long afflicted by dropsy and deeply affected by the defeat and capture of his son Francesco at the hand of Sforza at Montolmo in August 1444, Piccinino died on 16 October of the same year. He was 58 years old.

The duke ordered a solemn funeral in the Duomo of Milan. He also commissioned a funerary monument in Piccinino's honour. The monument was destroyed in 1455 by the new Duke of Milan, Francesco Sforza.[1]

1 Sources on Piccinino: G. Battista Poggio, *Vita di Niccolò Piccinino* (Perugia 1619); Pier Candido Decembrio, 'Vita di Niccolò Piccinino' in *Muratori Rerum Italicarum Scriptores* XX, 1053; C. Rendina, *I capitani di ventura* (Roma: Newton & Compton, 1999), pp.155–164; A. Fabretti, 'Biografie dei Capitani Venturieri dell'Umbria' in *Note e documenti da biografie dei Capitani Venturieri dell'Umbria* (Montepulciano: Angiolo Tumi, 1842), vol. II, pp.7–157; Lorenzo Spirito Gualtieri, *L'Altro Marte*, (Venezia: Leonardus Achates, 1489), p.39.

Francesco Piccinino

Francesco was Niccolò Piccinino's eldest son, and his actions were closely linked to those of his father for as long as the latter lived. Francesco was born in 1407 to Gabriella, the unfortunate woman whom her husband brutally killed out of jealousy.

He grew up among the Bracceschi troops commanded by his father. Together with Niccolò, he was taken prisoner in the Val di Lamone in 1425. Considering his son sufficiently mature for a military career, Niccolò sent him with 180 Bracceschi lances into the service of Pope Martin V. Francesco remained in papal employ until 1429.

In 1432, the Republic of Siena hired him with 450 cavalry and 100 infantry. He fought under Sienese colours at the Battle of San Romano.

Having returned to papal service under Eugene IV, he remained with him until December 1433. At that time, he commanded a force of 500 lances. In 1435, he assisted his father against Sforza. The following year, he was in the pay of the Aragonese against René d'Anjou.

In 1437, Francesco succeeded in defeating Count Francesco Sforza in the Marca. In February 1438, he persuaded the Italian Sforza captain from Friuli to change sides. Together, they plundered part of Umbria and then turned against Spoleto. After alternating fortunes, and with the support of other Umbrian cities, the two captains captured Spoleto on the night of 6 May 1438 and sacked it.

Shortly thereafter, the duke summoned them to Lombardy. Piccinino, however, stopped at Borgo Sansepolcro, which had rebelled against the pope, and occupied it.

In May 1439, Francesco fought in Romagna against the Sforzeschi. In 1440, he took part in the Siege of Città di Castello alongside his father. Still fighting at his father's side, he participated in the defeat of Anghiari.

After the battle, Niccolò entrusted him with the defence of Romagna together with Guidantonio Manfredi.

In 1442, Francesco commanded the Braccesco garrison of Bologna on behalf of the duke. During a popular uprising, the citizens captured him. He was released through a prisoner exchange in August 1443.

In 1444, he was entrusted with the command of the Milanese Army in place of his father. However, shortly thereafter, on 19 August, Sforza defeated him at Montolmo. Francesco was captured together with almost all his captains and 3,000 cavalry. Only his younger brother Jacopo managed to escape.

In November 1444, Francesco was released and once again given command of the army. Nevertheless, he suffered another defeat, this time at the hands of Micheletto Attendolo, the commander of the Venetian troops, who defeated him at Mezzano on 28 September 1446. Piccinino fled in disgrace with part of his troops. Crossing the bridge over the Po towards Parma, he abandoned 4,000 cavalry to Venetian capture.

Micheletto then began to ravage the wealthy territory of Milan. Visconti was forced to seek assistance from his son-in-law, Francesco Sforza. Meanwhile, Francesco Piccinino, together with Luigi dal Verme and Carlo

Gonzaga, attempted to stop Micheletto. The Venetian commander had advanced to the very gates of Milan. The Milanese forces were defeated once more at Monte Brianza. After this setback, the Venetians concentrated their efforts on the Siege of Lecco.

4. Filippo Maria Visconti. Drawing by Pisanello. (Public domain)

When Francesco Sforza arrived in Lombardy to intervene, Filippo Maria Visconti had already died in his castle at Porta Giovia. The Ambrosian Republic had already been set up in Milan. The Republic offered Sforza command of its forces under conditions more favourable than those granted by the late duke. He accepted the offer. Ancient hostilities were temporarily set aside, and Bracceschi and Sforzeschi united in defence of the Lombard capital. Their first success was the capture of the castle of San Colombano in the Lodi region. In December 1447, they took and sacked Piacenza. The Piccinino brothers particularly distinguished themselves on this occasion. In May 1448, they attacked Venetian positions along the River Adda. Finally, on 15 September, Sforza, aided by the Piccinino brothers, defeated Micheletto Attendolo in a major victory at Caravaggio.

Sforza now openly aspired to become Duke of Milan. For this reason, he soon came into conflict with the Ambrosian Republic. Meanwhile, Francesco Piccinino and his brother Jacopo kept watch over Sforza's actions. They regularly reported to the Milanese lordship, often exaggerating events to foster suspicion and distrust against him. At the same time, several cities of the duchy, including Pavia and Lodi, recognised Sforza as their lord. Lodi had been recaptured by Francesco Piccinino in October 1448. Meanwhile, Count Sforza hired William VIII of Montferrat and concluded an alliance with Venice. He ceded several cities to the Serenissima, including the recently conquered Bergamo and Brescia. In exchange, Venice agreed to support his attempt to seize Milan.

Sforza now resolved to march on Milan. The Piccinino brothers initially sided with him, only to betray him shortly thereafter. At the beginning of 1449, during the siege of Monza, they changed allegiance and supported the Ambrosian Republic. This intervention saved the city.

The two brothers were welcomed in Milan with public celebrations. They joined forces with Carlo Gonzaga, occupied Melegnano, and relieved Crema from a Venetian siege. Together with the Milanese militia, they assembled a large army and the Piccinino brothers then went into the territory of Varese and reached Lugano. Francesco died of dropsy on 16 October 1449.

Fabretti concludes his biography with the assessment: '... he was not always daring in battle, although he enjoyed the affection of his soldiers and was liberal and humane. Poggio writes that he was an imprudent man, inclined to excessive drinking. He married Camilla Fortebracci da Montone.'[2]

2 Sources: A. Fabretti, 'Biografie dei Capitani Venturieri dell'Umbria' in *Note e documenti da biografie dei Capitani Venturieri dell'Umbria* (Montepulciano: Angiolo Tumi, 1842), vol. II, pp.7–157; Lorenzo Spirito Gualtieri, *L'Altro Marte*, (Venezia: Leonardus Achates, 1489), p.74; C. Rendina, *I capitani di ventura* (Roma: Newton & Compton, 1999), p.430–431.

The Manfredi Brothers

Sons of Gian Galeazzo Manfredi, Lord of Faenza, and of Gentile Malatesta, Guidantonio was born in 1407 and Astorre in 1412. They had two other brothers: Carlo, the eldest, born in 1406 but who died in 1420 at the age of 14, and Gian Galeazzo, born in 1418.

In 1417, upon the death of their father, their mother Gentile became regent of the lordship, a position she held until 1428.

Guidantonio, also known as Guidaccio, embarked upon a military career at an early age. In 1424, at the age of 17, he allied himself with Duke Filippo Maria Visconti of Milan, who had already been at war with Florence for a year.

Florence dispatched an army across the Apennines to attack Romagna. The force was surprised and defeated by the inhabitants of the Lamone Valley, a territory under Manfredi control. Niccolò Piccinino and his son Francesco were captured, and Guidantonio brought them to Faenza. During his imprisonment, Piccinino succeeded in winning Manfredi's confidence and persuading him to side with Florence. In 1426, Manfredi signed a military contract with the city for 450 lances and 300 infantrymen.

In 1427, Venice hired Guidantonio. Serving under the commander general Carmagnola, he took part in the Lombard campaign and fought at the Battle of Maclodio. He remained in Venetian service until the Peace of Ferrara in 1428.

In 1430, he returned to the Florentine service with 400 lances and 200 infantrymen. He was accompanied by his 18-year-old brother Astorre. This decision proved unfortunate. Florence lost the War of Lucca, and Piccinino, now captain of the Milanese forces, defeated the Florentines at the Battle of Serchio in December 1430. During this engagement, Astorre was captured.

The following year, the two brothers entered the service of opposing powers. Guidantonio served Venice, while Astorre joined Milan. Despite fighting on opposite sides, they never became rivals. On the contrary, this alternation of allegiances often served to preserve their political standing.

In 1433, following the Peace of Ferrara, the two brothers returned to Faenza. In 1434, after Visconti occupied Imola, Forlì and Lugo, the pope, Florence and Venice formed a new anti-Visconti League against Filippo Maria. The Manfredi brothers joined this alliance. On 28 August 1434, they were defeated by Piccinino at Castelbolognese. Astorre was captured once again.

A short-lived peace followed in August 1435. In 1436, another anti-Visconti League was formed. The Manfredi brothers served in the pay of Venice during the Lombard campaign. In 1438, however, they again changed sides. Guidantonio entered Florentine service, while Astorre chose to support Visconti.

Meanwhile, Piccinino descended into Romagna and seized Bologna, Forlì, Imola and other cities in the region. These developments convinced Guidantonio to join the Milanese. According to some sources, he brought with him 600 lances; according to others, 1,500 cavalry. In return, Filippo Maria gave him the coveted lordship of Imola in 1439.

In 1440, Piccinino organised an expedition into Tuscany. Both Manfredi brothers took part in this campaign. This expedition ended in the defeat at Anghiari. Astorre was captured for the third time – this time by Niccolò da Pisa. He was handed over to Florence and imprisoned in the Stinche until the peace of November 1441.

On 6 February 1442, Astorre learnt that Niccolò da Pisa was in Bologna, then under Milanese control. He went there with a group of his men and murdered him in an act of personal revenge.

In 1442, amid renewed struggles in Northern Italy, Alfonso of Aragon entered the conflict. Fresh from his conquest of the Kingdom of Naples at Angevin expense, he had allied himself with Filippo Maria Visconti. In 1443, Alfonso advanced northwards against Francesco Sforza and reached Fano.

The Manfredi brothers initially supported the Visconti-Aragonese faction. Around 1446, however, they again changed allegiance and joined the Florentines.

Following Visconti's death in 1447, the brothers chose to serve Francesco Sforza. They fought for the Ambrosian Republic during the war in Lombardy and later returned to Faenza. The following year, Astorre returned to Lombardy with Sforza. Guidantonio, already ill, travelled to the Baths of Petriolo, where he died on 22 June 1448.

After his brother's death, Astorre retained Faenza and the Val di Lamone for himself and for their brother Gian Galeazzo. He assigned Imola to Taddeo, Guidantonio's son. For a time, Astorre served the Commune of Bologna. In 1450, he entered into his first conflict with his nephew Taddeo over the borders of their respective lordships. He seized several of his nephew's castles and then moved against Imola. Through the mediation of Francesco Sforza and Cosimo the Elder, the two agreed to a truce.

Between 1451 and 1460, Astorre enjoyed a prolonged period of peace. This was interrupted by renewed conflicts with Taddeo, who, supported by the Sforzas, attacked Faenza. Astorre occupied Riolo and Monte Battaglia. In 1462, thanks to the intervention of Pope Pius II, he stipulated an agreement with his nephew.

Astorre subsequently remained in papal service until 1463. In 1465, his brother Gian Galeazzo died, leaving Astorre as the sole Lord of Faenza.

In 1467, Manfredi was hired by the Republic of Florence. A few months later, he changed sides and joined Bartolomeo Coglioni, Captain General of the Venetian Army.[3] Florence, Milan and the Kingdom of Naples then

3 Modern texts refer to this captain as Colleoni, but in fifteenth century documents about him or his family, he appears as Coglioni. He is mentioned as Bartholomeus Coleus or *de Colionibus,* and Bartolomeo signed himself '*De Colionibus.*' In addition, the family coat of arms depicted three testicles, later censored with three lion heads or three upturned hearts. I favour the original name and coat of arms.

formed a league against Venice, under the command of Federico da Montefeltro. On 25 July 1467, the two coalitions clashed at the Battle of Riccardina, and Manfredi was present in the fighting.

Riccardina was to be his final military engagement, and he died on 12 March 1468.[4]

Micheletto Attendolo

'Lord Micheletto degli Attendolo of the Counts of Cotignola' appears under this title in the accounting records of his mercenary company, preserved in the archive of the Fraternita dei Laici of Arezzo.

He was probably the son of Bartolo, brother of the renowned Muzio Attendolo. The exact date of his birth is unknown, it is, however, known that he began his military career alongside Muzio under Barbiano, as many members of the Attendolo family had done before him.

In 1406, Micheletto was with Muzio at the Siege of Pisa fighting on behalf of Florence. Together with his cousin Lorenzo, he commanded 140 lances. In 1409, he entered the service of Niccolò III d'Este and assisted Muzio Sforza in the defeat and subsequent assassination of Ottobuono Terzi, Lord of Parma.

Micheletto later followed Muzio to the Kingdom of Naples. There, he entered the army of Queen Giovanna II. In 1415, when Muzio was captured by King James of Bourbon, Micheletto negotiated his release with the king's envoys. However, Muzio's family refused to recognise him as a legitimate emissary. After an agreement between Lorenzo Attendolo and the king, Micheletto left the Kingdom of Naples. He entered the service of Braccio Fortebracci da Montone with 400 cavalry and 200 infantry.

In Braccio's service, in 1419 he defended Jesi and Rocca Contrada. He was later forced to leave the company because of Captain Tartaglia, who had joined Fortebracci and fomented hostility against the Attendolo-Sforza faction. Niccolò Piccinino, his squadron commander, helped Micheletto escape this dangerous situation.

4 Sources on Manfredi: Piero Zama, *I Manfredi signori di Faenza* (Faenza: Fratelli Lega, 1954), pp.151–152, 176, 179–182, 185–186; Bartolomeo Righi, *Annali della città di Faenza* (Faenza: Montanari E Marabini, 1840), vol. II, pp.192–193, 197–198, 208, 211, 221–222, 224; Giulio Cesare Tonduzzi, *Historie di Faenza* (Bologna: Forni 1967), pp.482, 484, 486; Scipione Ammirato, *Istorie Fiorentine* (Torino: Cugini Pomba e comp, 1853), vol. V, pp.176, 216–218, 285, 293–296, 371–373; N. Capponi, 'Commentari' in *Muratori Rerum Italicarum Scriptores* XVIII, pp.1187–1188, 1192–1195; Anon., 'Corpus Chronicorum Bononiensium' in *Muratori R.I.S.* (Bologna 1922), XVIII, parte I, pp.103–104; Pier Candido Decembrio, 'Vita di Niccolò Piccinino' in *Muratori Rerum Italicarum Scriptores* XX, 1053; Giovanni Andrea Calegari, *Cronaca di Brisighella e Val d'Amone dalla origine al 1504*, (Bologna: Commissione per i testi di lingua, 1980), pp.50–52.

In 1420, Micheletto married Polissena of the Sanseverino, widow of Andrea Malatesta, Lord of Cesena. She brought him, as her dowry, 15 important fiefs. In the same year, Micheletto repeatedly served against the Bracceschi.

In 1422, with a force of 400 cavalry, he rescued Francesco Sforza, son of Muzio. Francesco had been endangered by a revolt of some of his own captains in Calabria.

In 1424, Micheletto took part in the Battle of L'Aquila. He contributed decisively to the victory over the Bracceschi by rescuing Jacopo Caldora at a critical moment.

Between 1425 and 1426, Micheletto signed a military contract under Pope Martin V. He returned to papal service again between 1430 and 1431. In the intervening period, in 1428, he fought against the Bolognese under Caldora. From April 1431, he entered the service of the Republic of Florence. Alongside Niccolò da Tolentino, he defeated the Sienese and Milanese at the well-known Battle of San Romano.

5. Nineteenth century portrait engraving of Francesco Sforza. (Public domain)

Attendolo later left the Florentine service and returned to that of the Church. Under Pope Eugene IV, from 1433 to 1434, he suppressed several rebellious nobles on behalf of papal authority. In October 1434, he occupied Rome, which had proclaimed itself a republic.

From 1435 to 1439, Micheletto was in the service of King René of Anjou, who appointed him Grand Constable of the Kingdom of Naples and Governor of Calabria, a title he held until 1438.

In May 1439, Micheletto entered the service of Francesco Sforza. He distinguished himself as one of the principal commanders in the victory at Anghiari in 29 June 1440.

In 1441, he was hired by the lordship of Venice as captain general. He replaced Gattamelata, and the contract would last for approximately eight years.

In September 1446, Micheletto defeated the Milanese forces commanded by Francesco Piccinino at Casalmaggiore. He then occupied the territory between the Rivers Oglio and Adda and advanced as far as the gates of Milan. Subsequently, he moved into the Cremonese and then into Brianza. There, on 19 August 1447, he again defeated Francesco Piccinino.

After the death of Visconti, Francesco Sforza came to the aid of the newly proclaimed Ambrosian Republic. On 15 September 1448, he defeated Attendolo at Caravaggio.

As a consequence of his defeat, Venice removed Micheletto from command of its army, and he was exiled to Conegliano.

In 1452, Micheletto, together with his sons Raimondo Vittorioso and Pietro Antonio, entered Florentine service. Because of his advanced age, however, he was assigned only marginal roles. In 1454, he moved to Lombardy. His sons entered the service of Duke Sforza, who granted them Pozzolo in the territory of Tortona. Micheletto settled there with his large family. He lived with his wife Isabella di Diano, whom he had married around 1432 after the death of Polissena. Micheletto Attendolo died in Pozzolo in 1463.[5]

Niccolò da Pisa

In *Dizionario Biografico degli Italiani* da Pisa is identified as Niccolò Gambacorti, born in Pisa presumably around the late fourteenth or the early fifteenth century. The *Dizionario*, however, specifies that the available documentation does not indicate any kinship with the well-known Pisan Gambacorti family.

Litta records a certain Bartolomeo di Niccolò Gambacorti, who was hired by the Florentines in 1402.

In two surviving documents, da Pisa appears under the name of Nicolaus de Gambacurtis de Pisis. The first is a letter dated 1435, addressed to Cosimo the Elder and preserved in the State Archives of Florence. The second is a letter of 1438 written by Gioacchino Valeri, in which he is mentioned as a captain serving under Sforza.[6]

Niccolò began his military career among the Bracceschi under Braccio Fortebracci da Montone. He is recorded at the Battle of L'Aquila in 1424 as one of the foremen.[7]

In 1430, he was in the pay of Pope Martin V, serving in Romagna under Captain Jacopo Caldora.

---

5 Sources on Attendolo: Paolo Giovio, 'Vita di Sforza Attendolo' in *Biblioteca storica italiana*, II (Milano: Libraro Franc Colombo, 1853), pp.20, 58, 86, 107–109; Scipione Ammirato, *Istorie Fiorentine* (Torino: Cugini Pomba e comp, 1853), vol. IV, p.387 and vol. V, pp.192–198 & 271; A. Minuti (G. Porro Lambertenghi ed.), 'Vita di Muzio Attendolo Sforza' in *Miscellanea di storia italiana*, VII (Torino: 1869), pp.153–154, 213; L. Botta, 'Una inedita cronachetta degli Sforza' in *Archivio storico per le province napoletane*, XIX (Napoli: Società napoletana di storia patria, 1894), pp.725–727, 731; C. Rendina, *I capitani di ventura* (Roma: Newton & Compton, 1999), pp.165–171; M. Del Treppo, 'Sulla struttura della compagnia o condotta militare' in *Condottieri e uomini d'arme nell'Italia del rinascimento*, (Napoli: Liguori, 2001), p.427; Francesco Guicciardini, *Le cose fiorentine*, vol. IV (Firenze: R. Ridolfi, 1945), pp.223–224; M. Nadia Covini, *L'esercito del duca: organizzazione militare e istituzioni al tempo degli Sforza: 1450–1480* (Roma: Istituto Storico Italiano per il Medioevo, 1998), pp.109–110.

6 Archivio di Stato di Firenze, 'Mediceo avanti il principato,' vol.1, filza 1, doc. 56;

7 The *capisquadra* (lit. foremen or fore-men) commanded multiple lances or companies of cavalry.

In 1432, Niccolò fought, with 100 lances, in the Battle of San Romano under the command of Niccolò da Tolentino. During the battle, he was taken prisoner by the Sienese. Luca degli Albizzi described the episode in his account of the battle: '*La sera fu preso Nicholò da Pisa in Capannole, che v'andò credendo co' parenti suoi rubellare il luogho*' (in the evening, Niccolò da Pisa was captured in the village of Capannole; he had gone there with his men to pillage the place).

He was captured again at the Battle of Castelbolognese on 28 August 1434. On this occasion, he fell into the hands of the Milanese troops commanded by Piccinino. At the time, he was serving in the army of the league formed by Florence, Venice and the Church. It appears that he was under contract with Patriarch Giovanni Vitelleschi.

The following year, still in the service of Vitelleschi, Niccolò fought against the Count of Poppi in Casentino.

In 1436, he signed a contract with the States of the Church. The heading of the contract reads: '*Nicchᴏlo da Pisa homo darme e conductiere di ducento cavallj*' (Niccolò da Pisa man-at-arms and commander of 200 cavalry).[8]

From 1437 onward, Niccolò served under Francesco Sforza. In February of that year, he was sent to Garfagnana with Piero Brunoro and Ciarpellone. Their task was to oppose Piccinino, who was besieging the castle of Barga. The three captains succeeded in driving the Milanese forces back into Lombardy.

In August 1437, Niccolò went to Fabriano with Giovanni Sforza, commanding 500 cavalrymen and 2,000 infantrymen. Francesco Piccinino, son of Niccolò, was threatening the city. On 11 September, Niccolò lifted the Siege of Ascoli.

The following year, da Pisa distinguished himself in Umbria and, together with Pietro Brunoro, he invaded the territory of Norcia, a city allied with Piccinino.

In November 1439, Niccolò da Pisa was in Northern Italy with Francesco Sforza to free Verona.

In 1440, he was in the force sent by Sforza to Tuscany in support of Florence against Niccolò Piccinino. He first distinguished himself in the Apennines, where he forced the Milanese to retreat at the Alpe di San Benedetto. Then, he took part in the Battle of Anghiari. During the battle, he captured Astorre Manfredi, and handed him over to the Florentines in exchange for 3,000 florins.

At the beginning of 1441, Niccolò da Pisa returned to Lombardy. Piccinino had launched a new offensive and forced Sforza to seek refuge in Verona. Gambacorti and Troilo da Muro joined Sforza, the general commander, there.

After a series of clashes won by the Milanese during the summer, peace was finally concluded at Cremona in December 1441.

---

8 Archivio di Stato di Roma, 'Commissariato sulle soldatesche e galere,' piece 80, anno 1436, f. 5r.

In February 1442, Francesco Sforza sent Gambacorti to Todi with 300 cavalry. While crossing the Bolognese territory without the permission of the city senate, he was intercepted and detained in Bologna.

The Bolognese authorities requested instructions from Piccinino. While awaiting his response, Astorre Manfredi and his companions arrived in Bologna in disguise. They entered the house where Gambacorti was being held, abducted him, killed him, and dismembered his body. The act was intended to avenge the events of Anghiari, when Gambacorti had handed Astorre Manfredi over to the Florentine Republic for 3,000 florins, despite Manfredi having offered 4,000 for his freedom.

Gambacorti died on 6 February 1442, and the Bolognese buried him in Basilica di San Petronio with full honours.[9]

Simonetto III Baglioni

Simonetto III of Castel di Piero[10] was the son of Pietromanno I di Giovanni, a member of the Baglioni family of Teverina Viterbese. He appears for the first time in local chronicles of 1409, when he assisted the militias of Viterbo in reconquering the city of Civita di Bagnoregio. The city had previously been seized by the Monaldeschi from Bishop Angelo I. In 1436, after several years spent in the service of Florence, Simonetto entered the pay of Pope Eugene IV. Acting in the pope's name, he besieged Lorenzo Colonna in Palestrina. In July 1438, Simonetto passed into the service of Patriarch Giovanni Vitelleschi. He was sent to fight Braccio and Malatesta Baglioni da Perugia, who had allied themselves with the captain of fortune Niccolò Piccinino in Umbria. In October 1438, the Church rewarded Simonetto for his services by granting him the town of Civita Lavinia.

Between 1436 and 1439, Simonetto took part in several military campaigns on behalf of the Church in Tuscany and Lazio. During these operations, he demonstrated considerable military ability.

9 Sources for Gambacorti: Pompeo Litta, *Famiglie celebri italiane* (Milano: Luciano Basadonna, *c.*1869): Gioacchino Valeri, 'Della Signoria di Francesco Sforza nella Marca secondo le memorie e i documenti dell'Archivio di Serrasanquirico' in *Archivio storico lombardo* (Milano: Libreria Editrice G. Brigola, 1884), vol. XI, p.279; Nicola Ciminello, *La guerra di Braccio: Poema* (Aquila: Tipografia Aternina,1903), p.133; Petra Pertici, 'Condottieri senesi e la rotta di San Romano di Paolo Uccello' in *Arch. Stor. Ital.* 1999, issue 581, p.560; F. Biondo, *Historie* (Venezia 1547), p.123; Anon., 'Corpus Chronicorum Bononiensium' in *Muratori R.I.S.* (Bologna 1922), XVIII, parte I, pp.103–104; Piero Zama, *I Manfredi signori di Faenza* (Faenza: Fratelli Lega, 1954), pp.185–186.

10 Now San Michele, Teverina, in the province of Viterbo.

In the spring of 1440, Simonetto da Castel di Piero hastened to assist the new papal legate, Cardinal Ludovico Scarampi Mezzarota. At the time, the cardinal was besieging Civitavecchia. Shortly thereafter, Simonetto fought in the Battle of Anghiari among the captains of the papal troops. On that occasion, he distinguished himself for his personal courage in battle.

Towards the middle of the fifteenth century, Simonetto returned to his native Teverina. There, he oversaw the renovation of his residence, the castle of Graffignano. This fortress was an important stronghold of the Patrimony of Saint Peter, controlling supply routes between Umbria, Viterbo and the Tyrrhenian Sea. Despite his attention to his estates, Simonetto never abandoned his principal occupation, the profession of arms.

In 1442, he entered the service of Francesco Sforza. The following year, he was hired by the Republic of Florence, in whose pay he remained until 1447. Later, Alfonso of Aragon hired him during the siege of Piombino in 1448. In 1451, Simonetto again served Florence, remaining under its command until 1460. In the spring of that same year, the Church hired him and sent him to Campania. There, he was tasked with assisting King Ferdinand I of Aragon, who engaged in the struggle against John of Anjou for control of the Kingdom of Naples. In July, Simonetto took part in the bloody Battle of the Sarno River on 7 July 1460. The battle ended in a disastrous defeat for the Aragonese army, and among the numerous casualties was Simonetto of Castel di Piero. With his death, the family branch of Simonetto III Baglioni became extinct. His only son, Pietro Francesco, had died in the same year.[11]

Ludovico Scarampi Mezzarota

Ludovico Trevisan, better known as Ludovico Scarampi Mezzarota, was born in Padua on 14 November 1401. He was the son of a physician named Biagio. He adopted the surname Scarampi, apparently derived from his mother's family. The additional surname Mezzarota, instead, was a fictitious one, used in his cardinal coat of arms.

In Padua, Scarampi devoted himself to his studies and graduated in medicine, following in his father's footsteps. Alongside scientific training,

11 Sources for Simonetto: C. Mancini, 'I Baglioni della Teverina: una famiglia al servizio dello Stato Pontificio' in *Per una storia delle famiglie delle Tuscia tardomedievale*, XVI Giornata di studio per la storia della Tuscia, Viterbo-Orte, 18–19 dicembre 2009; M. Signorelli, *Civita di Bagnoregio nella storia* (Viterbo, Agnesotti, 1979), p.22; Andrea da Mosto, 'Ordinamenti militari delle soldatesche dello Stato Romano dal 1430 al 1470' in *Quellen und Forschungen aus italienischen Archiven und Bibliotheken*, V 1902 pp.80–81; 'Commissariato sulle soldatesche e galere' Archivo Di Stato Di Roma, busta 80, anno 1436, ff. 2r–3v; Ignazio Ciampi, *Cronache e Statuti della Città di Viterbo: della R. Deputazione di Storia Patria* (Firenze, Viesseux, 1872), pp.174–175.

6. Patriarca Scarampi Mezzarota by Andrea Mantegna. (public domain)

he cultivated a strong passion for literature, which he never abandoned despite his marked predisposition for the profession of arms. Driven by ambition and the desire to gain honour and glory, he left Padua and moved to Rome.

In the early decades of the fifteenth century, Rome was deeply troubled by noble feuds, political discord, and local intrigues. In this environment, Scarampi entered the service of Cardinal Gabriele Condulmier as his personal physician. When Condulmier was elected pope in 1431, taking the name Eugene IV, Scarampi became his physician and secret chamberlain. Strengthened by the pope's trust, Scarampi began a rapid ecclesiastical career. In April 1435, he was appointed Canon of Padua, and on 7 September of the same year he became Bishop of Traù, in Dalmatia. Subsequently, he obtained the Archbishopric of Florence. In 1437, Pope Eugene IV entrusted him with a diplomatic mission to Venice. The purpose was to explain the reasons for transferring the council of Basel, convened by Pope Martin V, to the city of Ferrara in 1438. Scarampi's diplomatic skill and loyal service were rewarded on 9 December 1439, when he was appointed Patriarch of Aquileia, with an annual income of 4,000 ducats.

Giovanni Vitelleschi, who had instructed Scarampi in the art of warfare, died in 1440. After his death, Scarampi – described by contemporaries as 'a man of arms rather than of the Church' – was appointed captain general of the Papal Army and commanded the papal forces at the Battle of Anghiari.

Pope Eugene IV held the Paduan cardinal in exceptionally high esteem. In Rome, no major decision was taken without first consulting him. The accumulation of titles and influence within and beyond the Vatican soon made Scarampi one of the wealthiest men in Italy.

In 1455, Pope Callixtus III ascended to the papal throne. His primary objective was to organise a crusade against the Turks, who had taken Constantinople in 1453. With a bull dated 17 December 1455, the pope appointed Scarampi commander of the naval forces against the infidels.

In 1456, Scarampi travelled to Hungary to support the Christian cause against the Ottoman advance. In April, he reached the banks of the Danube, where he assembled more than 40,000 German troops. Among his captains was the renowned Count John Hunyadi. In July of the same year, Scarampi advanced to the gates of Belgrade at the head of the Papal Army and where he succeeded in defeating the Turks.

Ludovico Scarampi Mezzarota died in Rome in 1465. His death occurred shortly after the election of his bitter enemy, Cardinal Pietro Barbo, to the papacy as Pope Paul II. At his death, Scarampi left immense wealth to two of his relatives. However, the pope contested and annulled the will, ordering that Scarampi's goods and money be distributed to pious works.

Scarampi was buried in the church of San Lorenzo in Damaso in Rome.[12]

Pier Giovanpaolo Orsini

Pier Giovanpaolo was the eldest son of Ugolino Orsini of Manopello in Abruzzo. He belonged to the so-called 'southern' branch of the Orsini family.

He began his military career in the school of Braccio da Montone. Shortly thereafter, he entered the service of various powers – the pope, the King of Naples, the municipalities, and major landowners – motivated primarily by the pursuit of power and wealth.

In 1423, Braccio sent him to fight in the army of Alfonso of Aragon against Louis of Anjou. During this campaign, Orsini devastated the territories of Ortona and Chieti. The following year, he shared in the defeat of the Bracceschi troops at the Battle of L'Aquila.

In October 1427, Pier Giovanpaolo Orsini entered the service of the Duke of Milan, Filippo Maria Visconti. He was defeated at Maclodio by Francesco Bussone, known as Carmagnola, supreme commander of the Venetian forces.

On 28 August 1434, Orsini was hired by the Republic of Venice. Shortly thereafter, however, he was captured near Castelbolognese by Visconti forces led by Niccolò Piccinino. On that occasion, Niccolò da Tolentino – captain general of the Papal, Venetian and Florentine allied army – was also taken prisoner.

Two years later, in 1436, Orsini entered the service of Pope Eugene IV. During a clash with the troops of Francesco Sforza, he was ambushed and captured. Once freed, he sought revenge by sacking the city of Budrio, believing the town to have been responsible for his capture. In 1437, Orsini attempted to seize Imola from Guidaccio, Lord of Faenza. His advance was halted by Federico da Montefeltro, who inflicted a severe defeat on his army.

In 1439, the Republic of Florence hired Pier Giovanpaolo Orsini. As commander-in-chief, he played a leading role in the resounding Florentine victory at Anghiari on 29 June 1440 against the Milanese Army commanded by Niccolò Piccinino. Upon his triumphant return to Florence, Orsini deposited the captured enemy banners in Santa Maria del Fiore.

12 Consulted sources for Mezzarota: Giuseppe Vedova, *Biografia degli scrittori padovani*, vol. II (Padova: Minerva, 1836), pp.253–255; Giuseppe Cappelletti, *Storia della Repubblica di Venezia*, vol. 11 (Venezia: Antonelli, 1854), p.402; Scipione Ammirato, *Istorie Fiorentine* (Torino: Cugini Pomba e comp, 1853), vol. V, p.256; Pietro Prezzolini, *Storia religiosa del popolo fiorentino*, vol. II (Firenze: Galileiana, 1857), p.804; Jacobus Philippus Thomassini, *Elogia illustrium virorum iconibus exornata* (Patavii: 1630), p.12; Bernardini Scardeoni, *De claris civibus Patavinis* (Basilea: 1560), p.129.

Still in the service of the Church, in June 1442 he moved to the city of Tolentino, which had rebelled against the Sforza domination. He then moved into Umbria together with Piccinino, Ludovico Gonzaga, and Carlo da Montone. During this campaign, the captains captured and plundered several castles in the region.

Pier Giovanpaolo Orsini died in Monte San Savino in 1443.[13]

---

13 Sources consulted for Pier Giovanpaolo Orsini: Gustavo Brigante Colonna, *Gli Orsini* (Milano: Geschina, 1955), p.112; S. Romanin (ed.), *Storia documentata di Venezia*, vol. IV (Venezia: Pietro Noratovich, 1855), p.178; Giuseppi Colucci, *Dell'antichità Picene, Vita del conte Federico da Montefeltro duca II d'Urbino*, VII (Fermo: self-published, 1794), p.2.

3

Military Organisation of the Era

The Italian Cavalry in the Fifteenth Century

The Armour of the Knights

One cannot discuss cavalry in fifteenth century Italy without first examining the armour worn by knights of the period. This armour consisted primarily of steel plate, tempered through a cold-surface process that rendered the exterior compact, resilient and highly polished.

The finest armour of the time was produced in Italy, and more specifically in Milan. The city functioned not only as a manufacturing centre for the Italian peninsula but also as a major supplier for the whole of Europe, serving as a hub of technical innovation and artisanal excellence. Milanese armourers exported their products to England, Spain, France, Germany, and even as far as the Aegean. Foreign states frequently sent their smiths to Milan to learn the craft of armour-making and, at the same time, attempted to attract Milanese masters to their cities by encouraging the establishment of new workshops.[1]

Within Italy itself, these skilled artisans opened workshops in Brescia, Mantua, Modena, Ferrara, Venice, Urbino, Rome, and Naples.

The output of Milanese armourers contributed decisively to the international fame of the city. Among the most renowned families who founded true artisan dynasties were the Corio, the Vimercate, the Mondrone, and above all the Missaglia, who achieved exceptional recognition. In 1435, Filippo Maria Visconti knighted Tommaso Missaglia and, in 1450, Francesco Sforza granted him exemption from taxation.

1 Giovanni Treccani degli Alfieri, *Storia di Milano* (Milano: Fondazione Treccani degli Alfieri per la storia di Milano, 1958), XI, p.701.

Particularly notable was the efficiency of these armourers' workshops. For instance, following the defeat at Maclodio in 1427 – after which the Visconti troops were disarmed – two Milanese armourers managed, within a few days, to equip 4,000 cavalry and 2,000 infantry with new weapons and armour.[2] These craftsmen clearly did not work alone. Documentary evidence shows that the great armour-making families employed large numbers of workers, even involving entire villages in the mass production of armour.

Italian armour of the period was finely crafted and provided the mounted warrior with excellent protection while preserving a considerable degree of mobility. A harness typically weighed between 20 and 25 kilograms and offered remarkable resistance to blows. This resilience contributed significantly to the relatively low number of fatalities recorded in fifteenth century field battles.

Nevertheless, such armour had notable drawbacks. Poor ventilation, combined with the substantial weight, caused severe discomfort, particularly during Italian summer campaigns and battles, such as at the Battle of Anghiari. Another disadvantage was limited visibility when using fully enclosed helmets. As a result, many cavalrymen preferred open-faced helmets, a preference clearly attested to by contemporary iconography. A painted front panel depicting the Battle of Anghiari, preserved in the National Gallery of Ireland in Dublin, shows numerous cavalrymen wearing sallets with a T-shaped opening. The panel, part of a chest, dates to around 1460, and the armour and weapons represented therefore reflect equipment in use at that time. The sallet with a T-shaped opening only came into widespread use after 1450. At the time of the Battle of Anghiari, sallets were generally more open around the face.

Valuable information concerning the cost of armour and its individual components is preserved in the accounting records of the *condotta* of Micheletto Attendolo, held in the archives of the Fraternita dei Laici of Arezzo.

For example, a helmet known as a 'sparrow's beak', so called for its distinctive shape, could cost 4 ducats or even 6 florins.[3] At the time, ducats and florins were of nearly equivalent value. A sallet, by contrast, typically cost 2 florins.[4] A complete suit of armour ranged in price from 8 to 15 ducats, reaching up to 17 florins for particularly refined examples.[5] A breastplate – understood as the armour protecting the abdomen and thighs

---

2 Treccani, *Storia di Milano*, p.714; P. Levi Pisetzky, *Storia del costume in Italia* (Milano: Istituto Editoriale Italiano, 1964), vol. II, p.387.

3 F. Viviano, 'Registri della compagnia di Micheletto Attendolo.' in Fraternita dei Laici di Arezzo, libro 3574, f. 156v and libro 3569, f. 41.

4 Viviano, 'Registri della compagnia,' libro 3593, f. 37r.

5 Viviano, 'Registri della compagnia,' libro 3574, ff. 50r, 111r and 182v.

– cost between 1 and 3 florins.[6] A pair of rerebraces or greaves was valued at 6 florins, while iron gauntlets cost only 1 florin.[7]

The purchase of a complete suit of armour for Captain Micheletto amounted to 28 florins and 32 *bolognini*. It was acquired in Ancona from the shop of the Milanese armourer, Giovanni da Castelletto.[8] Given its relatively modest price, this armour was not particularly special, and it was the only set of armour owned by this *condottiero*, unlike that of some of his subordinate captains of *condotta*, such as Todero da Lecce, who had multiple pieces or set. Thus, after being wounded in the chest by a spear at Anghiari, and once fully healed three months later, Micheletto needed to travel to Florence to commission a new 'breastplate for his armour'.[9]

Prominent captains often owned multiple armour components to be used as replacements. For instance, in May 1439, the squadron commander Tartaglia d'Arezzo appraised a suit of armour together with two pairs of rerebraces at 6 florins. In June 1440, the same Tartaglia bought another suit of armour, iron gauntlets, and a pair of rerebraces for 86 *lire* and 12 *soldi*.[10]

The Armour in Use in 1440

This section analyses the types of armour in use at the time of the Battle of Anghiari. Unfortunately, very few complete suits of armour or individual pieces survive from this period; however, a substantial body of visual evidence is provided by contemporary works of art depicting battles and tournaments. Among the most important sources are paintings by Paolo Uccello and Pisanello, dating between 1436 and 1440. Paolo Uccello painted the Battle of San Romano in a series of panels now preserved in the Uffizi Gallery in Florence, the National Gallery in London, and the Louvre in Paris. Pisanello painted the fresco of the Tournament Battle of Louverzep, in the Ducal Palace of Mantua.

The types of armour depicted in these works are broadly similar, yet they do present clear and significant differences. According to scholars, the armour represented in the Battle of San Romano panels reflects a Florentine influence in its form, whereas that depicted in the Tournament of Louverzep reveals a Milanese influence. These differences are particularly evident in the helmets worn by the knights. In Uccello's paintings, the helmets are equipped with a ventail or visor which, when lowered to protect the face, leaves a visual opening between the visor and the lower edge of the front (see image 7 'Armour by Paolo Uccello'). This type of helmet is commonly

6 Viviano, 'Registri della compagnia,' libro 3574, ff. 48r. & 141v, and libro 3569, f. 51.
7 Viviano, 'Registri della compagnia,' libro 3574, ff. 77r & 108v, and libro 3593, f. 31v.
8 Viviano, 'Registri della compagnia,' libro 3593, f. 62v.
9 Viviano, 'Registri della compagnia,' libro 3574, f. 135r.
10 Viviano, 'Registri della compagnia,' libro 3561, f. 171v and libro 3574, f. 108v.

referred to as being in the 'Florentine style'. It appears in early fifteenth century inventory documents described as a 'helmet with the visor open'.

In Pisanello's fresco, by contrast, the helmets display a visor of the Milanese style, with the vision opening cut directly into the visor itself. This solution would gradually replace the Florentine type towards the end of the first half of the fifteenth century. A rare surviving example of a Milanese helmet of this type is in the collection of the Baron of Cosson.[11]

Piero della Francesca also depicted Milanese helmets in the fresco cycle *The Legend of the True Cross* in Arezzo. These works are clearer and more detailed than those in Mantua; however, they were made between 1452 and 1466. Old fashioned, della Francesca likely relied on earlier armour designs that he had previously drawn.

Further differences can be observed in the pauldrons. In Uccello's paintings, the right pauldron is concave both at the front and the back, facilitating the use of the spear. In Pisanello's representations, the rear edge of the pauldron is squared off.

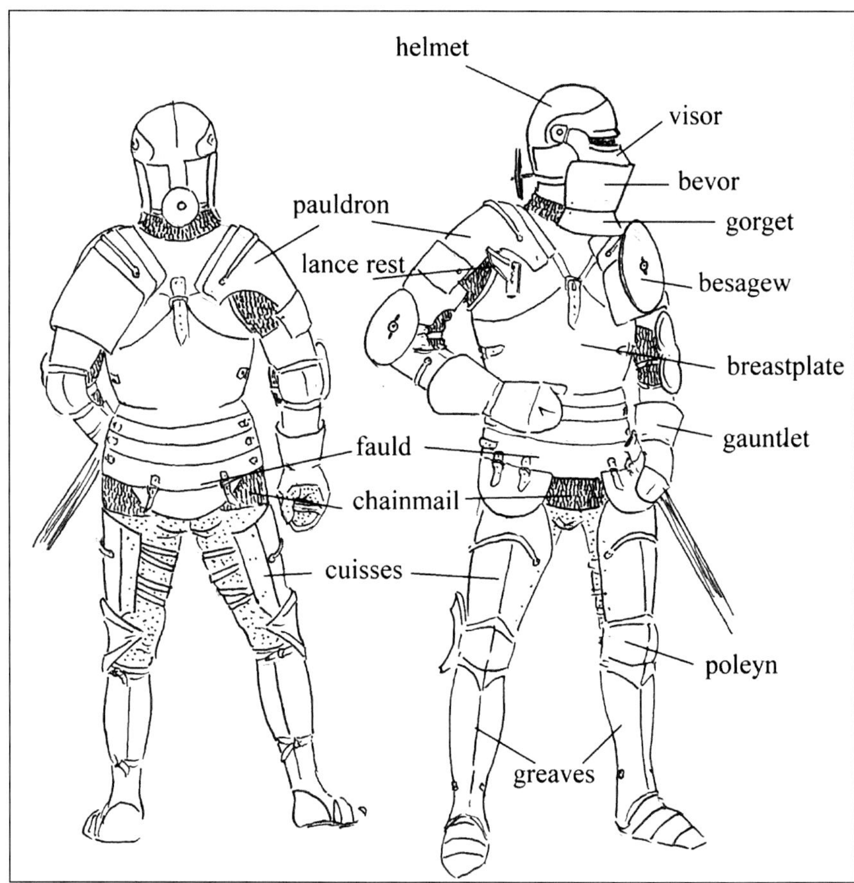

7. Type of armour for men-at-arms taken from the paintings of Paolo Uccello. (Artwork by author)

11 Sir Guy Francis Laking, *A Record of European Armour and Arms Through Seven Centuries* (London: G. Bell & Sons, 1920), vol. 2, p.81.

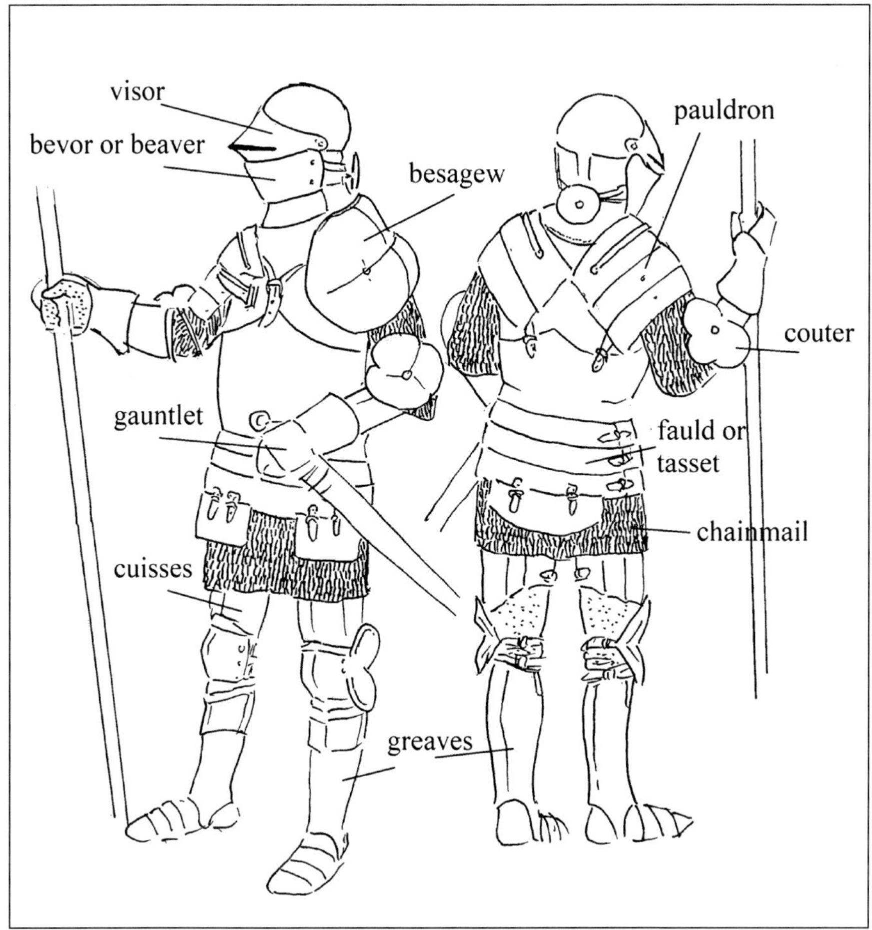

8. Type of armour for men-at-arms taken from Pisanello's paintings. (Artwork by author)

Clear differences can also be seen in the besagew (reinforcements applied to the front of the spaulders). Uccello depicts them as rounded, while Pisanello represents them in more complex, often concave shapes. These reinforcing elements are repeated on the couters. In Uccello's armour, reinforcements appear only on the right arm, and the left arm lacks such protection. The faulds also differ markedly. In Uccello's work, they consist of 4 or 5 lames, with narrow, convex lower edges, while in Pisanello's fresco, they are broader and rectangular in form. Finally, mail protections are more prominent and extensive in Pisanello's representations than in those of Uccello.

Additional important iconographic sources for this study include the 'Codice degli Uomini Illustri' preserved in the National Cabinet of Prints in Rome. This manuscript, dated between 1435 and 1440, presents a series of particularly informative depictions of armour. Further evidence is provided by the tombstone of Antonello Arcimboldi, who died in 1439, and by another work of Pisanello – the armour worn by St George in the fresco of Santa Anastasia in Verona.

With regard to surviving original pieces, two helmets for men-at-arms are of particular relevance. One is preserved in New York at the Metropolitan

Museum of Art (accession no. 29.158.5) and is dated 1435; it features a Florentine-type visor. Another helmet, dated between 1440 and 1445 and also with an open or Florentine visor, is preserved in Schluderns in the province of Bolzano. Both helmets were produced in Milanese workshops.

The final object of note is the well-known man-at-arms armour known as AVANT, preserved in Glasgow and dated between 1440 and 1445. This armour, of Milanese workmanship in both design and form, closely resembles the armour depicted by Uccello and is notably devoid of besagew.

The present analysis draws upon selected iconographic sources and armour discussed in Lionello Giorgio Boccia's study on Mantuan armour. Boccia was among the most important scholars of historical arms and armour and is widely regarded as the leading Italian authority in this field during the last century. This chapter also makes use of the researches of Maetzke and Righini.[12]

Company Structure, or *Condotta di Ventura*

The most authoritative studies on the structure of the Italian *condotta di ventura* – that is, mercenary companies – have been conducted by Michael Mallett, Mario Del Treppo, and Duccio Balestracci.[13]

The basic tactical and administrative unit of the company was the lance. Each lance was composed of three men: the first knight, *caput lancae* or *armiger* (lance leader), the second knight, *plattus* (flat), and finally, the *pagius* or *rigazzus* (page or boy.) Only the first two members of the lance were combatants. The page remained to the rear, ready to assist by replacing broken weapons or bringing fresh horses. In daily life and outside of battle, the page's duties were extensive. He was responsible for managing supplies, caring for the horses, cleaning weapons as well as a variety of other support tasks.

The leader of a lance also commanded a *condotta* composed of one or several lances. In this case, as attested in the accounting registers of Viviano, this figure is described as a corporal or companion.

In the registers, the entries 'three lances' and 'nine horses' are equivalent. However, lances were often incomplete due to death, desertion, or the individual hiring of knights. For this reason, the number of lances did not

12 L. G. Boccia, *Le armature di S. Maria delle Grazie di Curtatone di Mantova e l'armatura lombarda del '400'* (Milano: Bramante Editrice, 1982), pp.23–25 and 34–47; Guglielmo Maetzke, 'Armi e armature' in *Piero della Francesca* (Milano: Silvana Editoriale, 1998) pp.170–175; M. Righini, 'L'armatura da 'Homo d'arme' nell'Italia del '400' in *Ars Historiae*, July-September 2006.

13 Michael Mallett, *Signori e mercenari* (Bologna: Il Mulino, 1983); M. Del Treppo, 'Sulla struttura della compagnia o condotta militare' in *Condottieri e uomini d'arme nell'Italia del rinascimento*, (Napoli: Liguori, 2001); Duccio Balestracci, *Le armi, i cavalli, l'oro. Giovanni Acuto e i condottieri nell'Italia del Trecento*, (Roma: Ed. Laterza, 2003).

always correspond to exact multiples of three men. Consequently, the size and value of a *condotta* were calculated on the basis of the number of horses rather than the nominal number of lances.

Micheletto commanded numerous small *condotte*. In June 1440, for example, 21 of 44 *condotte* in his company consisted of fewer than 10 horses. At the same time, significantly larger contingents were also present. These included the *condotta* of Attendolo with 267 horses, that of the Lord of Carpi with 90 horses, Marco degli Attendolo with 111 horses, and Betuccio de Cortesi with 159 horses.[14]

The term man-at-arms generally referred to all armed knights listed in the registers. In practice, however, it was often used specifically to indicate the 'lance leader'. The term 'companion', by contrast, referred to the commander of a small *condotta*. This title implied a relationship of equality with the *condottiero* or squad leader.

The term *famiglio* (retainer) had a more specific meaning. It referred to a knight under the direct authority of the captain, belonging to his closest and most trusted circle and forming part of his personal household. For example, in 1439, Betuccio de Cortesi had 50 lances in his employ. Of these, 29 belonged to his 15 companions, while the remaining 21 formed part of his household of *famigli*. Similarly, in April 1440, Marco degli Attendolo, out of a total of 108 horses in his *condotta*, counted 50 *famigli*, while the remaining were horses belonging to his companions.

Betuccio de Cortesi and Marco degli Attendolo were squad leaders – that is, *condottieri* of companies selected directly by Micheletto. This status is clearly indicated by the large number of horses in their *condotte*. Not all squad leaders recorded in Viviano's registers are immediately identifiable. For instance, in book 3574, covering the years 1439 to 1441, Tartaglia d'Arezzo consistently appears with a *condotta* of only 18 horses – a small number for a squad leader. These horses, however, correspond to his *famigli*. A note at the bottom of folio 164v of the same register lists Tartaglia's companions in April 1440: Antonello di Lombardia, Mattioccio, Arrigo da Salerno, Cola Scrima, Giovanni Schiavo, Fraruffino, Jacopo di Fraruffino, and Stefano da Matera.[15]

Origin of the Knights Serving in the Companies of Fortune

The members of Italian companies of fortune in the fifteenth century were drawn almost entirely from the Italian peninsula, at least as far as cavalry was concerned. In this respect, Mario Del Treppo conducted a significant analysis of Micheletto Attendolo's company. Examining the registers of

14 See Chapter 6, table of Micheletto's captains at Anghiari.

15 The table in Chapter 6 lists almost all of these captains and their horses.

Viviano, he selected a sample of 450 captains, covering almost the entire lifespan of the company.[16]

This analysis reveals a remarkably limited foreign presence. Only 26 captains were of non-Italian origin: 10 Slavs, Albanians, and Greeks settled in southern Italy, while the remaining were French, Provençals, Germans, and Hungarians.

Among the Italian captains, 131 came from the Kingdom of Naples and 161 from the States of the Church. The latter included Lazio, Umbria, the Marche, Romagna, and Emilia. The remaining 142 captains came from Tuscany and Northern Italy. The regions with the highest number of origins were Lombardy, with 64 men, followed by Romagna and Campania with 51 captains each. Tuscany accounted for 43 captains, Emilia for 38, and Umbria for 36. Lombardy ranked first among the northern regions. However, the majority of captains came from the countryside of Bergamo and Brescia, areas that had been under Venetian influence for many years. A substantial number of soldiers also came from the Kingdom of Naples. This can be explained by Micheletto's long military career in those territories, where he had also been invested with feudal lordship. Finally, a significant number came from Romagna. In particular, cities such as Cotignola, Bagnacavallo, Barbiano, Lugo, Granarolo, and Brisighella recur frequently – towns closely connected geographically and historically to the Attendolo family.

A useful comparison with this analysis can be drawn with the historical adversaries of the Attendolo, namely the Bracceschi. More specifically, this concerns Francesco Piccinino's *condotta* of 1432 under the Republic of Siena.[17] This contract is entirely organised by lances. Each page of the register records the three members composing each lance.

The opening page lists the *condottiero* Francesco Piccinino himself, together with his *piatto,* Nicolò Gioacchino da Gubbio, and his *pagius*. The contract records the name and place of origin of the first two cavalrymen of each lance. For the pages, however, it usually notes only the physical characteristics of their mounts, most commonly a rouncey.

The company thus comprised a total of 449 horses and 100 infantrymen. The mounted forces consisted of 300 captains and *piatti* and 149 pages.

If one considers only the knights – whose personal data are recorded – it is possible to analyse their geographical origins, following the same method applied by Del Treppo to Micheletto's company.

In this case, the number of foreigners rises slightly to 30. Most originated from Northern Europe: 10 Germans, 8 Hungarians, and 5 Frenchmen. Among Italian regions, Lombardy is the most represented, with 48 cavalrymen. Of these, 11 came from the city of Milan. Umbria follows closely with 44 men, 20 of whom were from the city of Perugia. The

16 M. del Treppo, 'Gli aspetti organizzativi economici e sociali di una compagnia di ventura Italiana' in *Nuova rivista storica,* 69°, 1985, pp.253–275.

17 Archivio di Stato di Siena, Biccherna 261, 1432, 'Ruolo della compagnia di Francesco di Niccolò Piccinino.'

remaining regions, in descending order, are Emilia with 21 cavalrymen, Romagna with 16, Tuscany with 15, and Lazio with 14.

Out of 300 cavalrymen, nearly one-third was from Lombardy and Umbria. This distribution is likely the result of Piccinino's long-standing service under the Visconti, as well as the Perugian origins of the Bracceschi Company.

An Italian company of fortune was not composed solely of soldiers. It also included a large body of non-combatants responsible for the daily functioning of the company, such as administration, provisioning, and so on.

They included secretaries, notaries, treasurers, and *spenditori* charged with the financial management of the *condotta.* In addition, there were numerous service personnel, including cooks, bakers, undertakers, carters and mule drivers, blacksmiths, and other specialised craftsmen. Doctors, barbers, priests, servants and often women – wives or even entire families of captains – also formed part of the company establishment.

A detailed study of these non-combatants is provided in Duccio Balestracci's work on Giovanni l'Acuto.[18] A corresponding list drawn from Viviano's registers is included in the present volume in Chapter 7.

Pay

With regard to the pay within a *condotta*, two documentary sources drawn from Viviano's registers are particularly informative.

The first document is preserved in envelope 3604, which contains several unnumbered documents. It refers to a contract concluded under the company of Francesco Sforza in May 1439. The engagement was stipulated to be for a period of three months at a rate of 6 florins per lance. Although the document does not explicitly state so, the sum was almost certainly intended as a monthly payment. The same record also notes a subsequent renewal of the contract at a higher rate of 8 florins per lance.

The second document is taken from Mario del Treppo's comprehensive publication concerning the period of Micheletto Attendolo's *condotta* in Venetian service in 1444–1445. The text of the document specifies the following monthly salaries:

> A *lancia* (lance) receives 50 lire per month; the *capo de lancia* (lance leader) receives 22 lire and 10 *soldi* per month; the *piatto* receives 16 lire and 10 *soldi* per month; the rouncey receives 11 lire and 0 *soldi* per month.[19]

18 Balestracci, *Le armi, i cavalli, l'oro,* pp.56 – 61.
19 Treppo, 'Sulla struttura della compagnia,' p.418.

By the middle of the fifteenth century, the value of one florin corresponded to approximately 5 lire.

The Use of Heraldry: the Company of Micheletto Attendolo as a Case Study

All companies of fortune of the period carried a banner in battle and during parades, displaying the 'device' of their commander.

Micheletto Attendolo's company bore a flag featuring blue and silver waves quartered with a device on a red field. A document preserved in Viviano's registers records that it was entirely made of silk purchased from a merchant named Mattia by the master Luca Setaiolo, and manufactured by the banner maker Antonio Banderaro. On the red quarters was an emblem, painted by the Florentine workshop of Pesello; the document does not specify its subject, but it was most likely a unicorn or quinces (see Plate C, image 1 and image 5).

Taking into account both materials and workmanship, the total cost of the flag amounted to around 44 florins.[20]

In addition to their own standards, companies also carried those of the cities or lordships that employed them. Between 1431 and 1433, corresponding to Micheletto's two *condotte* under Florence, the registers record several references to standards and banners bearing lilies. In October 1432, the Signoria bestowed upon Attendolo – probably in recognition of his actions at the Battle of San Romano – '*una bandera collo giglio, un almetto collo giglio, un chavallo covertato di chermosy e brochato d'oro*' (a flag with the lily, a helmet with the lily, and a horse with a caparison of crimson and gold brocade).[21]

Other banners were mounted atop the campaign pavilions. These were not made of taffeta like those described above, but of blue *boccaccino* (a cotton fabric) with a yellow lion, which unmistakably represented the Attendolo coat of arms.[22]

The pavilions themselves could be made of white *pannolino* (linen), painted red and blue or decorated with quinces, or alternatively of canvas painted entirely red.

Another type of cloth widely used in the armies of the time was the trumpet banner, used primarily by trumpeters belonging to the lord's household.

Micheletto employed several such trumpeters. Around the time of the Battle of Anghiari, three banners are recorded in the registers. After 1441, with his entry into Venetian service and the consequent increase in

20 Viviano, 'Registri della compagnia,' libro 3593 f. 71v.
21 Viviano, 'Registri della compagnia,' libro 3591 f. 106v.
22 Viviano, 'Registri della compagnia,' libro 3593 f. 79v.

the number of horses in his *condotta*, the number of trumpeters probably increased. Register 3593, which records the expenditures of Micheletto's household between 1439 and 1446 – including the first 6 years under Venetian service – mentions several purchases of trumpet banners: 4 in 1441, and 6 in 1445.

Like the principal banners, trumpet banners were made of silk and displayed the lord's device. Crimson or grain-coloured taffeta was used for the red field, while white taffeta and *alexandrino* (a variegated blue-and-gold fabric) was used for the waves.[23] In some cases, the registers also mention yellow or gold fabric, probably used for the emblem – most likely the quinces – on the red field. In 1445, the 6 banners mentioned above cost a total of 87 florins.

Trumpeters, however, were not the exclusive prerogative of *condottiero* alone; even prominent subordinate captains could have them within their own company.

On 8 June 1440, Betuccio de Cortesi paid 8 florins for '*a tronbetta collo lione*', (a trumpet banner displaying the lion). This lion does not represent Cortesi's impresa rather the Attendolo coat of arms. [24] This and similar cases, in which subordinate captains adopted the commander-in-chief's device, are further analysed below.

With regard to the emblems or symbols of recognition worn by individual captains, Viviano's registers provide particularly valuable evidence. The unicorn impresa appears frequently in the records on *giornee* belonging to the commander-in-chief Micheletto degli Attendolo. In 1441, he commissioned three *giornee* of crimson velvet with unicorns for his three sons – Jacopo Sforza, Raimondo Vittorioso and Pietro Antonio – using the same unicorn motif from one of his older *giornee*.[25]

These unicorns in fine gold were applied not only to *giornee* but also to the lord's combat spears, and were painted on the shafts.

A second emblem used by Attendolo was the dragon, used as a helmet crest. This impresa is discussed in the heraldry chapter on heraldry below in connection with two flags bearing the dragon depicted on two painted chests illustrating the Battle of Anghiari.

Another captain whose emblems are documented in the registers is Marco degli Attendolo, known as Marchetto, a relative of Micheletto and a member of the company from 1431 to 1446. Viviano records that Marchetto bore three imprese on his *giornea*. The first, mentioned in 1433, consisted of three silver rays.[26] The other two date to the period around the Battle of Anghiari: one depicting traps and the other lanterns[27] (see Plate C, figure 2 where only the lanterns are present). Finally, Viviano records a *giornea*

23 Viviano, 'Registri della compagnia,' libro 3593 ff. 72v, 110v and 205r.
24 Viviano, 'Registri della compagnia,' libro 3574 f. 134r.
25 Viviano, 'Registri della compagnia,' libro 3593 f. 68v.
26 Viviano, 'Registri della compagnia,' libro 3558 f. 138r
27 Viviano, 'Registri della compagnia,' libro 3574 ff. 77r and 118r.

bearing Micheletto's device made from three and a half *bracci* of grain rose and three *bracci* of white and blue cloth; this was in fact the device of the Attendolo family, to which Marchetto belonged. The same red, white, and blue colours were also used to decorate the hose of his principal *famigli*.[28]

Unfortunately, the accountant does not record the impresas of other captains, limiting himself instead to describing the colours of their *giornee* and fringes. For example, Betuccio de Cortesi da Cotignola adopted the Attendolo device; the *giornee* worn by the footboys of his household were decorated in red, white, and light blue.[29] This strongly suggests that Betuccio's *famigli* also wore the same device. Betuccio was an old companion of Micheletto and had followed him since 1431. He commanded the most numerous company after that of the captain himself and belonged to a Cotignola family closely connected to the Attendolo.

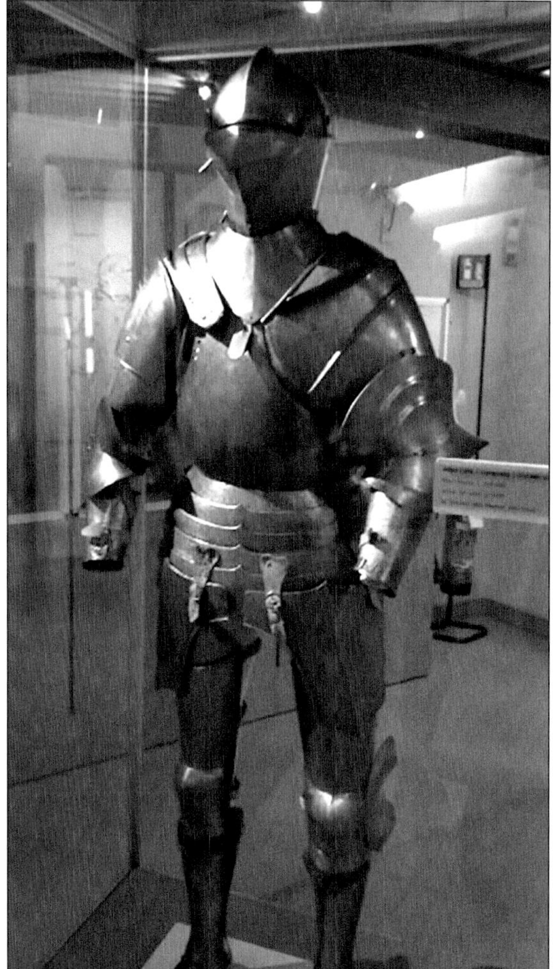

9. Armour *c.* 1450, preserved in the Sanctuary of the Madonna delle Grazie in Mantua. (Photograph by the author)

Other captains wore the Attendolo device despite not belonging to the family, such as Bagnacavallo of Bagnacavallo, near Cotignola, and Moschino with his companion Antonio, whose place of origin Viviano does not specify.[30]

Many other captains appear in the registers with their own devices. Tartaglia d'Arezzo, for instance, equipped his *famigli* with scarlet and white cloth *giornee*. Antonello and Francesco Seguro, as well as Carnecina and Ragazzino, likewise wore red and white.[31]

Orso Orsini wore a *giornea* (see below) with the fringe in the colours of his device – crimson, green, black and gold – while Raffaello di Vramonte, Lord of Carpi, had the fringe of his *giornee* in silver.[32]

Paolino da Barbiano owned *giornee* and hose made in his livery colours from 14½ *braccia* of fine cloth, divided as follows: 12 *braccia* of white, 1½ *braccia* of red and 1½ *braccia* of green (although the total exceeds 14 *braccia* by ½ *braccia*).[33]

---

28 Viviano, 'Registri della compagnia,' libro 3574 f. 160.

29 Viviano, 'Registri della compagnia,' libro 3574 f. 195r.

30 Viviano, 'Registri della compagnia,' libro 3574 ff. 53r and 152v.

31 Viviano, 'Registri della compagnia,' libro 3573 f. 147v and libro 3574 ff. 61r and 168v.

32 Viviano, 'Registri della compagnia,' libro 3574 ff. 33r and 105r.

33 Viviano, 'Registri della compagnia,' libro 3574 f. 173r. A *braccio* in fifteenth century Italy varied from city to city. It ranged from approximately 50cm to 60cm.

Turquoise hose, by contrast, identified Marino's household of Bologna, while light blue hose were worn by Renzo of Rome and his household.[34]

Viviano records an interesting note from January 1441 concerning the manufacture and supply of 22 *giornee* in the livery colours of Seguranza da Vico. Although the colours are not specified, the number itself is significant: at the time, this captain commanded a company of 21 horses, meaning that all his men – including pages – sported his emblem on their *giornee*.

The *giornea* (plural *giornee*) was a predominantly male and military garment, worn over armour and open at the sides to allow free movement of the arms, similar to the English tabard or surcoat. (see Plate C figure 4). It was usually made of silk, velvet or wool and could be full-length, short, or a half-*giornea*, which covered only the shoulders and was especially favoured in combat. Many knights preferred the half-*giornea* because, unlike the full-length version, it left the chest free, preventing spear blows from catching on the cloth rather than sliding harmlessly over the steel of the armour (see Plate C figure 2). The Dublin Chest depicting the Battle of Anghiari shows numerous cavalrymen on both sides wearing half-*giornee*.

The emblem could be sewn, embroidered, or even painted onto the *giornea*. In register 3593, recording the expenditures of Micheletto's household, there are numerous references to *giornee* 'with the lord's device' or 'for *famigli*' – expressions that indicate the same typology of garment.

In May 1439, a Florentine tailor named Giovanni di Buonaiuto was paid to manufacture 130 *giornee* bearing a device, at a total cost of 460 florins.[35]

Thanks to the Viviano's documents, it is possible to gain a fairly precise understanding of the role played by the device on the clothing worn by the cavalrymen of companies of fortune.

A significant part of the troops wore the livery of their *condottiero*. In Micheletto's company, all *famigli* belonging to his household sported the Attendolo emblem, as did the *famigli* of Betuccio and Marchetto, along with several smaller companies.

On the basis of Viviano's registers, it is possible to calculate how many cavalrymen wore this device. Micheletto commanded 267 horses, all of which – including pages – most likely displayed his colours. Added to these were Betuccio's 63 *famigli*, Micheletto's own 50 *famigli*, and the small companies of Moschino and Antonio, Bagnacavallo and Conrado Alemanco, amounting to 25 horses, all recorded as wearing the Attendolo colours. Finally, the Constables Francesco da Bibiena and Cristofano da Cremona, members of the lord's household, controlled – beside the infantry – a total of 27 horses.

The total therefore amounts to 452 cavalrymen out of approximately 1,120, or roughly 25 percent of the entire company.

The numerous small *condotte* commanded by companions generally wore different liveries in the colours of their own leaders. Nevertheless,

34 Viviano, 'Registri della compagnia,' libro 3574 ff. 73v and 50r.

35 Viviano, 'Registri della compagnia,' libro 3593 f. 11v.

not every soldier owned a *giornea:* as contemporary paintings show, many fought without any visible symbol of recognition over their armour. Many corporals lacked the means to clothe their subordinates and were therefore the only ones to wear a *giornea* bearing their device, while numerous lance leaders could not afford even this distinction.

Another important sign of recognition consisted of the plumes mounted on top of helmets and sallets, which were far more widely used than crests made of boiled leather, cotton or wool. Only captains, companions, and the lord's *famigli* were entitled to wear these plumes, which usually consisted of ostrich feathers dyed in the colours of the commander-in-chief.

The number of feathers composing each plume varied considerably. At the beginning of register 3593, under the date of September 1439, there is a list of 17 *famigli* of Micheletto, each of whom was given a plume. These plumes could consist of as few as two feathers – as in the case of Antonello da Baschi – of 10 feathers, as worn by Agostino di Francalancia, of 22 feathers, like Giovanni da Crema, and up to 25 feathers, as in the case of Antonaccio.

The record also mentions Micheletto's own two plumes: one composed of 30 ostrich and five peacock feathers, and another of 16 ostrich and seven peacock feathers (see Plate C, figure 4). The latter was mounted on a helmet surmounted by a dragon crest.[36]

Beyond the number of plumes, the colour combinations of the feathers also varied significantly. In envelope 3604, containing several unnumbered loose documents, two lists of captains' plumes are preserved. Among these appears Carnecina, who had 17 white plumes, 2 red, and 6 blue; Cola Scrima with 7 white plumes, 3 red, and 15 blue; and Olivo da Barbiano, with 50 white plumes, 5 blue, and 5 red.[37] These captains adopted Attendolo's colours. Other captains, however, are listed with different colour schemes, not always corresponding to their heraldic device. Fraruffino had 8 white plumes, 8 red, 8 green, and 1 blue; Giovanni da Casale had 25 white plumes; Ruggeri Picinino had 10 green and white plumes and 10 red; Tartaglia d'Arezzo had 8 white, 8 black and 8 green plumes.

From both the variability in number and the colour diversity of the plumes, it can be inferred that each was highly personal, differing also in form, as confirmed by contemporary iconographies. Their function was not merely decorative: above all, plumes served as high-visibility sign of recognition in the midst of battle. They acted almost as small flags, allowing observers to track the movements of the individual captains of a *condotta* during combat.

Some modern historians have suggested that plumes and crests were largely pictorial conventions favoured by contemporary artists rather than objects actually used in battle. Micheletto's registers, however, contradict

36 Viviano, 'Registri della compagnia,' libro 3593 ff. 3r and 4v.

37 Olivo da Barbiano owned 60 feathers likely divided into several plumes. The registers report a maximum of 25 or 35 feathers, as in Micheletto's case.

this interpretation. In book 3574, Viviano records on 25 June – only four days before the Battle of Anghiari – the payment for supplies of plumes for 13 captains and some of their companions.[38] Although no one in the League Army encamped at Anghiari could have known that a battle would occur within four days, the proximity of the Milanese Army – Piccinino had pitched camp between Città di Castello and Borgo Sansepolcro – made a battle highly likely. These preparations were therefore clearly intended for combat, not for a tournament or parade.

Another important category of visual identification consisted of horse harnesses and caparisons, which were usually painted with the heraldic symbols of the captains. In contemporary battle paintings – particularly on painted wedding chests – these richly decorated harnesses are prominently depicted. In the records, they are variously described as horse blankets, vestments or even horse armour. They could be made of leather or velvet, as in the case of Micheletto's own caparison, which was fashioned from blue velvet and gold brocade and cost 208 florins.[39]

Other caparisons were far less expensive, e.g. '*ducati otto furono duno paro di covertte dipintte per Francalancia da Pisa*' (eight ducats for a pair of painted blankets for Francalancia da Pisa), or '*fiorini 10 per uno paro di coverte dipinte per Bagnacavallo da Bagnacavallo*' (10 florins for a pair of painted blankets for Bagnacavallo da Bagnacavallo).[40] Book 3593 also lists individual pieces of barding with their respective costs: flanchard, crupper, reins, and peytral, all in red leather, for a total of 16 florins.[41]

The documents nevertheless make clear that full barding was a privilege reserved for captains and some of their companions. In book 3561, which records the *condotta* under King René of Anjou between 1435 and 1439, five captains – Marco degli Attendolo, Betuccio de Cortesi, Colella da Castellaneta, Villano di Bemba, and Francesco da Bibiena – and three companions – Actor, Antonello da Capodistria and Bersichella – are noted as having received a pair of white horse coverings. Each covering cost only five florins, suggesting that these items would probably be decorated at a later stage.[42]

A similar list is among the loose documents in envelope 3604, which records 15 captains owning one or even two pairs of horse coverings. Among them is Micheletto himself, who possessed no fewer than nine pairs, as well as a certain Braccio, who is recorded as owning a horse armour.

Beyond these entries, the company records provide little further detail regarding horse protection. From the available data, it can be inferred that

38 Viviano, 'Registri della compagnia,' libro 3574 ff. 103v, 120r, 135v, 144v, some examples.
39 Viviano, 'Registri della compagnia,' libro 3593 f. 93v.
40 Viviano, 'Registri della compagnia,' libro 3560 f. 121r and libro 3557 f. 12r.
41 Viviano, 'Registri della compagnia,' libro 3593 f. 52r.
42 Viviano, 'Registri della compagnia,' libro 3561 ff. 14v, 62r, 90v, 156r and 164v.

fully barded horses were relatively rare in fifteenth century companies of fortune, the vast majority being equipped only with simple harnesses.

This lack of protection undoubtedly contributed to the heavy horse losses recorded in contemporary battles, such as at Anghiari, where 600 horses were killed.

Viviano mentions a single heraldic caparison with an emblem belonging to a Captain Corrado *todescho* (German), who owned a horse armour decorated with lions at a cost of 4 florins and 28 *bolognini*.[43] These lions most likely correspond to the lions on the Attendolo coat of arms.

Finally, it is noteworthy that the records also mention some red-painted coverings intended for mules employed as beasts of burden.[44]

To conclude this chapter on barding and *giornee*, used both as protective elements and as garments for the display of emblems, it is necessary to mention a significant passage by Cennino Cennini from 'Il libro dell'arte', written at the end of the fourteenth century. In the chapter '*Come dei lavorare coperte da cavalli, divise e giornee per torneamenti e per giostre*' (How to make horses blankets, devices, and *giornee* for tournaments and jousts), Cennini explains that the emblem or device should be painted onto a layer of carefully prepared wool paper, which was then applied or sewn onto *giornee* and horse coverings. However, Cennini specifies that these *giornee* and coverings were intended for use in tournaments or jousts and makes no reference to their employment in battle.[45]

10. Milanese helmet by Piero della Francesca. (Public domain)

43 Viviano, 'Registri della compagnia,' libro 3574 f. 86r.

44 Viviano, 'Registri della compagnia,' libro 3356 ff. 20r and 47v.

45 Cennino Cennini (Franco Brunello ed.), *Il libro dell'arte* (Vicenza: Neri Pozza, 1982), p.176.

Undated list of plumes for the captains of Micheletto's *condotta*, preserved in envelope 3604:

Olivo 50 white, 5 blue and 5 red feathers; 60 feathers in total

Aniballe Bentivoglio 12 blue and 12 white feathers, 24 feathers

Fraruffino 8 white, 8 red, 8 green and 1 light blue feathers; 25 feathers

Ruggeri Picinino10 white and 10 red feathers; 20 feathers

Feathers in the livery colours: 200

Torso has 20 feathers: 20 half white and half red feathers

Bosio Sforza 40 feathers: 14 red, 13 white, 13 blue for a total of 40 feathers

Marchetto, 16 feathers: 16 white feathers

Tartaglia d'Arezzo, feathers: 8 white, 8 black, 8 green, for a total of 24

Iacomo dalla [?]. 26 white feathers

Beatasilo, Marchetto's man-at-arms, has 25 feathers

17 white, 3 green and 5 red, for a total of 25

The Infantry

From the beginning until approximately the middle of the fifteenth century, the infantry of the companies of fortune was divided into three main categories: long-spearmen, shield or pavise-bearers, and crossbowmen. In the *condotta* stipulated made during this period by the Republic of Florence and preserved in the State Archives under the series called the *Dieci di Balìa* – the enrolled infantrymen are consistently divided into these three categories, usually in equal numbers. For example, in December 1439, the city hired the Constable Lorenzo di Giovanni da Pisa with a force of 120 infantrymen, specifically 40 crossbowmen, 40 soldiers armed with long spears, and 40 pavise-bearers.[46]

A similar tripartite division is also found in the documents of the Republic of Siena concerning the enlistment of Francesco Piccinino's *condotta* consisting of 449 horses and 90 infantrymen for the campaign of 1432, which culminated in the Battle of San Romano. In the Engagement Register, the infantry led by Constable Giovanni Giacomo da Roma is divided into three specialties, although not in equal numbers. 31 men are armed with spears; 30 are 'shooters', subdivided into 22 armed with large

46 Archivi di Stato di Firenze, 'Dieci di Balìa, Deliberazioni condotte e stanziamenti,' lib. 18, f. 33r.

11. The Battle of Anghiari by Leonardo da Vinci (detail). (With permission from the Museo Arqueologico de Madrid)

crossbows, four with small crossbows, and four archers; 18 are shield-bearing infantrymen, 14 equipped with *targoni* and four with *rotelle*. The remaining men consist of four subordinate captains serving under the constable, four infantrymen armed with brown bills (usually designated as corporals), and four *paghe* (unclassified infantrymen).[47] The recording of specialties within this *Biccherna* is particularly detailed, reflecting the precision of the Sienese enrolling accountants.

Andrea da Mosto, in his study on the soldiers of the Papal State around 1456, describes infantry employed before the middle of the century as: spearmen armed with long or short spears, crossbowmen equipped with simple or windlass-spanned crossbows, archers, pikemen, bearers of *rotelle* or *targhe*, and gunners.[48]

By contrast, the *Nuove disposizioni* (New Provisions) of the Venetian Republic's pay bank of 1434 provide an exceptionally detailed description of the vast array of armament owned by these infantrymen. The text reads:

> Infantrymen must be armed in the following manner.
>
> Constables must possess a breastplate, sallet, vambraces, *armisias* [leg defences], sword, guisarme, axe or *glavarina*, and a *targone*.
>
> Corporals must have the aforementioned weapons and must not employ boys under the age of fourteen to carry a *targone*.
>
> Infantrymen with only one *famiglio* must have at least a sallet, right vambrace, sword, greaves, and targone, and must carry a spear which they may pass to the familiar when handing him their *targone*.
>
> Infantrymen with more than one *famiglio* must be armed in the aforementioned manner, holding the spear and passing it to the *famiglio* who bears the *targone*.[49]

47 Archivi di Stato di Siena, Biccherna 261, 1432, 'Ruolo della compagnia di Francesco di Niccolò Piccinino,' ff. 77–87.

48 Andrea da Mosto, 'Ordinamenti militari delle soldatesche dello Stato Romano dal 1430 al 1470' in *Quellen und Forschungen aus italienischen Archiven und Bibliotheken*, 1902, V, p.21.

49 'Nuove disposizioni del banco degli stipendiari del 1434,' Archivi di Stato di Venezia, Commemoriali, reg. XII, ff. 136–139.

12. Long spears from 'Hesperis'. (Artwork by the author)

13. Long spears and *palvesari* from 'Hesperis'. (Artwork by the author)

Beyond the more familiar defensive equipment – such as breastplates, sallets, and shields – the infantry also used vambraces (sometimes only one) and *armisias* – which were thigh defences. These forms of protection are depicted in contemporary images, notably in Paolo Uccello's *Battle of San Romano*, painted around 1440 and in Gentile da Fabriano's *Adoration of the Magi*.

Infantrymen also wore greaves, and their use was widespread and not limited to *palvesari* (pavise-bearers), as evidenced by numerous contemporary iconographies, and their use continued throughout the fifteenth century into the early sixteenth century. Representations of greaves can be seen on the two chests depicting the Battle of Anghiari, preserved in the National Gallery of Ireland in Dublin and in the Archaeological Museum of Madrid (see image of a detail of the Madrid Chest), as well as in Pesellino's chest depicting *David and Goliath*, held at the National Gallery in London. They also appear in the miniatures of the 'Hesperis' and in the works of Biagio di Antonio, Antonello da Messina, Pinturicchio, and others.

As offensive weapons, the brown bill appears frequently, particularly associated with constables or corporals, and is visible in the works of Paolo Uccello, Piero della Fancesca, and many other contemporary iconographies. Another offensive weapon, now little known, was the *glavarina*, also called *chiavarina* or *lanzotto*, a throwing weapon similar to a javelin.

The primary role of infantry was defensive. In battle, spearmen, together with pavise-bearers, formed a protective wall behind which the cavalry could regroup and reorganise. Infantrymen were also essential in the defence, siege, and assault of fortified places.

The fighting style of the Italian infantry is well illustrated in the miniatures of the 'Hesperis', a Latin poem by Basinio da Parma recounting the wars waged by Sigismondo Malatesta on behalf of Florence against Alfonso of Aragon between 1448 and 1453. Most of these illuminations depict the Aragonese Siege of Piombino in 1448 and its subsequent liberation by Malatesta.[50]

Combat between infantry units is especially revealing. The miniatures show soldiers armed with long spears occupying the front ranks, directly facing their opponents. In these images, the infantry is shown without armour, wearing only doublets, hose, and hats. In the Anghiari chest and other iconography of the time, however, infantrymen are depicted with at least a sallet for protection. Their spears were approximately 4 metres long, and in the 'Hesperis' miniatures, these infantrymen outnumber other types of soldier (see image 12). Behind and among them appear the pavise-bearers armed with spears, as well as infantry equipped with small shields and one, or more often two, javelins acting in a supporting role. The pavise-bearers carry oval shield protecting them from neck to knee and wear open

50 Basinio da Parma, 'Hesperis', three preserved illuminated works: Paris, Bibliothèque de l'Arsenal, 630; Bodleian Library, Ms. Canon. Class. Lat. 81; Biblioteca Apostolica Vaticana, Vat. Lat. 6043

sallets, as seen in Paolo Uccello's panels. They wear greaves only on the right leg, and their spears are shorter, sometimes taking the form of partisans (see image 13).

The other infantrymen, known as javelinmen (*lanciotti*), are shown advancing, running, and lowering, often in the front line, preparing to throw the javelin – *lanciotto* or *chiavarina* – while protected by a small shield.[51] These shields are rectangular, though some, known as *rotelle*, are round. Alongside the *lanciotti* are the *famigli*, young boys who assisted infantrymen in much the same way as a page assisted a knight, by carrying reserve spears. One such boy is clearly depicted in an illumination: smaller than the others, armed with a knife at his waist, he waits tensely, his expression betraying a hint of fear (see image 14).

14. *Lanciotto* with *famiglio*, young boys, from 'Hesperis'. (Artwork by the author)

Behind the infantry, and sometimes intermingled with them, are crossbowmen, 'shooters', and even archers, all depicted while loading their weapon or aiming at the enemy. Crossbowmen are shown using a belt hook-spanned crossbow. The crossbowman engaged the spanning mechanism into the rope, placed his foot in the bracket, and straightened his body to draw the prod (see image 15). Notably absent in all these miniatures are polearms such as brown bills or spetums, which are nevertheless attested for Italian infantry in several images of the time.

Infantry formations appear neither compact nor orderly in these representations. Behind the spearmen there is a dense crowd of shield-bearers,

51 Mario Troso, *Alla ricerca del dardo mistero e fascino di un'antica arma da lancio* (Mariano del Friuli: Edizioni della Laguna, 2014), p.21.

15. Crossbowmen from 'Hesperis'. (Artwork by the author)

crossbowmen, *lanciotti,* and others, seemingly without rigid order. In practice, however, each soldier performed a specific role according to his weapon. It is important to note that these images depict combat between infantry factions; the apparent lack of compact formation was likely intended to avoid presenting easy targets to enemy missile troops.

Against cavalry, by contrast, infantrymen closed ranks tightly, forming a barrier of shields and long spears. The same tactic was employed during assaults on the fortifications, where shield-bearers formed a protective wall behind which crossbowmen and handgunners fired at defenders positioned high on the battlements, while other infantrymen and cavalry prepared ladders for the assault (see image 16 assault). Siege warfare was therefore a specialised and central task of the infantry, both in offence and defence. This is further confirmed by the *condotta* contracts stipulated by the Republic of Florence – known as *Dieci di Balìa* – prior to the Battle of Anghiari.[52] Among the forces hired by the Republic during this period, infantrymen outnumbered cavalrymen. For example, between September 1439 and April 1440, contracts were stipulated or renewed for approximately 5,525 infantrymen, compared with about 2,139 cavalrymen. This imbalance reflects Florence's need to secure its territory from the threat posed by Piccinino's army, garrisoning border fortresses and castles with infantry, especially crossbowmen.

Hand Cannon

It is necessary to consider handgunners separately.

The hand cannon can be traced back to the late thirteenth century and, during the following century, was sporadically used in warfare, primarily by infantry during sieges. It was only in the fifteenth century that this primitive firearm became firmly established on the battlefield.

The hand cannon consisted of an iron, brass or bronze barrel mounted on a wooden handle. The powder charge and the projectile were rammed to the bottom of the barrel using a wooden rod. A small quantity of priming powder was then poured into the chamber positioned above the breech and ignited manually. During the second half of the fifteenth century, manual ignition was progressively replaced by the serpentine mechanism.[53]

52 'Dieci di Balìa, Deliberazioni condotte e stanziamenti,' Archivi di Stato di Firenze, lib. 18.

53 A. Angelucci, *Gli schioppettieri milanesi nel XV secolo* (Milan: S. Radegonda,1865), pp.35–36.

16. An assault on a fortress from 'Hesperis'. (Artwork by the author)

The hand cannon was difficult to operate effectively in combat, and for this reason handgunners were regarded as specialist. Around 1440, groups of expert 'shooters' began to appear in Italy.

A significant example is provided by the records of Micheletto Attendolo's company concerning the *condotta* under Francesco Sforza between 1439 and 1441. In May 1440, Micheletto hired 12 handgunners commanded by a certain Giovanni Colonna, described as constable of 'our handgunners'.[54] These men are recorded individually rather than collectively like the rest of the infantry or cavalry, whose numbers are usually given without names. Each handgunner is listed by name, weapon, and place of origin, following the same documentary practice reserved for captains of *condotta*. This treatment highlights the importance attributed to handgunners at the time. Furthermore, they are designated by the term 'our', indicating that they served directly under their *condottiero* and therefore most likely wore his colours – that is, Attendolo's colours – on their hose.

Their geographical origin is particularly noteworthy. Of the 12 handgunners, nine were Germans, two were Istrians from the city of Koper, and only one – Arigho Nero – has no recorded place of origin. Michael

54 F. Viviano, 'Registri della compagnia di Micheletto Attendolo,' in 'Fraternita dei Laici di Arezzo', book 3574, ff. 128r–133v, 137r.

Mallett notes that during this period many Germans were employed as handgunners in Italian armies, while emphasising that this military specialty was not exclusive to them.[55]

In battle, handgunners were typically deployed at the outset of an engagement, either to provoke the clash, disrupt enemy formations, or support cavalry charges. The destructive impact of bullets was terrifying even to mounted men, whose armour frequently proved inadequate against firearms.

Among notable casualties inflicted by handgunners were Leone Sforza, mortally wounded during the siege of Caravaggio in 1440, Luigi dal Verme, who died from the effects of a gunshot wound in 1449, Gentile da Leonessa, killed by wounds sustained at the Siege of Manerbio in 1453, and Rodolfo Gonzaga, shot at the Battle of Fornovo in 1495.

Feared and deeply resented, handgunners were usually denied quarter when captured. This occurred, for example, after the Battle of San Giorgio di Piano in August 1443, when Milanese handgunners taken prisoners were executed by the Bolognese forces of Annibale I Bentivoglio. The 'Cronica di Bologna' records the event thus: '*Furono presi de' nemici 236 uomini d'arme di riputazione, e undici Capi di squadra, due mila cavalli, e il Carriaggio del Conte, come quello di tutto il campo; e tutti gli schioppettieri, che furon presi, furono morti*' (The enemy lost 236 men-at-arms of repute, 11 squadron commanders, 2,000 horses, and the baggage train of the Count,[56] as well as that of the entire camp; and all captured handgunners were killed).[57]

Both iconographic and documentary sources indicate that the protective equipment of handgunners was minimal. At most, they wore a sallet and, if they could afford it, a breastplate. Otherwise, their attire consisted of ordinary contemporary clothing: hat, shirt, doublet, and hose. The hose was often decorated in the livery colours of the commander or the colours of their city.

---

55 Michael Mallett, *Signori e mercenari* (Bologna: Il Mulino, 1983), p.162; *L'Organizzazione militare di Venezia nel '400*, Jouvence 1989, p.107.

56 Count Luigi dal Verme, commander of the Milanese forces.

57 'Cronica di Bologna' in *Muratori Rerum Italicarum Scriptores* XVI II, 672.

4

The Battle of Anghiari in Art

Few battles of the fifteenth century have been celebrated in literature and painting as extensively as the Battle of Anghiari. The reasons undoubtedly lie in the strategic significance of the Florentine victory: from that moment onward, the 'City of the Lily' definitively freed itself from the Milanese (Visconti) influence in Tuscany, which had persisted since 1390.

In literary sources, numerous poems and short compositions glorify the military achievement, such as *La Fuga del Capitano* and *La rotta del Piccinino*,[1] while in painting the battle was frequently represented on wedding chests.

Domestic furnishings at the time were few and essential: beds, tables, chests, folding chairs, and stools. Wardrobes did not yet exist as independent pieces of furniture and were instead created from recesses and protrusions within the structure of the house walls. Folded garments were therefore stored in chests, which constituted the principal item of household furniture.

Among wealthier families, chests were lavishly decorated with painted panels or carved ornamentations crafted by the finest artistic or artisanal workshops of the time. Their painted panels typically featured mythological subjects, festive scenes, tournaments, or romantic scenes; nevertheless, episodes drawn from contemporary military history were not uncommon, as in the case of the Battle of Anghiari. A wedding chest, used to contain the bride's dowry, was customarily adorned with the coats of arms of the two spouses on its lateral panels, as will be discussed further below.

At present, three pictorial representations of the battle are known: one preserved at the National Gallery of Ireland in Dublin, one at the Archaeological Museum in Madrid, and a third in the Bryce Collection in London.[2]

---

1 See 'La Fuga del Capitano' in A. Fabretti, *Note e documenti da biografie dei Capitani Venturieri dell'Umbria*, vol. Unico (Montepulciano: Angiolo Tumi, 1842), pp.249–276; Angelo Ascani, 'La rotta di Niccolò Piccinino' in Angelo Ascani, *Anghiari dalle origini all'anno 1440* (Città di Castello: Città di Castello, 1973), pp.286–293.

2 The Battle of Anghiari at the National Gallery in Dublin is dated to around 1460.

The Dublin panel (cat. N 778) is undoubtedly the best preserved representation, and also the most accurate from a historical standpoint. It decorates the front panel of a chest measuring 0.61cm x 205cm (see Plate I). The painting narrates the events of the engagement with a level of detail comparable to that of a contemporary chronicler. On the left is the city of Borgo Sansepolcro, depicted with its two gates, one of which bears the Visconti *biscione*; indeed, since 1438, the Biturgians (inhabitants of Borgo) had been loyal allies of Milan.[3] Nearby is shown the initial deployment of Piccinino's troops, while slightly below appear the Milanese forces at two successive moments of the battle: first massed before the bridge over the Tiber, and later in disordered retreat.

On the right hand side of the composition is the town of Anghiari, identifiable by the Florentine lily displayed above its gate. The victorious troops of the League are shown entering the city, leading prisoners and carrying captured enemy flags. At the bottom of the scene, the initial formation of the League is represented, with the captains arrayed before the so-called Ponte delle Forche, a stone bridge at the foot of the hill of Anghiari, spanning a narrow, steep banked stream.[4]

The central section of the panel depicts the final and decisive clash: a chaos of men and horses set against the backdrop of Città di Castello. Contemporary chronicles report that until this point the fighting had taken place on the Ponte delle Forche or on the slopes of the hill of Anghiari; in the final phase, however, the Milanese, were driven back onto the plain between the two bridges and attempted a last assault in an effort to reverse the outcome. The painting thus shows the allied forces of Florence and the Papacy, now victorious, seizing the enemy flags.

As already noted, the painting is in a good state of preservation. Aside from a general yellowing probably due to the ageing of protective varnishes, the colours, however, remain vivid with the exception of certain hues that have darkened to black, particularly on many emblems and imprese.

In heraldry, the colour black (sable) was traditionally used sparingly, except in cases such as the black and silver (white) carving of the Capponi family. This coat of arms appears in the painting, quartered with other emblems on a shield (image 75), which are examined in detail below.

With the exception of this original use of black, the darkened colours visible elsewhere are the result of chromatic alteration: pigments originally blue or green – both notoriously unstable – have oxidised and darkened over time. A clear example is provided by the barry wavy of the Attendolo-Sforza. This impresa is visible on the shield shown in image 75 and again in image 38, among the League's flags, quartered with quinces, the emblem of the Attendolo di Cotignola. It is well established that the waves was

3 Lorenzo Coleschi *Storia della città di Sansepolcro* (Atessa: Spalding, 1982), p.77.

4 Capponi, 'Commentari', p.1195; Giovanni Simonetta, 'Rerum gestarum Francisci Sfortiae' in *Muratori R.I.S.* XXI p.293.

originally blue and silver, but here the blue has turned to black.[5] The same oxidation on the blue wavy of the Attendolo-Sforza can be observed in numerous contemporary paintings, most notably in the flag of Micheletto Attendolo in Paolo Uccello's *Battle of San Romano*, now in the Louvre in Paris (see Plate N). In that work, one may also observe the alteration of green pigments in the background foliage, which – apart from the fruits – have darkened markedly.[6] This pictorial phenomenon recurs in all the panel paintings examined below.

The artist of the Dublin panel remains unknown. Some scholars, including Schubring and Weisbach, and more recently Hughes, have attributed it to the so-called Master of Anghiari, while others, such as Polcri and Scalini, consider it a product of the workshop of Apollonio di Giovanni.[7]

Turning to the second painting of the Battle of Anghiari, preserved in the Archaeological Museum of Madrid (inv. no. 51936) (see Plate L). This panel is less well preserved than the Dublin example. Polcri, who first published a study on this work, noted numerous similarities between it and the third, now lost chest from the Bryce Collection in London (Plate M).[8] In both cases, the setting of the battlefield is identical: Borgo Sansepolcro on the left, with the Visconti standard on its walls, and Anghiari on the right marked by the lily flag. In the background is Città di Castello, while in the foreground there is only one bridge – the Ponte delle Forche – unlike the Dublin Chest, which also includes the bridge over the Tiber. On the Bryce Chest, the battle is shown at its climax, with the Milanese engaging the League's cavalry immediately beyond the bridge, on the slopes of the hill of Anghiari. In the Madrid panel, on the other hand, the fighting has already ended: on the left the defeated Milanese flee, while in the centre and on the

5 Sforza's coats of arms and imprese: G. Cambin, *Le rotell Milanesi Giornico, 1478* (Farvagny, Vétroz, and Bern: Società Svizzera di Araldica, 1987), pp.122–123 & 208–218; Canterina Santoro, *Gli Sforza* (Milano: Dall'Oglio 1968), pp.405–406; Pompeo Litta, *Famiglie celebri italiane* (Milano: Luciano Basadonna, *c.*1869), vol.16.

6 This pictorial similarity has been observed by: Cambin, *Le rotelle milanesi*, p.279; L. G. Boccia, 'Le armature di Paolo Uccello' in *L'Arte*, III 1970, p.77; M. Scalini, 'Divise e livree, araldica quotidiana' in 'Leoni vermigli e candidi liocorni, Comune di Prato' in *Quaderni* 1, 1992, p.54:

7 Paul Schubring, Paul, *Cassoni: Truhen und Truhenbilder der italienischen Früh-Renaissance. Ein Beitrag zur profanmalerei im Quattrocento* (Leipzig: K.W. Hiersemann,1923), p.243; W. Weisbach, 'Eine darstellung der letzten deutschen Kaiserkronung' in *Rom, Zeitschrift fur bildende kunst*, XXIV, 1912/13, pp.261–262; Graham Hughes, *Renaissance Cassoni* (London: Art Books International, 1997), pp.104–105; F. Polcri, 'La battaglia di Anghiari dipinta sui pannelli di tre cassoni preleonardeschi' in *Pagine Altotiberine* 13; M. Scalini, 'Divise e livree', p.61.

8 F. Polcri, *La battaglia di Anghiari*, pp.136–138; There is only one reproduction of the Bryce Collection chest in Schubring, Paul, *Cassoni: Truhen und Truhenbilder der italienischen Früh-Renaissance. Ein Beitrag zur profanmalerei im Quattrocento* (Leipzig: K.W. Hiersemann,1923), pp.106–107.

right, the victorious Florentines advance towards Anghiari, dragging the captured enemy flags along the ground.

The composition, architecture, flags, and weaponry are similar in the two works, suggesting that they were produced within the same workshop, which Polcri again identifies as that of Apollonio. The execution of the Madrid panel, however, can be dated with relative certainty thanks to its patrons, whose coats of arms appear painted in the central pillars of the chest's front (see image 17). As was customary in the fifteenth century, these arms identified the two spouses for who's wedding the chest was commissioned.

The coat of arms on the left – gules, a griffin or – belongs to the Florentine Martelli family,[9] while that on the right is the arms of the Noceto family of Lucca: or an uprooted walnut vert impaling bendy argent and gules.[10] In the second half of the fifteenth century, two young members of the Martelli family married young women of the Noceto family, as recorded by Litta in volume 21 of *Famiglie Italiane*. In Plate II, Litta mentions Niccolò Martelli, son of Antonio, who married Angela, daughter of Piero of the Lords of Noceto (without specifying the date). In Table III, he records another Niccolò Martelli, son of Ugolino, who in 1458 married Ginevra, also daughter of Piero of the Lords of Noceto. Research in the State Archives of Florence has yielded a manuscript giving the date of the first marriage: 'Niccolò, born in 1444 .... married Agnola, daughter of Piero of the Counts of Noceto, 1466.'[11]

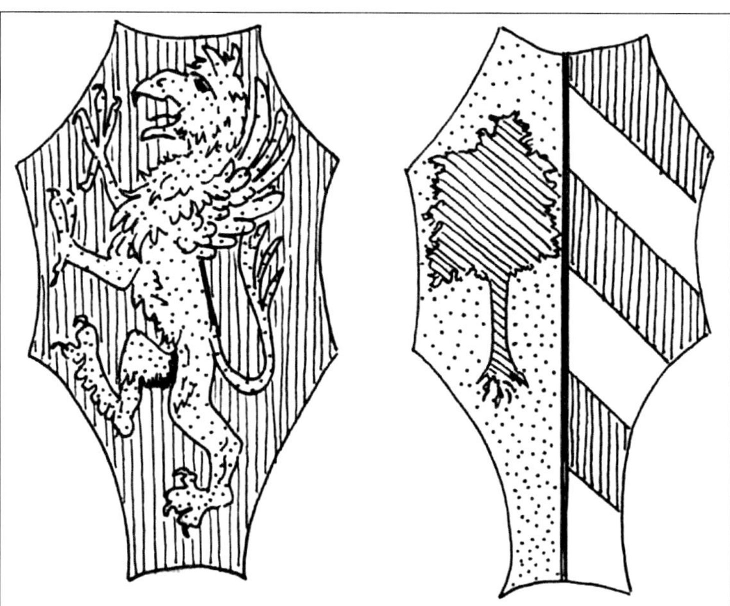

17. Martelli and Noceto family coats of arms. (Artwork by the author)

9 Pompeo Litta, *Famiglie celebri italiane* (Milano: Luciano Basadonna, *c.*1869), vol.21, tav.I.

10 Guelfo Guelfi Camajani, *Dizionario araldico* (Milano: Ulrico Hoepli, 1921), p.449.

11 ASFi, Manoscritti, 397, ins.26, f. 87r.

It is therefore plausible that the Madrid Chest – most likely together with the Bryce example – was painted and presented as a wedding gift to one of these two couples, either in 1458 or in 1466.

Another representation of the battle, executed with tempera on wood, is preserved in the chapel of the sacristy of Santa Maria del Carmine in Florence. This work, a predella panel of the Florentine school from the second half of the fifteenth century and formerly attributed to Pesellino, is entitled *Giovanni Dazzi, the apparition of Saint Andrew Corsini and the Battle of Anghiari* (see image 18). From the perspective of military heraldry, the painting is of limited value, as the cavalrymen bear few identifiable emblems, apart from three banners: the Florentine lily, the Church's keys, and the Visconti *biscione*. To this author, the remaining symbols on caparisons and shields appear imaginary. Nevertheless, the predella illustrates the Florentine victory as divinely assisted by Saint Corsini.

According to the narrative depicted, the saint appears to Giovanni Dazzi, one of the *Dieci di Balìa*, who in 1440 had gone to Corsini's tomb to seek counsel against the Milanese threat. The saint urges an attack on the Milanese Army on the feast of Saints Peter and Paul. Dazzi fails to relay the message to the *Dieci,* and is struck by illness as punishment; after praying, he recovers and this time delivers the vision to the Florentines who do not believe him and imprison him. Despite this, the *Dieci* dispatched an expedition against Piccinino, and on 29 June the Florentine army, guided by Saint Andrew, defeated the Milanese.[12]

18. Giovanni Dazzi, the apparition of Saint Andrew Corsini and the Battle of Anghiari. (Artwork by the author)

12 Elio Conti et al, *La civiltà fiorentina nel quattrocento* (Firenze: Vallechi Editore, 1993), p.280; Mario Carniani, *Santa Maria del Carmine* (Firenze: Becocci,

More recently, further hypotheses have been advanced concerning additional pictorial representations of the battle. Among these, the most intriguing involves none other than the most renowned battle painter, Paolo Uccello. In his celebrated triptych of the *Battle of San Romano*, several scholars have noted significant differences between the two panels now in Florence and London and the third preserved in Paris, suggesting that the latter may in fact represents the Battle of Anghiari (see Plate N).

In a study published in 1970, Boccia observes that the Paris panel differs from the other two in its superior state of preservation, the larger scale of figures, and the distinctive details of the horses.[13] The horse harnesses in the Paris panel are more elaborate and consistently include a crupper, absent in the other two. The bits are thinner and straighter, and the reins simpler, whereas in the Florence and London panels the bits are heavy and curved, and the bridles double, with broad and richly decorated false reins. Moreover, the armour worn by the cavalry in the Florence and London panels can be dated to between 1435 and 1440, while that depicted in the Paris panel appears later, around 1450.

Pietro Roccasecca, in his studies, has proposed that the Florence and London paintings were executed around 1436, while the Paris panel, depicting Micheletto da Cotignola, dates to 1451 – after the *condottiero*'s death.[14] Roccasecca further emphasises not only the difference in proportions between them but also divergences in execution, perspective, and, above all, heraldry. In the Paris panel, all identifying symbols, such as flags or the colours of the infantrymen's hose, can be traced to Attendolo livery, whereas in the other two panels the heraldry is more varied and often associated with Niccolò da Tolentino.[15]

Roccasecca also identifies in the Paris painting two possible imprese of the Bartolini Salimbeni family: the 'withering poppies' on the hat of a trumpeter in the centre of the scene, and the 'halved almonds' bordering two infantry shield, reminiscent of the gold lozenges on a red field in the Salimbeni arms. Originally a prominent Sienese lineage, a branch of the family settled in Florence in the early fourteenth century, adopting the name Bartolini Salimbeni. Through these imprese, Roccasecca supports recent publications suggesting that the three panels were commissioned not by the Medici, as has long been believed, but by the Bartolini Salimbeni, from whom Lorenzo the Magnificent later seized them by force. On this basis, he proposes alternative titles: *The Rout at San Romano* for the London and Florence panels, and *The Rout of Niccolò Piccinino* for the Paris panel, which

---

*c.*1990),pp.81–82.

13 L. G. Boccia, 'Le armature di Paolo Uccello' in *L'Arte*, III 1970, pp.68 and 79.

14 P. Roccasecca, *Paolo Uccello e le battaglie* (Milano: Electa, 1997), pp.9 &14–21.

15 P. Roccasecca, 'La rotta di San Romano e la rotta di Niccolò Piccinino,' *Bulletin de L'Ahai* 2005, pp.11 & 13.

he considers 'nothing more than another way of referring to the celebrated Battle of Anghiari.'[16]

Petra Pertici has furthered questioned why Micheletto appears twice: once in the London panel, to the right of Niccolò da Tolentino, identifiable by the *giornea* bearing the Attendolo arms and a second time in the Paris panel, entitled *Il Micheletto da Cotignola*.[17] Attendolo played only a secondary role in San Romano and such representation seems excessive unless the Paris panel was executed later, perhaps to commemorate and glorify the Battle of Anghiari, in which Micheletto played a decisive role.

Finally, one of the most interesting theories concerns the identification of the Battle of Anghiari with a fresco by Piero della Francesca.[18] This is the episode of the *Victory of Constantine over Maxentius* from the cycle of the *Legend of the True Cross* (*c.* 1452–1466) in the church of San Francesco in

19. The Battle of Ponte Milvio. (Artwork by the author)

16 Roccasecca, 'La rotta di San Romano,' pp.12–17.

17 Petra Pertici, 'Condottieri senesi e la rotta di San Romano di Paolo Uccello' in *Arch. Stor. Ital.* 1999, issue 581, pp.548–549.

18 Guglielmo Maetzke, 'Armi e armature' in *Piero della Francesca* (Milano: Silvana Editoriale, 1998), p.127; Fabrizio Fabbrini, *Piero della Francesca e i suoi tempi* (Arezzo: Alberti & C., 2006), pp.99–100; Oreste del Buono, *L 'opera completa di Piero della Francesca* (Milano: Rizzoli Ed., 1967), p.95; Giuseppe Centauro, *Piero della Francesca committenza e pittura* (Poggibonsi: Lalli ed. 2000), p.173; Marco della Ratta, *La storia e la croce* (Fiorentina: Società Editrice Fiorentina, 2005), p.42.

Arezzo (see image 19), also known as *The Battle of Ponte Milvio.* The fresco depicts Emperor Constantine leading his army as the forces of Maxentius flee across the Tiber, defeated by the mere presence of a small cross. The scene lacks actual fighting or death and resembles a victorious parade more than a battle. Many critics have noted that the landscape does not correspond to the Tiber near Rome, but rather to the plain between Anghiari and Borgo Sansepolcro. The river bends, houses, and mill may reflect places familiar to Piero from childhood, as he was born in Borgo Sansepolcro and signed his works 'Petri de Burgo'. In this interpretation, Maxentius does not drown in the Tiber but instead assumes the features of Piccinino, retreating to the left back of the river to seek refuge within the walls of Borgo Sansepolcro. A red flag bearing a green dragon may allude to the Visconti *biscione*, while the armour, except for the helmets – predominantly fifteenth century in style, though mixed with pseudo-Roman elements – has been dated to around 1455.

On this point, Guglielmo Maetzke observes that the helmets depicted by Piero della Francesca:

> ... appear to lack a front and feature a Milanese-style visor, in which the sight is cut directly into the visor itself, rather than formed by the space between the lower edge of the front and the upper edge of the visor, as in the Florentine style – a type that replaced the former towards the end of the first half of the fifteenth century.

He further notes their resemblance to helmets painted by Pisanello in the fresco of the tournament at the Ducal Palace of Mantua, dated 1435.[19]

20. Battle of Heraclius against Khosrow. (Artwork by the author)

19 Guglielmo Maetzke, 'Armi e armature' in *Piero della Francesca* (Milano: Silvana Editoriale, 1998), pp.170–175.

Image 20 illustrates similar Milanese-style helmets from Piero's *Battle of Heraclius against Khosrow,* part of the same cycle of the *Legend of the True Cross*. This raises the question of how Piero came to depict helmets much older than the armour they accompany. Some scholars have suggested that he may have witnessed the Battle of Anghiari first hand, or that he stayed in Borgo Sansepolcro during the Milanese occupation between 1438 and 1440, using the opportunity to sketch such equipment for later use in his future frescoes.[20]

Indeed, Piero's artistic chronology reveals a documentary gap between 1439 and 1442. In September 1439, he is documented in Florence, mentioned in the payments to Domenico Veneziano as his collaborator for the frescoes in the choir of Sant' Egidio; thereafter, nothing is known until 1442, when he is recorded as eligible among the *consiglieri popolari* of Borgo Sansepolcro. He most likely continued working with Veneziano, though not until the completion of the cycle, as in 1441 his position as collaborator was taken over by Bicci di Lorenzo.[21]

20 Edgardi Ferri, *Piero della Francesca* (Sebreate: Mondadori 2001).

21 A. Paolucci & C. Bertelli (eds), *Piero della Francesca e le corti italiane* (Arezzo: Skira, 2007), pp.21–22 & 258.

5

Background to the Battle

Having failed to capture Brescia and having lost Verona, Niccolò Piccinino, with the consent of Duke Filippo Maria Visconti, sought to alter the strategic balance by opening a new front in Tuscany. This diversion had a clear intent: by invading central Italy, Piccinino hoped to draw Francesco Sforza away from Lombardy.

On 5 February 1440, the Bracceschi commander crossed the Po with 6,000 'horses' – a term commonly used in the chronicles to indicate 'cavalrymen'. He left the command of the Milanese forces in Lombardy to Gianfrancesco Gonzaga, Marquess of Mantua, assisted by Italiano del Friuli, Luigi di Sanseverino, and Luigi dal Verme. These captains were instructed to continue the encirclement of Brescia and to counter the Sforzeschi in the region of Riva del Garda and Verona, where Count Francesco Sforza was.[1]

Despite the winter conditions of snow and ice, Piccinino advanced rapidly southeast. After brief halts in Piacenza and Parma, he reached Bologna on 1 March. The exact size of his army is disputed. Neri di Gino Capponi and Francesco Viviano report 6,000 horses; Giovan Battista Poggio speaks of 5,000 cavalry and infantry combined; Angelo Pezzana suggests 4,000 horses plus 2,000 Malatesta troops; Nicola della Tuccia writes of 5,000 cavalry and 5,000 infantry.[2]

Meanwhile, Florence, alarmed by reports of a Milanese descent into Tuscany, dispatched the commissioners Giuliano Davanzati and Neri Capponi to Venice to negotiate military support with the doge from Francesco Sforza. When they reached Ferrara on 9 February, they learnt that Piccinino had already left Lombardy. The doge proved reluctant, and Neri

1 F. Biondo, *Historie* (Venezia 1547), p.121.

2 N. Capponi, 'Commentari' in *Muratori Rerum Italicarum Scriptores* XVIII, col. 1191; F. Viviano, *Registri della compagnia di Micheletto Attendolo*, in Fraternita dei Laici di Arezzo, book 3574, flyleaf; Giovan Battista Poggio, *Vita di Niccolò Piccinino* (Perugia: 1619), p.252; Angelo Pezzana, *Storia di Parma* (Parma: Dalla Ducale Tipografia,1842), II, p.426; Nicola della Tuccia, *Cronaca di Viterbo* (Firenze: G.P. Vieusseux, 1872), p.171.

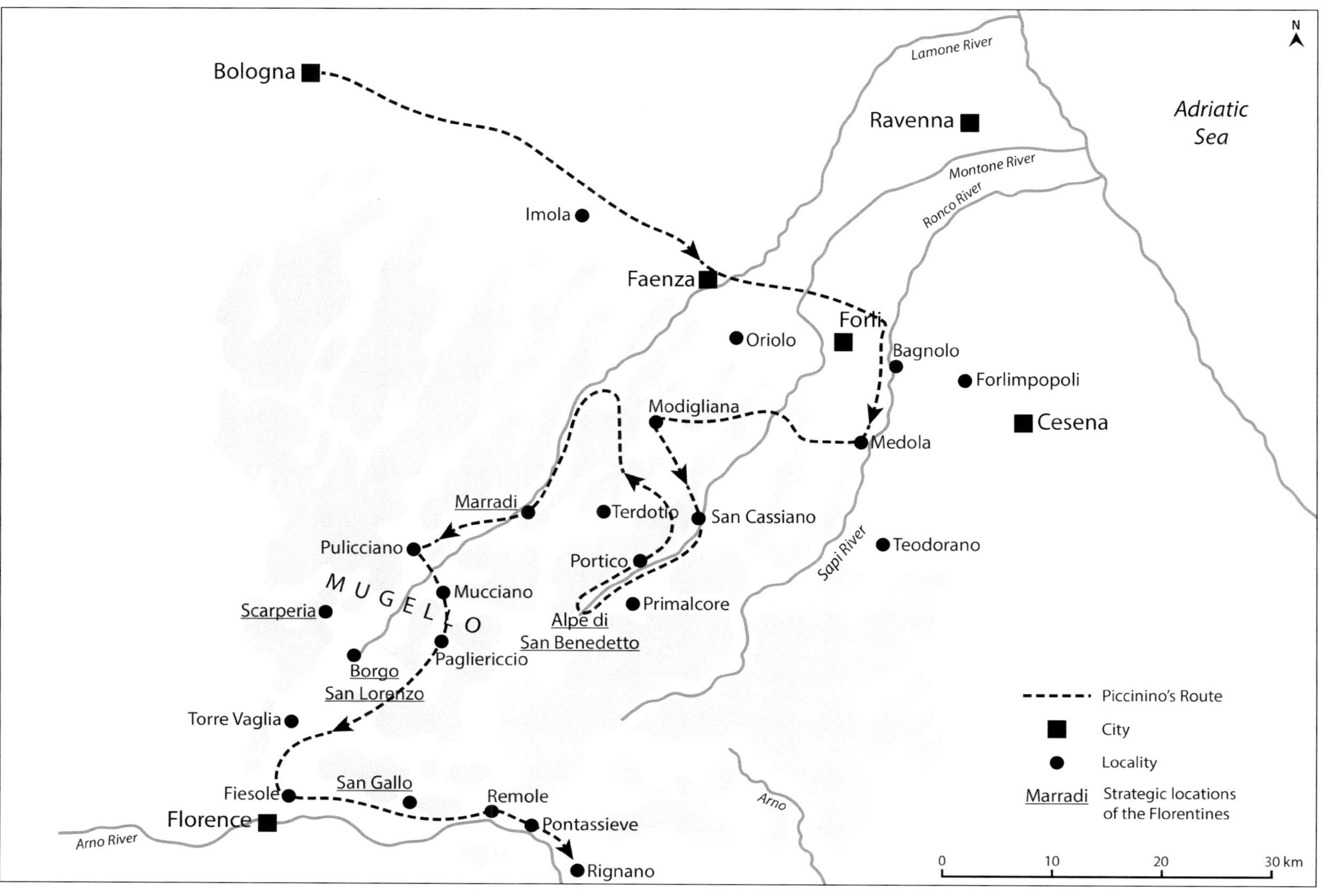

21. Piccinino's movements leading up to the battle.

therefore went to Verona to negotiate directly with Count Sforza. There, he met another Florentine envoy, Commissioner Bernadetto de' Medici.

On 1 March, Piccinino arrived in Bologna, where he collected 20,000 ducats from the citizens. He then moved on to Forlì and Cesena, territories controlled by Malatesta and allies of the League, and where Pier Giovanpaolo Orsini commanded a force of Florentine infantry.[3] Unable to cross the swollen Sapi River because of the thaw, Piccinino camped on 12 March at Medula, a possession of Malatesta Novello, and opened the siege of it.[4] After six days, he captured the town and then sacked several weak castles on the Apennines – including Teodorano in the district of Forlì, which he successfully captured.[5]

Given this unfavourable beginning for the League, on 18 March, the Malatesta brothers – Sigismondo Pandolfo, Lord of Rimini,[6] and Malatesta Novello, Lord of Cesena – reached an agreement with Piccinino to return the castles they had seized. The accord went further: having become allies of the Milanese, on 26 March, the Malatesta made peace with Guidantonio da Montefeltro, Count of Urbino – until then their bitter enemy but already aligned with Milan.[7] Sigismondo joined Piccinino, while Malatesta Novello remained to defend his territories. Deprived of their allies, the Florentines feared for the fate of their captain Pier Giovanpaolo Orsini, who was in Malatesta lands with a *condotta* of 400 lances and 200 infantrymen.[8]

Francesco Sforza, concerned about developments in Tuscany – particularly the risk of losing influence in the Marca – went to Venice to persuade the doge to allow him to march south and oppose Piccinino. Doge Francesco Foscari refused, arguing that if Sforza crossed the Po, Lombardy would be endangered, and whoever prevailed in Lombardy would ultimately win the war – the doge persuaded him to remain.

A dramatic development came about on 19 March with the arrest of Giovanni Vitelleschi da Corneto, Patriarch of Alexandria, at the bridge of Castel Sant'Angelo. Vitelleschi was commissioner of the Church's Army of 4,000 horses and 2,000 infantry. A powerful military leader, he had restored papal authority in the States of the Church by subduing local rebellious lords that had been threatening the Papal States for years. However, he was suspected by the Florentine authorities of secret negotiations with Niccolò Piccinino – they had intercepted some letters between the two in Montefiascone. Acting on Pope Eugene's orders, Antonio Rido da Padova,

3 Capponi, 'Commentari', 1191; Biondo, *Historie*, p.121.

4 The Sapi River mentioned by Biondo is today's Bidente.

5 Lorenzo Spirito Gualtieri, *L'Altro Marte*, (Venezia: Leonardus Achates, 1489), cap. 58; 'Cronache Malatestiane dei secoli XIV e XV', in *Muratori Rerum Italicarum Scripores* XV col. 937.

6 Pandolfo is said to have had a condotta of 200 lances, cf Capponi, 'Commentari', 1192.

7 'Cronache Malatestiane dei secoli XIV e XV', col. 937; Anon., 'Diario del Graziani' in *Arch. Stor. Ital.* XVI 1, 1850, p.449; Gaspare Broglio Tartaglia (A. G. Lucani, ed.), *Cronaca Malatestiana del secolo XV* (Rimini: Bruno Ghigi, 1982), p.66.

8 Capponi, 'Commentari', 1192.

Castellan of Castel Sant'Angelo, arrested him by a stratagem. Vitelleschi died – or was killed – in prison on 2 April, much to the relief of the Florentines.[9]

Meanwhile, Piccinino, reinforced by Sigismondo Malatesta and Guidantonio Manfredi, prepared to cross the Apennines. Malatesta brought with him 800 horses and 400 infantry, though he returned to Rimini in May. Manfredi, Lord of Faenza and a seasoned captain of fortune, led approximately 500 horses and 300 infantry. Having long served Florence, he had recently entered Milanese employ; his brother Astorre was already in Piccinino's army.[10]

On 6 April, the Captain of Perugia took the area of Modigliana; there, the Milanese took prisoner the whole company and a constable of the Republic of Florence, Gregorio or Grigoro d'Anghiari, who had arrived with 300 *paghe* (a term used in accounting records to indicate infantrymen) to relieve the town.[11] At the same time, the Visconti commander seized other towns and castles: San Cassiano, Montevecchio, Portico, Mutiliana, Bagnolo, Terdotio, and Oriolo.[12] He then advanced towards Tuscany through the Montone Valley, attempting to cross the Apennines at the Alpe di San Benedetto. There he encountered Niccolò da Pisa, recently appointed captain of the infantry by Florence. According to Biondo, da Pisa repelled the Milanese and relieved the castle of Primalcore.[13]

Piccinino therefore went along the Lamone River, led by Florentine exiles who cleared the way from the snow to the Marradi Pass.[14] There, the general commissioner of the municipality of Florence Bartolomeo Orlandini was stationed. Shortly before the enemy's arrival, however, he abandoned his position and fled with his men. Giovanni Cavalcanti recounts this episode, describing Orlandini as '... *uomo molto valoroso contro i più deboli di lui, ma pavido contro i più forti*' (... brave only against those weaker than

9 Biondo, *Historie*, p.122; Capponi, 'Commentari', 1192-1193; Tuccia, *Cronaca di Viterbo*, pp.169–172; Giovanni Cavalcanti, *Istorie Fiorentine* (Fiorenze: all'insegna di Dante, 1839), vol. II, book XIV, ch. III.

10 D. Buoninsegni, *Storia della città di Firenze* (Florence: 1673), p.71; *Cronache Malatestiane*, col. 937; Giulio Cesare Tonduzzi, *Historie di Faenza* (Bologna: Forni 1967), 1675, pp.484 – 485. In the text, Guidantonio is said to have many more cavalrymen.

11 G. d'Anghiari, 'Memorie dall'anno 1437 al 1481', Bibl. Naz. Fir. Ms. II. II. 127, f. 38r; Arch. Stat. Fir. Dieci di Balìa, *Deliberazioni condotte e stanziamenti*, n. 18, f. 20r.

12 Visconti donated most of these places to Guidantonio Manfredi as a prize for having conquered them, cf. Tonduzzi, *Historie*, p.486; A. Messeri, *Faenza nella storia e nella arte*, 1909, p.154; Piero Zama, *I Manfredi signori di Faenza* (Faenza: Fratelli Lega, 1954), pp.179–180.

13 Niccolò Machiavelli, *Istorie Fiorentine* (Milan: Società Anonima Notari or Alpes, 1928), vol. 2, p.81; Scipione Ammirato, *Istorie Fiorentine* (Torino: Cugini Pomba e comp, 1853), vol. V, p.257; Biondo, *Historie*, p.123.

14 Poggio, *Vita di Piccinino*, p.252; Pier Candido Decembrio, 'Vita di Niccolò Piccinino' in *Muratori Rerum Italicarum Scriptores* XX, 1080, when the Milanese crossed the mountains and suffered deaths among men and horses due to the cold and snow.

himself, but fearful against those stronger). According to Palmieri's *Annali*, he commanded about 1,000 Mugello farmers. A small vanguard was sent to secure the pass, while Orlandini followed on horseback with the remainder. When the infantry vanguard reached the summit and saw the large number of enemy ascending the slopes, they ran back in alarm. Seeing them retreat and misunderstanding their cries, Orlandini assumed the pass had already fallen and ordered a general withdrawal. He shouted, '*Adoprate le gambe per più di ottime armadure; campate, perchè noi abbiamo alle coste i nemici*' (Use your legs rather than fine armour; save yourselves, for the enemy is upon our heels) and fled as far as the village of San Lorenzo. Cavalcanti concludes: '*... e così furono perdenti senza esser vinti*' (... and thus they were losers without being defeated).[15]

On 10 April, Piccinino arrived in Mugello and, as the chronicler records, ranged throughout the country raiding, taking prisoners, and allowing his soldiers, *saccomanni*,[16] and Astorre da Faenza, to rape many women.[17] In this regard, Cavalcanti adds: '*Ma bene era vero che da Astorre da Faenza, con tutte le miserie, erano cerche infino ne'luoghi nascosti e coperti: ma io credo, pittosto a dipregio di Comune che a speranza di preda il facesse*' (It was indeed true that Astorre da Faenza sought women everywhere, even in the most hidden and secluded places; yet I believe that he did so more out of contempt for the *Comune* (Florence) than to rape them).[18]

Meanwhile, another Milanese force under the command of Francesco Piccinino, Niccolò's son, was already stationed in Borgo Sansepolcro, a town on the border with Umbria near Anghiari. The city had rebelled against papal rule in June 1438 and had surrendered to the Milanese, who had entered it under Francesco Piccinino. From that moment onward, the Biturgians (inhabitants of Borgo Sansepolcro) remained loyal to Milan.

From Borgo Sansepolcro, mounted troops launched raids into Umbria.[19] According to Graziani's *Cronaca di Perugia*, on 12 April they entered the Perugian countryside with 1,000 horses and 1,000 infantrymen under various captains. Among them were the Perugians Giovanni di Sesto, Francesco di Ranieri, and Rodolfo Signorelli; also present were Federico da Montefeltro, son of count Guido; Lodovico Gonzaga, son of Gianfrancesco, Lord of Mantua, the son of Bernardino della Carda degli Ubaldini; and Tartaglia da Torsciano.[20]

---

15 M. Palmieri, 'Annales,' in *Muratori Rerum Italicarum Scripores Bologna* 1922, volume XXVI, appendix, p.147; Cavalcanti, *Istorie Fiorentine* Book XIII, Ch. II.

16 *Saccomanni*: soldiers in charge of services, the supply train and the looting in the armies of the period.

17 Buoninsegni, *Storia*, p.71.

18 Cavalcanti, *Istorie Fiorentine*, Book XIII, Ch. III.

19 Lorenzo Coleschi *Storia della città di Sansepolcro* (Atessa: Spalding, 1982), p.77; Tuccia, *Cronaca di Viterbo*, p.173; *Diario del Graziani*, p.451.

20 Alternatively, according to 'La Fuga del Capitano' in A. Fabretti, *Note e documenti da biografie dei Capitani Venturieri dell'Umbria*, vol. Unico (Montepulciano: Angiolo Tumi, 1842), p.82, the captains were Giovanni Scotti, Francesco Montelmini,

After encamping at Ponte San Giovanni, near Perugia, these units set out on 13 April to raid the territory of Cortona. They captured 150 prisoners and livestock and returned in the evening to Monte Cologna near Magione. The city of Perugia immediately dispatched ambassadors to protest against the depredations. The following day, the captains restored part of the booty, sending some back to Borgo Sansepolcro and the remainder to its place of origin.

Meanwhile, the Florentine commissioners led by Neri Capponi had reached an agreement with Venice and Francesco Sforza regarding military assistance. It was decided that Count Francesco would remain in Lombardy to continue the war on behalf of Venice, which paid him 81,000 florins. Capponi instead secured from Sforza 1,000 horses under the captains Troilo da Rossano, Pietro Torelli, and Niccolò da Pisa, who was already in the Apennines. With these forces, the Florentine commissioner crossed the Po towards Florence on 18 April.

The following day, 19 April, Pier Giovanpaolo Orsini arrived in Florence with a contingent of 600 horses. On 4 April, he had fled Forlimpopoli, evading enemy watch.[21]

Meanwhile, in Mugello, Piccinino had laid siege to Pulicciano, while his men captured Monte di Prete, Paglierriccio, Feriuolo, Monte Ritono, Mucciano, and Torre a Vaglia (all locations recorded by Cavalcanti). The *condottiero* then crossed the entire region towards the mountains of Fiesole and Ponte a Sieve, even crossing the Arno and advancing to within three miles from Florence.[22]

During these raids, Cavalcanti recounts a curious episode near Fiesole, where Madonna Giovanna, widow of Niccolò Pintore, lived, '*la quale era donna volubile e leggera d'intendimento e padrona di un piccolo podere*' (a fickle and light-minded woman who owned a small estate). She was persuaded – by whom is unknown – that her soul would be saved if she donated her property to the canons of Fiesole. Shortly thereafter she fell gravely ill. In the final days of her illness, the Milanese arrived to sack Fiesole. The inhabitants, warned by the ringing of the bells, fled in terror. Amid the confusion, Madonna Giovanna rose with what little strength she had, fled with the others, recovered from her illness, and lived for many years thereafter. Cavalcanti comments: '*Il dottore guarisce gli infermi e li vede, Niccolò invece guarì Madonna Giovanna senza vederla*' (The doctor heals the sick by seeing them; Niccolò instead healed Madonna Giovanna without seeing her).[23]

Ridolfo Signorelli, Tartaglia da Torgiano, and the sons of Count Guido, Berardino della Carda and the Marquess of Mantua.

21 Capponi, 'Commentari', 1193; Niccolò Machiavelli, *Istorie Fiorentine* (Milan: Società Anonima Notari or Alpes, 1928), vol. 2, p.80; Scipione Ammirato, *Istorie Fiorentine* (Torino: Cugini Pomba e comp, 1853), vol. V, p.259; *Cronache Malatestiane*, col. 937.

22 Capponi, 'Commentari', 1193; Machiavelli, *Istorie Fiorentine*, vol. 2, p.82; Ammirato, *Istorie Fiorentine* vol. IV p.259; Cavalcanti, *Istorie Fiorentine*, Book XIII; Ch. IV.

23 Cavalcanti, *Istorie Fiorentine*, Book XIII, Ch. V.

At that time, fear seized Florence. Armed guards were posted at the gates; citizens stood day and night with weapons in hand; and 100 cavalrymen were kept ready to escort Cosimo the Elder to safety if necessary. The newly arrived reinforcements were deployed: Pier Giovanpaolo at San Gallo; Niccolò da Pisa and Pietro Torelli at Borgo San Lorenzo; Agnolo d'Anghiari at Scarperia; and Troilo approaching from Modena with a Sforza company.[24] News arrived that Ludovico Scarampi, Patriarch of Aquileia, who had replaced Vitelleschi, was assembling papal forces to intervene, while Micheletto Attendolo had departed the Marche with the same intention.[25]

Meanwhile, the Milanese, while maintaining camp and the siege at Pulicciano, sent a contingent across the Arno near Remole, where they plundered and captured prisoners, including 120 *saccomanni* from the Florentines, and whom they brought within the walls of the town. Shortly thereafter, Neri Capponi and Pier Giovanpaolo with approximately 1,000 infantrymen and other foreign troops retook Remole and freed the *saccomanni*.[26]

Agnolo d'Anghiari also launched a sortie directly against the Milanese camp at Pulicciano. Giusto d'Anghiari, Agnolo's prosecutor, records in his 'Diary' that on the night of 17 April the Anghiarese captain, with his men-at-arms, *saccomanni,* and part of Bernardo Duti's infantry, attacked the men of Astorre da Faenza, capturing 60 horses and numerous plackarts, cuirasses, *giornee,* and silver-adorned helmets.[27]

At this point, Piccinino changed his strategy. He realised the limited military value of Mugello and that order prevailed within Florence. Encouraged by the promises of the Florentine exiles led by Rinaldo degli Albizzi, he had hoped for an internal revolt that never happened. Consequently, he withdrew to Casentino to lure the Florentines, with Francesco Guidi, Count of Poppi, a trusted ally of Albizzi who had until then faked his loyalty to the Florentine Republic.[28]

Palmieri wrote that the Milanese abandoned the camp at Pulicciano on 18 April after 10 days of siege.[29] It is not known if Piccinino managed

24 Cavalcanti, *Istorie Fiorentine,* Book XIII, Ch. VI, Biondo, *Historie,* p.123; d'Anghiari, 'Memorie', f. 38r.

25 Micheletto Attendolo da Cotignola had served under Francesco Sforza since 1439. Given Piccinino's clear intentions of attacking Tuscany and not the Marca, Sforza ordered Attendolo to help the Florentines. On p.450 of his 'Diary' Graziani recalls the passage of Micheletto with 800 cavalrymen through Assisi and towards Todi on April 9.

26 Capponi, 'Commentari', 1193; 'La Fuga del Capitano' in A. Fabretti, *Note e documenti da biografie dei Capitani Venturieri dell'Umbria,* vol. Unico (Montepulciano: Angiolo Tumi, 1842), vol. I, p.81. Fabretti, on the other hand, writes that the 1,000 infantry were 1,000 Sforzeschi cavalry.

27 d'Anghiari, 'Memorie', f. 38v.

28 Machiavelli, *Istorie Fiorentine,* vol. 2, p.83; Ammirato, *Istorie Fiorentine,* vol. IV, p.259; Capponi, 'Commentari', 1193.

29 d'Anghiari, 'Memorie', f. 38v; Buoninsegni, *Storia,* p.72; M. Palmieri, *Annales,* p.148.

to take Pulicciano, since historians do not agree. Decembrio and Biondo agree on Piccinino's capture of the town· Biondo states: '... *in capo di 28 giorni il Piccinino hebbe Montepulciano in mano*' (... after 28 days Piccinino had taken Montepulciano).[30] Giovan Battista Poggio also writes of these 28 days at Pulicciano but does not report its capture. Ammirato and Poggio Bracciolini, by contrast, are of a completely different opinion and declare that the Milanese tried to take Pulicciano but in vain due to the obstinacy of the defenders.[31] Other historians are silent or vague. Given the chronology of the Milanese movements, however, a 28-day siege at Pulicciano appears unlikely.

In the same days, a regrettable episode occurred, recounted in detail by Cavalcanti. Madonna Bartolomea, wife of Francesco Gianfigliazzi, one of the Florentine exiles, was in Siena when she learnt that her son Baldassarre, sheltered in Bologna, had fallen gravely ill. Disguised as a humble pilgrim, she passed through Florence and reached her son safely. After his recovery, she attempted to return to Siena, where she had left her daughter-in-law in the care of her sister-in-law. During the journey back, still dressed as a pilgrim, she had to stop in Florence, and a whistle-blower recognised and denounced her to the Florentine authorities as the wife of Francesco Gianfigliazzi. Arrested on 27 April, she was tortured and interrogated, and on 4 May, was confined in the Stinche prison by the *Berrovieri*[32] and '... *messa nelle obbrobriose abitazioni le quali sono deputate per le disoneste femmine, e io ne vidi in sua compagnia più pubbliche meretrici*' (... placed in the shameful cells reserved for dishonest women, and I saw her there in the company of prostitutes). Cavalcanti was an eyewitness, having been imprisoned in the infamous Stinche for nearly 10 years for failure to pay taxes to the republic.[33]

Meanwhile, Piccinino entered Casentino via San Leolino (modern Rignano sull'Arno), where he joined Count Guidi, who supplied men and bombards for a siege. Guidi, with numerous infantry and some cavalry, moved throughout the countryside and seized Cetica, taking prisoners, raping women, and sacking the city.

On 24 April, Piccinino took Bibbiena by agreement with the inhabitants, who, learning of the Count of Poppi's defection, chose submission in order to preserve their lives and property.[34]

Two days later, Rocca Rizzarda and Romena fell, and San Niccolò was put under siege.[35]

30 Decembrio, 'Niccolò Piccinino' 1080; Biondo, *Historie*, p.124.

31 Poggio, *Vita di Piccinino*, p.253; Ammirato, *Istorie Fiorentine*, vol. IV, p.259; Poggio Bracciolini, *Historia Fiorentina*, Venice 1715, p.340.

32 *Berrovieri*: armed men employed by the republic in police-type actions.

33 Cavalcanti, *Istorie Fiorentine*, Book XIV, Ch. IV.

34 Ammirato, *Istorie Fiorentine*, vol. IV, p.260; Capponi, 'Commentari', 1193; Cavalcanti, *Istorie Fiorentine*, Book XIV, Ch. II & Ch. VII.

35 I. Masetti-Bencini, 'La bataglia di Anghiari' in *Rivista delle biblioteche e degli archivi*, Luglio-Agosto 1907, p.113; Ammirato, *Istorie Fiorentine*, vol. IV, p.260; Capponi, 'Commentari', 1193.

Meanwhile, in Mugello, after the departure of the Milanese, numerous Florentine infantry '... *veterani e novelli, e con soldo e senza soldo ...*' (veterans or novices, with pay or without pay), as Cavalcanti specifies – rushed to the fortresses that had previously fallen to the enemy and laid siege to Torre a Vaglia. They compelled the garrison to surrender by threatening a massacre while promising to spare their lives; yet once the fortress had been taken, the Florentine infantry violated the agreed terms and everyone within was killed, including the young commander Leonardo di Antonio Raffacani.[36]

When Piccinino learnt of this, he resolved upon retaliation. During the capture of Romena, he had taken prisoner 22 infantrymen from Pistoia, whom Neri Capponi had dispatched to defend the position. According to Cavalcanti, he ordered that one faction, the Cancellieri, be hanged, while the Panciatichi were released. These represented the two rival political factions of Pistoia: the Panciatichi were Ghibellines and therefore inclined towards Milan, whereas the Cancellieri were Guelphs. Piccinino further ordered that their commander, Bartolomeo del Bolognino, also of Pistoia, be executed in a particularly brutal fashion: he was placed on a catapult and hurled into the castle of San Niccolò.[37]

The castle stood at the foot of the mountains dividing Casentino from the Val d'Arno and occupied a naturally strong and difficult position (see

22, San Niccolò Castle. (Photograph by the author)

36 Cavalcanti, *Istorie Fiorentine*, Book XIV, Ch. VI.

37 Ammirato, *Istorie Fiorentine*, vol. IV, p.260; Capponi, 'Commentari', 1193. Cavalcanti, *Istorie Fiorentine*, Book XIV, Ch. VIII. The *briccola* was a catapult. Bartolomeo del Bolognino is not mentioned in the contractual documents that the Republic of Florence signed in that period among the various condotte, that is, in the Deliberations and Condotte of the 'Dieci di Balìa'.

image 22). The Milanese had a hard time taking it. Its garrison consisted of 120 infantrymen under the command of Morello Perla da Poppi. The fortress would withstand assaults, artillery fire, and bombardment by *briccola* (catapult) for 31 days.[38]

Cavalcanti, characteristically attentive to marginal yet vivid anecdotes, refers to the siege on several occasions in his chronicle. In order to undermine the defenders' morale, Count Guidi had Morello's mother – Perla, who resided in Poppi – brought in chains beneath the castle walls so that her son might see her. The count offered her life in exchange for surrender. Morello refused, stating proudly that he would never betray the Republic. Cavalcanti records his words:

> *La vita è breve, e di poca duranza ai giovani: adunque agli antichi è brevissima; ma la buona nominanza è perpetua. Adunque, io eleggo pittosto perpetualità di fama, che la transitoria della materna vita, veduto avere a essere così corta. Tiratevi indietro, e dite al conte che io eleggo pittosto che egli viva in tra gli uomini ingiusti e crudeli, che io sia detto traditore e cattivo.* (Life is short and of brief duration for the young: for the old it is briefer still. But good fame is everlasting. Therefore, I choose perpetual renown over the fleeting remainder of my mother's life. Withdraw, and tell the count that I prefer he lives among unjust and cruel men rather than I be called a traitor and coward).

Unfortunately, Cavalcanti does not record what ultimately befell Morello's mother.[39]

From that point onward, the siege intensified. Many of the besieged attempted to escape, but the Milanese, acting on Piccinino's orders, maintained a vigilant guard and captured numerous fugitives. They were first interrogated and then placed upon a catapult and hurled back into the castle. Cavalcanti reports that, in this manner, 37 people – 'men, women and children' – were killed, 25 in a single night.[40]

Meanwhile, Milanese detachments plundered the surrounding territory, capturing and sacking Borgo a Stia, Palagio, Ortigiano, Giugatojo, and Orzano. When they reached Reggiolo, they found the position naturally strong and easily defensible, though the buildings were roofed in thatch. A *masnadiere* (a soldier of fortune of low social extraction) discharged flaming *rocchetta*[41] from his crossbow: the arrow struck the straw roof and, aided by the wind, the fire spread rapidly consuming the houses and eventually the

38 Ammirato, *Istorie Fiorentine*, vol. IV, p.260; Capponi, 'Commentari', 1193; Palmieri, 'Annales,' p.148; Arch. Stat. Fir. Dieci di Balìa, f. 32v.

39 Cavalcanti, *Istorie Fiorentine*, Book XIV, Ch. XV.

40 Cavalcanti, *Istorie Fiorentine*, Book XIV & XIV, Chs XVI & XXI.

41 *Rocchetta*: a sort of long distaff-like stick with one end wrapped in tow or other flammable materials, which was shot from a crossbow or thrown by hand onto houses to set them on fire.

castle itself. In the conflagration, 150 men, women, and children perished. Reggiolo thus remained untaken by either Milanese or the Florentines.[42]

By mid-May, the Florentines concentrated their men-at-arms and commanders at several points in the Valdarno. According to Machiavelli, they fielded 3,000 cavalry under Pier Giovanpaolo Orsini, Neri Capponi, and Bernadetto de' Medici.[43] Capponi and Ammirato, however, give a figure of 2,200 cavalry, composed of the troops of Micheletto Attendolo[44] and two Sforza squadrons under Bosio Sforza and Troilo Orsino,[45] all under the authority of the commissioners Neri Capponi and Piero Guicciardini.

The troops were stationed at Figline and at Leone (modern Pergine Valdarno), to the considerable detriment of those communities. Cavalcanti, more precise than other chroniclers, relates about the discord between the commanders Micheletto Attendolo and Giovanpaolo Orsini and describes the depredations committed by their soldiers. These behaved like enemies rather than allies, plundering the lands of the Republic and killing peasants who resisted. They even seized and pillaged the castle of Trappola, belonging to the Florentine Ricasoli family: '*...e quella, ad onta degli abitanti, presero, e la roba sortirono tra loro: e così per niuno si conosceva qual si fusse più l'amico che il nemico...*' (...and they captured it disregarding the inhabitants and plundered it, so that no one recognised the friend from the enemy...).[46]

In that moment, Borso d'Este, son of Niccolò, Marquess of Ferrara, ostensibly came to Florence's aid with 1,500 cavalrymen. He was accompanied by the Florentine Angelo Acciaioli, who had engaged him on behalf of the Republic for 15,000 florins. Yet upon reaching Modena, Borso abruptly abandoned Acciaioli and turned towards Lombardy, declaring that he would serve Duke Filippo Maria Visconti, who offered better pay – although he retained the Florentine money.

Florence, however, was compensated by better fortune elsewhere: Genoa, a member of the League, dispatched 400 veteran crossbowmen as help. They entered Florence on 21 May and were received with great rejoicing.[47]

The following day, 22 May, seven men arrived from San Niccolò to request assistance from the commissioners encamped in Valdarno.[48] Neri

42 Cavalcanti, *Istorie Fiorentine*, Book XIV, Ch. IX; Palmieri, 'Annales,' p.148.

43 Cavalcanti, *Istorie Fiorentine*, Book XIV, Ch. XI; Machiavelli, *Istorie Fiorentine*, vol. 2, p.84.

44 From the records of Micheletto's company we also learn that the company set up camp in Vacheria di San Giovanni Valdarno (7km from Figline) from 18 May to around 4 about Jun. See: Viviano, *Registri della compagnia*, libro. 3574, ff. 115v, 115r, 118r, 121r & 123r.

45 Capponi, 'Commentari,' 1193; Ammirato, *Istorie Fiorentine*, vol. IV, p.260. Bosio or Buoso was Francesco Sforza's brother.

46 Cavalcanti, *Istorie Fiorentine*, Book XIV, Ch. XI. The chronicler also writes that only Niccolò da Pisa did not participate in these lootings.

47 Cavalcanti, *Istorie Fiorentine*, Book XIV, Ch. XVIII; Ammirato, *Istorie Fiorentine*, vol. IV, p.260; Biondo, *Historie*, p.124; Buoninsegni, *Storia*, p.72.

48 According to Cavalcanti, these men formed part of a delegation from the besieged city and were granted safe-conduct by Piccinino. After conferring with the lords of

Capponi and Piero Guicciardini marched with the entire force to relieve the castle, though they had only 2,200 cavalrymen – scarcely a third of the Milanese strength. Moreover, they were disadvantaged by terrain: San Niccolò stood upon elevated ground, and the ascent from the Valdarno side was steeper and harder to traverse than that faced by Piccinino, whose main forces were placed more favourably. The Braccesco commander had also constructed a defensible earthwork above the castle, commanding a clear view of enemy approaches.

For these reasons, and owing to discord within the Florentine people, it was resolved not to risk the army and the relief force withdrew without helping the castle, awaiting the arrival of papal reinforcements.[49]

When the defenders of San Niccolò perceived that no help would come, they opened the gates to the Ducheschi. On 24 May, after a month of siege, Niccolò Piccinino took possession of the castle. The chroniclers are silent regarding the fate of the prisoners, yet it appears that Piccinino honoured his word and released them. Evidence lies in the renewal of Morello da Poppi's *condotta* with the *Dieci di Balìa* on 29 May 1440 and in letters of 25 June documented by Masetti-Bencini. The only executions were those of two Milanese *saccomanni* who had deserted and sought refuge in the castle; Cavalcanti writes that, once recognised, Piccinino ordered them hanged as traitors.[50]

At this point, according to Cavalcanti, the Florentines appointed Giovanpaolo Orsini as Captain General of the Army of the Republic, whereupon he promptly reorganised the forces. The *Deliberazioni e condotte dei Dieci di Balìa* indicate, however, that Orsini had already been engaged as captain general a month earlier, on 25 April 1440.[51]

Meanwhile, Piccinino advanced to Rassina, encamped there, and after eight days captured it along with Bienzina and other minor positions. He then seized Chiusi. The Count of Poppi, seeking to exploit Milanese support to conquer neighbouring territories, urged Piccinino to station his troops between Chiusi, Caprese, and Pieve, and await the enemy's movement in order to strike if they appeared in Casentino, Valdarno, or Valtibertina. Piccinino, observing the rough terrain, replied that his horses did not feed upon stones and instead marched towards Borgo Sansepolcro to join his son Francesco.[52]

---

the Republic, they returned to the castle. Cavalcanti, *Istorie Fiorentine* Book XIV, Ch. XX e XXII.

49 Capponi, 'Commentari', 1194; Ammirato, *Istorie Fiorentine*, vol. IV, pp.260-261; Machiavelli, *Istorie Fiorentine*, vol. 2, p.85; Palmieri, 'Annales,' p.148; Cavalcanti, *Istorie Fiorentine*, Book XIV, cap. XXII.

50 Dieci di Balìa, *Deliberazioni e condotte*, f. 32v; Masetti-Bencini, 'bataglia di Anghiari', p.113; Cavalcanti, *Istorie Fiorentine*, Book XIV, cap. XXII.

51 Cavalcanti, *Istorie Fiorentine*, Book XIV, Ch. XXIV; Dieci di Balìa, *Deliberazioni e condotte*, f. 34v.

52 Buoninsegni, *Storia*, p.72; Palmieri, 'Annales,' p.148: Ammirato, *Istorie Fiorentine*, vol. IV, p.261; Capponi, 'Commentari', 1194; d'Anghiari, 'Memorie', f. 39r.

On 8 June, the Milanese passed through Pieve Santo Stefano but did not occupy it, because of the defence mounted by Leale d'Anghiari on behalf of Florence. They proceeded to Borgo Sansepolcro, where they were well received, then moved to Città di Castello and opened a siege. The following day, Niccolò entrusted the siege to his son Francesco and set out for Perugia, his hometown.[53] He hoped to obtain its lordship, as Fortebraccio had once done. Encamping five miles from the city, he negotiated with leading political citizens and, on 10 June 1440,[54] entered Perugia with only 400 cavalry[55] and was received with great honour.[56] He lodged in the Palazzo dei Priori and the next day accompanied the Priors to the papal legate, who governed the city in the name of the Church. Under the pretext of negotiation, Piccinino sent the legate to Florence to confer with the pope.[57] Once the legate departed, he placed the city's government nominally in the hands of the Priors. Within days, however, the citizens, perceiving his ambition to assume the lordship and induced him to accept 8,000 florins on the condition that he departed. On 15 June, he withdrew with his men towards Cortona, hoping to seize it by stratagem.

Meanwhile, other events unfolded in Tuscany. The Count of Poppi, since Casentino was free of armies, organised a large infantry expedition and ravaged Valdarno, carrying off its livestock. On the other side, the Florentines, encamped at Anghiari, sacked Monte Agutello, part of the Lordship of Madonna Anfrosina.[58] This madonna was the Lady of Citerna and Monterchi, born to the Lords of Montedoglio and widow of Bartolomeo di Maso de' Tarlati di Pietramala. Since Piccinino's arrival in Romagna, she had sided – like other Ghibelline families – with the Ducheschi.[59] After the Battle of Anghiari, Anfrosina lost her lordship to the Republic.

---

53 Machiavelli, *Istorie Fiorentine*, vol. 2, p.85; Lorenzo Taglieschi, (Daniele Finzi & Matteo Parreschi eds), *Delle memorie istoriche e annali della terra di Anghiari* (Anghiari: Sansepolcro, 1991); p.169; d'Anghiari, 'Memorie', f. 39r; Poggio, *Vita di Piccinino*, p.253.

54 400 horses according to Capponi and Ammirato, 200 according to Lorenzo Spirito, 500 according to Battista Poggio and Biondo, but only 40 according to Machiavelli.

55 On the previous day, 9 June, Graziani, in his *Cronaca di Perugia*, reports that the son of the Marquess of Ferrara joined Piccinino with 240 lances; see *Diario del Graziani*, p.456. This man was possibly Borso d'Este, who abandoned Acciaioli for Filippo Maria Visconti – or it may have been his brother Lionello? Graziani is the only source to mention this episode.

56 *Diario del Graziani*, pp.454 –455; Capponi, 'Commentari', 1194; Poggio, *Vita di Piccinino*, pp.254–255; Machiavelli, *Istorie Fiorentine*, vol. 2, p.86; Ammirato, *Istorie Fiorentine*, vol. IV, p.261.

57 According to Biondo, this was the Bishop of Naples, although he does not give his name; Biondo, *Historie*, p.127.

58 d'Anghiari, 'Memorie', f. 39r; Cavalcanti, *Istorie Fiorentine*, Book XIV, Ch. XXVII and XXVIII.

59 In his *Cronica*, Benedetto Dei lists the pro-Milanese Florentine families in that war: Strozzi, Peruzzi, Gianfigliazzi, Degli Albizzi, de' Rossi, Lanberteschi, Guadagni, and Barbadori in Benedetto Dei, *La Cronica dal anno 1400 alle anno 1500* (Firenze: Papafava, 1984), p.56.

Meanwhile, Piccinino arrived in Cortona but failed in his design. He could not take the city because his secret treaty, concluded with certain citizens, had been discovered. One evening, Bartolomeo di Senso, an eminent citizen, intended to guard one of the city gates. He was stopped by a friend, another citizen of Cortona, who warned him not to go, as he would be killed. Thus, in this way, he became aware of the conspiracy. He informed the captain of the city, who arrested the conspirators and doubled the guards at the gates. Piccinino therefore withdrew to Città di Castello.[60]

Finally, in mid-June, Papal forces arrived under the command of Ludovico Scarampi Mezzarota, Patriarch of Aquileia and Papal legate who, as already mentioned, had replaced Vitelleschi in command of the army. According to Capponi and Ammirato, he led 3,000 cavalry and 500 infantry; according to Biondo, he led 4,000 cavalry and 2,000 infantry; while for Palmieri the Papal reinforcements amounted to only 2,000 cavalry.[61] Among the *condottieri* were Simonetto da Castel di Piero, Everso d'Anguillara, Paolo della Molara, and Angelo Roncone. These troops similarly camped near Anghiari and joined the Florentines, inflicting severe damage upon the town, as recorded by Giusto d'Anghiari.[62]

On 24 June, St. John's Day, news reached Florence that Florentine forces had retaken Castel San Niccolò thanks to the cunning of its inhabitants. A San Niccolò blacksmith, Marco d'Elia, approached the castellan appointed by the Count of Poppi to guard the fortress. He suggested that, for better defence, the catapult – that bloody war machine of Piccinino still positioned outside the walls – should be brought within the castle, so that it might not be used by any enemy. The castellan accepted the suggestion, opened the gates, and ordered his men to bring the heavy machine inside. The astute Marco, seeing the gates opened, blocked them with a *briccola* and signalled to the Florentine troops hidden nearby. They entered and seized the poorly defended fortress. Leonardo Aretino comments: '*... un mese intero stette Piccinino per conquistare quel castello, i nostri lo recuperarono in pochi giorni*' (... Piccinino spent a whole month in taking that castle; our men recovered it in a few days).[63]

The news that Florence had regained San Niccolò also reached the Count of Poppi. Enraged, he ordered a raid on Borgo alla Collina, a village near San Niccolò. He carried off a great deal of spoil and cruelly had all the men hanged: '*Avvenga dio che tutti quegli uomini, non facendo più riserbo d'uno che d'un altro, per la gola impiccò*' (He hanged all those men, sparing none).[64]

60 Machiavelli, *Istorie Fiorentine*, vol. 2, p.86; Ammirato, *Istorie Fiorentine*, vol. IV, p.261; Capponi, 'Commentari', 1194.

61 Capponi, 'Commentari', 1194; Ammirato, *Istorie Fiorentine*, vol. IV, p.261; Biondo, *Historie*, p.123; Palmieri, 'Annales,' p.148.

62 d'Anghiari, 'Memorie', f. 39v.

63 Cavalcanti, *Istorie Fiorentine*, Book XIV, Ch. XXIX; d'Anghiari, 'Memorie', f. 39v; L. Aretini 'Commentarius' *Muratori XIX*, col. 941.

64 Cavalcanti, *Istorie Fiorentine*, Book XIV, Ch. XXX.

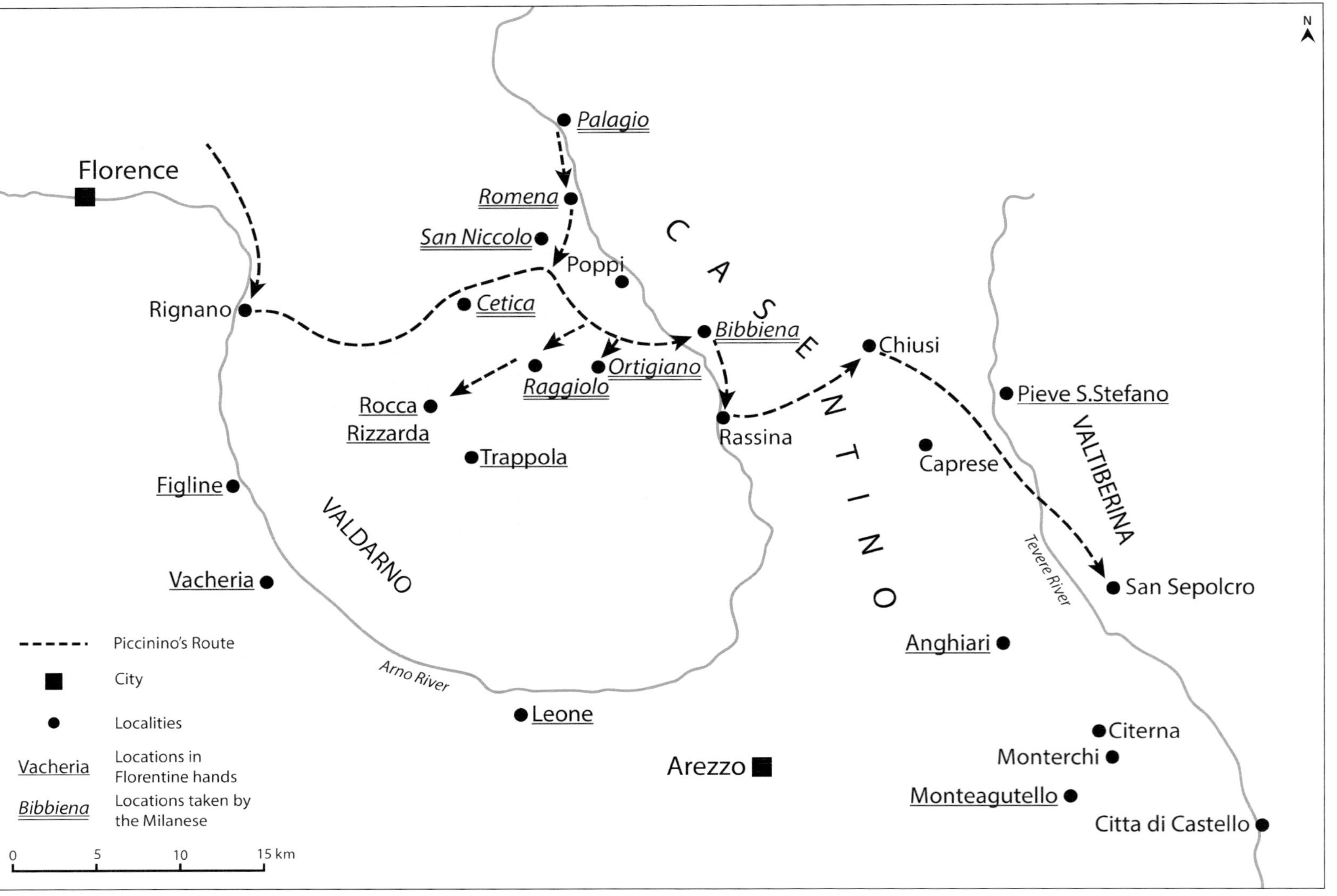

23. Piccinino movements towards San Sepolcro.

Meanwhile, Niccolò Piccinino had returned to the Siege of Città di Castello, a difficult place to take, since it was protected on one side by a high, steep slope and on the other by the River Tiber. Within the city, provisions were now scarce, as the only accessible supply route was controlled by the enemy. The citizens were divided; one faction sought negotiation with the Milanese, the other appealed to the Florentines for aid.

The Patriarch of Aquileia and the other captains of the League, concerned for the city, dispatched Troilo with 100 lances and Molara with 80, together with some infantry and 30 handgunners.[65] According to Capponi and Ammirato, in the ensuing clash, the Milanese captured all of the infantry and the handgunners. According to della Tuccia, however, they captured only seven men-at-arms of Molara's company, after which the Florentines defeated the enemy, captured about 70 horses, and entered the city. Biondo, for his part, writes that the Florentines entered Città di Castello unharmed, passing through the enemy camp.[66]

Thus, the city was resupplied, and Piccinino realised that he had gained little strategic advantage over the summer, despite his efforts. Moreover, with the arrival of papal reinforcements, the Florentines could now hope to prevail in open battle against the Milanese.

More importantly, news arrived that Count Francesco Sforza had defeated the Milanese at Soncino in Lombardy and was threatening Milan itself.[67] Duke Filippo Maria Visconti urged Piccinino by letter to return with all haste. Within his army – consisting largely of Lombards – murmurs began to spread that Lombardy should not be abandoned and many openly declared their wish to return home.

The Braccesco commander implored his soldiers to remain calm and promised to lead them back within a few days. Yet, he resolved to first strike the army of the League by surprise. This plan was supported by Rinaldo degli Albizzi and the Florentine exiles, as well as by Manfredi – that is, by those within Piccinino's army whose interest lay not in Lombardy but in Tuscany. Piccinino also wanted to attack out of a sense of pride and a desire for revenge against his hated rival Francesco Sforza. Additionally, as a seasoned professional soldier, he had observed through careful reconnaissance of the enemy camp that a surprise attack offered a strong prospect of success.

For these reasons, on the morning of 29 June, he readied his army to attack the League camp at Anghiari.

---

65 Capponi, 'Commentari', 1194; Ammirato, *Istorie Fiorentine*, vol. IV, p.261. According to Biondo, *Historie*, p.127, Troilo and Molara commanded 300 selected cavalrymen, whereas according to Tuccia, *Cronaca di Viterbo*, p.175, they were at the head of 700 cavalrymen.

66 In the *Vita Nerii Capponii, Muratori R.I.S. XX*, col. 500, Bartolomeo Platina states that Troilo had 300 cavalrymen and an equal number of infantrymen. The cavalry managed to enter the city, whereas the infantry, being slower, were all captured.

67 Biondo, *Historie*, p.127; Machiavelli, *Istorie Fiorentine*, vol. 2, p.87; Ammirato, *Istorie Fiorentine*, vol. IV, p.262; Buoninsegni, *Storia*, p.73; Decembrio, 'Niccolò Piccinino', 1081.

6

The Opposing Armies

It is always difficult to calculate the number of soldiers deployed in a fifteenth century battle, particularly because contemporary chroniclers and later historians frequently provide conflicting accounts. Many reported inaccurate figures, whether because of unreliable sources or because they deliberately exaggerated the strength of the enemy for propaganda purposes, in order to magnify their victory.

Another factor is that Renaissance armies, like those of the Middle Ages, were accompanied by numerous non-combatants; auxiliaries, servants, *saccomanni*, or simple camp followers. These individuals were rarely counted or declared in the administrative records of the various *condotte*, yet, owing to their light equipment and exposure, they constituted the majority of casualties in battle.

Their number must have been considerable. An example of their proportion in relation to effective combatants may be found in Capponi's 'Commentari' concerning the Aragonese expedition to Tuscany of 1448.[1] The Florentine chronicler states that Alfonso V of Aragon, King of Naples, had approximately 15,000 men: 7,000 cavalry, 4,000 infantry, and the remainder described as 'useless people'. Thus, out of 15,000 men, 11,000 were combatants and 4,000 non-combatants. The latter therefore represented almost 30 percent of the total personnel present with the army – a considerable proportion.

Capponi also reports the strength of the opposing forces, stating that the Florentines fielded about 5,000 cavalry and 2,000 infantry and that, including non-combatants, their number rose to 8,000 men. In this case, however, the non-combatants constituted roughly 12 percent of the total.

These differing percentages provide an insight into the marked disparity in the presence of such 'unnecessary' forces among various armies. Their functional use within each army was nonetheless significant. Alfonso's army, operating hundreds of kilometres from its homeland, required a

1 N. Capponi, 'Commentari' in *Muratori Rerum Italicaruma Scriptores* XVIII, col. 1204.

greater number of *saccomanni* to secure provisions through plunder, unlike the Florentines, who were campaigning within Tuscany.

Further important information in this regard may be found in a collection of ordinances dated 1434 and drafted by the Republic of Venice, containing the provisions of the *banco degli stipendiari*.[2] This *banco* was essentially a table at which Venetian officials, known as *collaterali*, enrolled and paid mercenaries. These ordinances, divided into 56 paragraphs, detail the obligations – including loyalty and probity – that soldiers were required to observe upon entering Venetian service. In additional unnumbered sections, the equipment prescribed for cavalrymen and infantrymen is described (see chapter The Infantry).

These documents reveal that, in addition to captains, constables, and men-at-arms, infantry corpsmen and *palvesari* were accompanied by boys and *famigli* who carried their *targoni* or spears in battle. Such individuals were never recorded in the registers of the companies of fortune nor in the contracts stipulated with the lordships. Consequently, they may reasonably be included among the so-called 'useless people'.

In the chronicles concerning Piccinino's expedition to Tuscany and the Battle of Anghiari, little information is provided about the number of auxiliaries. They are mentioned primarily in connection with acts of plunder.

Giusto d'Anghiari, who served in Agnolo Taglia's company as prosecutor, refers to *saccomanni* as being employed both to procure supplies and in combat, as when they took part in the night attack against Astorre Manfredi's squadron. Cavalcanti, characteristically outspoken, mentions them repeatedly in relation to their atrocities – such as rapes or the burning of Reggiolo – or in connection with the execution of two *saccomanni* ordered by Piccinino in San Niccolò. Only Capponi, more precise and arguably among the most reliable chroniclers, reports that 120 *saccomanni* on the Florentine side were captured by the Milanese near Remole.[3]

But let us turn to the actual combatants. Numerous documents survive concerning the *condotte* stipulated by Florence at the time, and these provide an almost complete picture of the number of soldiers employed I refer in particular to the 'Deliberazioni condotte e stanziamenti of the Dieci di Balìa' preserved in the State Archive of Florence, as well as to the 'Commissariato delle soldatesche e galere' held in the State Archive of Rome, and the 'Registri della società di ventura di Micheletto Attendolo' preserved in the Fraternita dei Laici of Arezzo.

---

2 State Archives of Venice, 'Commemoriali 12,' ff. 10 and 11.

3 G. d'Anghiari, *Memorie dall'anno 1437 al 1481*, Bibl. Naz. Fir. Ms. II. II. 127, ff. 38r and 39r; Giovanni Cavalcanti, *Istorie Fiorentine* (Fiorenze: all'insegna di Dante, 1839), vol. II, Book XIII, Ch. III, Book XIV, Ch. IX and Ch. XXII; Capponi, 'Commentari', 1193.

Unfortunately, no comparable body of documentation survives for calculating the Milanese forces, since only a few records of the period survived the near-total destruction of the Visconti archives during the Ambrosian Republic. Therefore, for the strength of Piccinino's army, we must rely on discordant historical sources, as already noted in the previous chapter on the historical background of the battle.

Let us therefore examine the reports in detail.

Capponi, who lived through these events, states that Piccinino crossed the Po and began the campaign with 6,000 cavalry. The same figure is given by Bartolomeo Platina and Giovanni Cambi, his contemporaries, as well as by Francesco Viviano, accountant of Micheletto Attendolo's company – although the latter refers specifically to the Battle of Anghiari.[4]

Machiavelli and Ammirato, writing in the sixteenth century, also attribute to him 6,000 horses, as does Sismondo Sismondi, who, however, wrote in the nineteenth century. Flavio Biondo, secretary to Pope Eugene IV, records that before the battle Piccinino had 6,000 cavalry and 3,000 infantry; whereas Giovan Battista Poggio reports a total of 5,000 cavalry and infantry combined.[5]

Niccolò della Tuccia, a fifteenth century historian from Viterbo, states that the forces leaving Lombardy were 5,000 cavalry and 5,000 infantry. Angelo Pezzana, in his *Storia di Parma* written in the nineteenth century, claims that the Milanese cavalry numbered 4,000, to which must be added a further 2,000 supplied by the lords of Rimini and Cesena[6]. Matteo Palmieri, a contemporary Florentine chronicler, reports 5,000 cavalrymen and 1,000 Milanese infantrymen in Mugello. Bracciolini, by contrast, does not specify the number of horses with which Piccinino began his campaign; he merely notes that they were elite cavalry, together with 1,500 infantrymen.[7]

In the *Trophaeum anglaricum*, Leonardo Dati states that, on the morning of the battle, Piccinino had with him an *ordinanza* of 40 elite lances and 2,000 infantrymen, of whom 300 were handgunners, 300 shield-bearers,

4 Capponi, 'Commentari', 1191; B. Platina, *Vita Nerii Capponii*, Muratori Rerum Italicarum Scripores XX col. 499; B. Platina, *Hist. Mantuane*, Muratori R.I.S. XX col. 833; G. Cambi, *Istorie* in *Delizie degli Eruditi Toscani*, 1785, volume 20, vol. I, p.226; F. Viviano, *Registri della compagnia di Micheletto Attendolo*, in Fraternita dei Laici di Arezzo, libro 3574, foglio di guardia.

5 Niccolò Machiavelli, *Istorie Fiorentine* (Milan: Società Anonima Notari or Alpes, 1928), vol. 2, p.76; Scipione Ammirato, *Istorie Fiorentine* (Torino: Cugini Pomba e comp, 1853), vol. V, p.255; J. C. L. Simondo Sismondi, *Storia delle repubbliche italiane* (Capolago: 'Italia' 1846), vol. VI, p.69; F. Biondo, *Historie* (Venezia: 1547), p.128; Giovan Battista Poggio, *Vita di Niccolò Piccinino* (Perugia: 1619), p.252.

6 These two lords were Sigismondo and Novello Malatesta, but the number of their cavalrymen is exaggerated.

7 Nicola della Tuccia, *Cronaca di Viterbo* (Firenze: G.P. Vieusseux, 1872), p.171; Angelo Pezzana, *Storia di Parma* (Parma: Dalla Ducale Tipografia,1842), II, p.426; M. Palmieri, *Annales*, Muratori Rerum Italicarum Scripores Bologna 1922, volume XXVI, appendix, p.147; P. Bracciolini, *Historia Fiorentina* (Venice: 1715), p.338.

300 crossbowmen, and an equal number (though this seems unlikely) of archers.[8]

Cavalcanti and Simonetta both assert that the Visconti commander departed Lombardy with half of his army, leaving the other half stationed in Brescia, though neither provides precise figures.[9] Finally, two contemporary but anonymous poems describing the Battle of Anghiari – *La rotta di Niccolò Piccinino* and *La Fuga del Capitano* – offer further numerical estimates. In the first, the Milanese are said to have fielded 6,000 cavalrymen; in the second, 4,000 cavalrymen and 2,000 infantrymen.[10]

The opinions of the writers are varied. For the cavalry, the figures range from 6,000 – a number given by more than half of the chroniclers – to 4,000 men. For the infantry, however, only about half of the authors provide any estimate at all, and each gives a different figure, ranging from an improbable 5,000 to as few as 1,000 soldiers.

The most reliable sources are those chroniclers who either lived at the time of the battle – such as Biondo, Platina, and Poggio – or who directly participated in the battle, such as Capponi and perhaps Viviano. The majority of these authors converge on a cavalry strength of approximately 6,000 men.

The Venetian chronicler Marin Sanudo confirms this figure in *Vite dé Duchi di Venezia*, written at the end of the fifteenth century. He calculates the cavalry forces serving in the Italian armies in 1439, distributing them according to their respective commanders, specifying the cavalry strength of each company – figures generally regarded as reasonably accurate.[11] He estimates the total Milanese cavalry at 19,750 cavalrymen and, beginning with the captain general Niccolò Piccinino, lists all the other captains for 53 companies in total. From this list, it is possible to identify those companies that later participated in the Tuscan campaign, since the names of their captains recur in the chronicles. However, the figures refer to 1439 – one year before Anghiari – and it is possible that, with the intensification of hostilities, these numbers increased rather than diminished.

According to Sanudo, Piccinino's forces consisted of 2,500 cavalrymen, together with 600 *lance spezzate*[12] and 600 ducal *famigli*. These companies

8 L. di Piero Dati, 'Dal Tropheum anglaricum' in *Giornale Storico della Literatura Italiana* (Torino: Ermanno Loescher, 1890), vol. XVI, p.52.

9 Giovanni Cavalcanti, *Istorie Fiorentine* (Fiorenze: all'insegna di Dante, 1839), vol. II, Book XII, Ch. XII; Johannis Simonetae, 'Vita Francisci Sfortiae,' *Muratori R.I.S.* XXI, col. 286.

10 Angelo Ascani, 'La rotta di Niccolò Piccinino' in Angelo Ascani, *Anghiari dalle origini all'anno 1440* (Città di Castello: Città di Castello, 1973), p.288; 'La Fuga del Capitano' in A. Fabretti, *Note e documenti da biografie dei Capitani Venturieri dell'Umbria*, vol. Unico (Montepulciano: Angiolo Tumi, 1842), vol. I, p.251.

11 M. Sanudo, 'Vite dé duchi di Venezia' in *Muratori R.I.S.*, XX col. 1089; Michael Mallett, *Signori e mercenari* (Bologna: Il Mulino, 1983), p.122.

12 In companies of fortune, the cavalrymen who for various reasons were without *condottiero* were known as *lance spezzate* (lit. broken spears).

were under the direct command of Piccinino in his capacity of captain general.[13] In addition, there was the company of Count Carlo[14] with 200 cavalrymen, that of Don Sacramoro[15] with 300, and that of Don Rinaldo di Monte Albotto[16] with 100.

This brings us to a subtotal of 4,300 cavalrymen. To this must be added the 500 cavalry of Guidantonio Manfredi – whom Sanudo designates 'the Lord of Faenza' – who would join the Milanese in Romagna, as well as the 600 of Francesco Piccinino, who, at time of his father's departure from Lombardy, was already in Tuscany.[17] The resulting total is therefore 5,400 cavalrymen.

However, no figures are provided for several other important captains.[18] For example, Sanudo does not indicate the strength of Astorre Manfredi's company, nor that of other captains such as Antonello della Torre, Tartaglia della Guancia, and others who will be discussed in the chapter on casualties.

If we assume that these additional companies may each have numbered several hundred men, the overall cavalry strength would plausibly have approached, if not exceeded, 6,000 men, which corresponds to the figure most frequently cited by the chroniclers.

Unfortunately, the number of infantry can only be estimated approximately. Nevertheless, Flavio Biondo's estimate of 3,000 infantrymen appears to be the most credible.[19]

The strength of the pro-Florentine forces – which were divided into three components: troops hired directly by the Republic, the papal contingent, and the forces of Sforza – is more complex to assess, yet at the same time more precise owing to the abundance of surviving documentation.

According to Biondo, the army of the League numbered 6,000 cavalrymen and 3,000 infantrymen – thus equalling the Milanese strength. Palmieri reports the same number of cavalry but raises the infantry to 4,000.[20]

---

13 Maria Nadia Covini, 'Per la storia delle milizie viscontee: I familari armigeri di Filippo Maria Visconti' in L. Chiappa Mauri & P. Mainoni (eds), *Il dominio di Milano fra XIII e XV secolo* (Milano: La Storia, 1993), p.42.

14 Carlo Fortebracci, Count of Montone, son of the famous Braccio. He was 18 at the time.

15 Sacramoro Visconti, illegitimate son of Barnabò Visconti.

16 Probably the same Monte Albotto mentioned after the battle among the Milanese prisoners, see Chapter 9, Casualties of the Battle.

17 When Niccolò Piccinino arrived in Mugello in April 1440, his son Francesco was already in Tuscany in Borgo Sansepolcro, a city that had surrendered to him in 1438. In 1438, Francesco was commanding a company of 1,000 cavalrymen and 300 infantrymen. See: Tuccia, *Cronaca di Viterbo*, p.163; 'Diario del Graziani,' Arch. Stor. Ital. XVI 1, 1850, p.433.

18 Litta, *Famiglie*, Manfredi Family, tav. VI: in 1435, Astorre was with Piccinino and 200 cavalrymen.

19 Biondo, *Historie*, p.128.

20 Biondo, *Historie*, p.128; Palmieri, *Annales*, p.148.

The German historian Willibald Block, who produced an important study of the battle in the early twentieth century, states that both sides fielded 3,500 cavalrymen and 2,000 infantrymen[21]. However, the origin of these figures remains unclear.

Poggio Bracciolini asserts that a total of 8,000 cavalrymen fought in Anghiari on both sides combined, whereas Sismondi maintains that 8,000 or 9,000 cavalrymen belonged to the League alone.[22]

Finally, the two poems offer further figures. *La rotta di Niccolò Piccinino* attributes 5,000 cavalrymen to the Florentines, while in *La Fuga del Capitano* they are said to have 4,000 cavalrymen and 2,000 infantrymen, the same numbers as those given for the Milanese.[23]

Thanks to the *condotta* contracts stipulated by the Republic of Florence – preserved in the State Archives under the *Dieci di Balìa*[24] – detailed information survives concerning the forces hired by the Republic at that time. These contracts provide precise data on recruitment, including the name of the commander or captain, the strength of his army, the date of engagement, salary, and related conditions.

They register every company, from the smallest – consisting of only three infantrymen or even a single cavalryman described as '*cum una equa*' – to the largest formations numbering hundreds of men. From these records it is therefore possible to reconstruct the number of men enlisted in the months immediately preceding the battle and to derive several noteworthy conclusions. For example, between September 1439 and April 1440, contracts were stipulated or renewed for approximately 5,525 infantrymen and 2,139 cavalrymen. This imbalance reflects Florence's need to secure its territory by garrisoning border fortresses and castles with infantry, particularly crossbowmen.

The registered infantry is consistently divided into three categories: crossbowmen, spearmen, and *palvesari* (infantry armed with pavises, known as Pavisers), generally in equal proportions. For instance, in December 1439, the city engaged a certain Lorenzo di Giovanni da Pisa with 120 infantrymen – 40 crossbowmen, 40 spearmen and 40 *palvesari.*[25]

This tripartite proportion appears regularly in larger companies. By contrast, smaller companies – numbering few than 10, eight or even as few as three infantrymen and far more common in the registers – consist exclusively of crossbowmen.

It is also significant to observe the marked increase in contracts as the conflict intensified, particularly as the Milanese threat drew nearer. In the

21 Wilbald Block, *Die Condottieri: Studien uber die sogenannten 'unblutigen Schlachten'* (Berlin: Emil Ebering, 1919), p.71.

22 Bracciolini, *Historia*, p.349; Sismondi, *Storia*, vol. VI, p.75.

23 *La rotta di Niccolò Piccinino*, p.289; *La Fuga del Capitano*, p.257.

24 Archivi di Stato di Firenze, *Dieci di Balìa, Deliberazioni condotte e stanziamenti*, lib. 18.

25 *Dieci di Balìa*, 18, f. 26r.

three months from January to March 1440, 29 captains stipulated contracts for a total of approximately 1,362 infantry. In April of the same year alone – on 10 April Piccinino was already at Mugello – 28 captains signed or renewed contracts amounting to 2,611 infantry.

Unfortunately, the contracts of the *Dieci di Balìa* are not always easy to interpret, as they are handwritten in fifteenth century Latin and heavily abbreviated. Because of orthographic irregularities, the names of certain captains may be illegible or incomplete; in some cases, the number of troops is entirely omitted, or the dates are incorrect. At times, the foliation itself becomes inconsistent: in one volume I consulted, after folio 34v. the numbering returns to 34r and proceeds again to 34v. Finally, some pages may even be missing.

Let us return to the calculation of troop numbers. As indicated in the previous paragraphs, infantrymen were roughly twice as numerous as cavalrymen. Leonardo Aretino states that by the end of May more than 4,000 infantrymen had been hired[26]. However, given their responsibility for territorial defence, it is unlikely that all of them were present at the Battle of Anghiari.

Let us attempt a calculation regarding these infantry at Anghiari. Pier Giovanpaolo Orsini, captain general, in addition to his lances, had 300 infantrymen with him,[27] while the constable Pazzaglia Guasparini da Pistoia commanded 500 infantrymen.[28] A further 400 crossbowmen arrived from Genoa under Bernardo di Duti. These infantrymen do not appear in the records of the *Dieci*[29] but are mentioned in several chronicles.[30] Finally, the Anghiarese constables Gregorio[31] and Leale[32] commanded respectively 300 and 80 infantrymen; according to the local historian Lorenzo Taglieschi, they most likely took part in the battle.[33]

Other constables mentioned in connection with the battle include Baldaccio d'Anghiari – who was in Piombino at the time – and Pietro

---

26 L. Aretini, 'Commentarius', *Muratori Rerum Italicarum Scripores*. XIX, col. 941.

27 *Dieci di Balìa*, 18, f. 34v.

28 *Dieci di Balìa*, 18, f. 32v; I. Masetti-Bencini, *La bataglia di Anghiari*, Rivista delle biblioteche e degli archivi, Luglio-Agosto 1907, p.121; *La Fuga del Capitano*, p.252, in this poem, Pazzaglia has 1,000 *paghe*.

29 Probably, they were not registered in the records because they were allies, thus paid directly by the Republic of Genoa.

30 d'Anghiari, 'Memorie', f. 38v; Cavalcanti, *Istorie Fiorentine*, Book XIV, Ch. XVIII; D. Buoninsegni, *Storia della città di Firenze* (Florence: 1673), p.72; Masetti-Bencini, 'bataglia di Anghiari', p.121.

31 *Dieci di Balìa*, 18, f. 20r: Gregorio di Vanni da Anghiari with 300 infantrymen: he is the same Gregorio who had been captured by the Milanese with his company in Modigliana and then redeemed, as Taglieschi recounts on p.171.

32 *Dieci di Balìa*, 18, ff. 26v and 33r: he has 60 infantrymen and, three months after, another 20 of reinforcement.

33 Lorenzo Taglieschi (Daniele Finzi & Matteo Parreschi eds), *Delle memorie istoriche e annali della terra di Anghiari* (Anghiari: Sansepolcro, 1991), p.172.

Brunoro, erroneously included by Benedetto Dei, as he was then in Lombardy.[34]

The total number of infantrymen thus amounts to 1,580.

Let us turn to the cavalry. Orsini commanded the largest cavalry contingent, with 1,200 cavalrymen – that is, the 400 lances recorded by the *Dieci*. Capponi and Palmieri report the same figure, whereas Sanudo attributes to Orsini 1,500 cavalrymen.[35]

The second largest contingent was that of Agnolo d'Anghiari, with 302[36] cavalrymen – in Florentine service since 1437 – followed by the 90 lances of a certain Antonio di Antonio Stefano, about whom nothing is presently known apart from his contract with the *Dieci*.[37]

There were also several smaller companies consisting of only a few lances each. It is certain that only Orsini and Agnolo were present at Anghiari; therefore, the Republic likely fielded approximately 1,500 cavalrymen and a comparable number of infantrymen.

As for the League, we begin with the contingent of the State of the Church. Here again, historians and chroniclers provide divergent figures.

Poggio Bracciolini and Taglieschi state that the Patriarch of Aquileia brought 4,000 cavalrymen into Tuscany. Biondo and Sismondi agree with this number, adding that he also had 2,000 infantrymen. According to Capponi and Ammirato, the army consisted of 3,000 cavalrymen and 500 infantrymen, whereas Aretino and Palmieri reduce the figure to 2,000 cavalrymen. Finally, Broglio and Graziani report that Patriarch Luigi Scarampi commanded 1,500 cavalrymen and 1,000 infantrymen.[38]

It is plausible that Bracciolini and Biondo, as well as Taglieschi and Sismondi, were referring to the total papal forces previously under Giovanni Vitelleschi, Scarampi's predecessor. In fact, Cardinal Vitelleschi commanded 4,000 cavalrymen and 2,000 infantrymen at the time of his arrest. These troops then passed to Scarampi, who first consolidated his power within the territories of the Church before departing to help the Florentines. However, as della Tuccia recounts, Scarampi left part of his forces to guard the Patrimonium (the State of the Church): namely 1,000 cavalrymen and

---

34 Romualdo Cardarelli, *Baldaccio d'Anghiari e la Signoria di Piombino nel 1440 e 1441* (Roma: Stabilimento Tipografico Leonardo da Vinci, 1922); Benedetto Dei, *La Cronica dal anno 1400 alle anno 1500* (Firenze: Papafava, 1984), p.56; Sanudo, 'Vite,' col. 1094.

35 *Dieci di Balìa*, 18, f. 34v; N Capponi, 'Commentari,' 1192; Palmieri, 'Annales,' p.148; Sanudo, 'Vite,' col. 1089.

36 *Dieci di Balìa*, 18, f. 24r; d'Anghiari, 'Memorie,' f. 35v; Sanudo states that they are 600 cavalrymen, col. 1089.

37 *Dieci di Balìa*, 18, f. 34r.

38 Bracciolini, *Historia*, p.345; Taglieschi, *Delle memorie*, p.171; Biondo, *Historie*, p.123; Sismondi, *Storia*, vol. VI, p.72; Capponi, 'Commentari,' 1194; Ammirato, *Istorie Fiorentine*, vol. IV, p.261; Aretini, 'Commentarius,' col. 941; Palmieri, 'Annales,' p.148; Gaspare Broglio Tartaglia (A. G. Lucani, ed.), *Cronaca Malatestiana del secolo XV* (Rimini: Bruno Ghigi, 1982), p.71.

600 infantrymen under Ludovico Micheletti da Perugia, Antonello della Sene, and other captains. Then, he joined Simonetto da Castel Pietro in Tuscany with 2,000 cavalrymen and numerous infantrymen.[39]

Even in the case of the papal troops, it is possible to reconstruct part of the personnel in greater detail thanks to several documents of varying reliability.

The accounts of the battle indicate that Lodovico Scarampi Mezzarota, Patriarch of Aquileia, was the supreme commander, while command in the field was entrusted to Simonetto da Castel di Pietro. Other captains included Count Averso of Anguillara, Paolo della Molara, Cristoforo da Farnese, and Angelo Roncone; no additional captains are mentioned in the sources.[40]

The same captains are listed in the registers of *condotte* hired by the Papal State, preserved in the State Archives of Rome under the inventory of *Soldatesche e galere*. These documents pertain to 1439, as the volume for 1440 is missing.[41] The registers, comparable in structure to those of the *Dieci di Balìa*, record the following figures: Simonetto as captain of 400 cavalrymen; Count Averso of 230; Count della Molara and Count Roncone of 150 each; and Count Farnese of 100.[42]

In the previously examined list of captains of fortune for 1439, Sanudo includes two of these names: Simonetto, to whom he attributes 600 cavalrymen, and Averso.[43] The latter appears both as Count Anguillara with 400 cavalrymen and as Count of Anversa with 600 cavalrymen; these two references most likely designate the same person.

On the basis of the forces listed in the Archive of Rome – probably more reliable – the total reaches slightly over 1,000 cavalrymen; specifically, 1,030. However, to this number must be added other captains listed in the Roman registers but not mentioned in the battle chronicles, such as Pandolfo Savello, Rinaldo Orsini and Carlo di Tartaglia da Lavello.

We must also include the *lance spezzate* from the company of Angelo Tartaglia, incorporated into the Papal Army after the *condottiero*'s death in 1421. These cavalrymen are identifiable in the depiction of the Battle of Anghiari on the Dublin Chest by the distinctive Tartaglia knot impresa. They are discussed further in the chapter devoted to heraldry.

It is therefore reasonable to conclude that Scarampi's forces at Anghiari most likely amounted to approximately 2,000 cavalrymen and 1,000 infantrymen.

39 Tuccia, *Cronaca di Viterbo*, pp.173–174.

40 Tuccia, *Cronaca di Viterbo*, p.175; *La rotta del Piccinino*, p.289.

41 Archivio di stato di Roma, *Commissariato delle soldatesche e galere*, busta 80, libro 1439.

42 *Soldatesche e galere*, ff. 8, 49, 57, 61, 1; Regarding Farnese, he is reported as Cristofano in *La rotta del Piccinino*, but in Chapter 1 of the *Soldatesche e galere* he is called Agnolo de Ranuccio da Farnese; perhaps, these two names do not refer to the same person.

43 Sanudo, 'Vite,' col. 1088.

The Sforza Forces and the Third Formation of the Pro-Florentine Army

Count Francesco Sforza dispatched several companies to assist the Florentines. According to Niccolò Capponi, an initial group consisted of 1,000 cavalrymen under the command of Troilo Orsino[44] and Bosio Sforza,[45] Francesco's brother. Ammirato, who clearly drew extensively upon Capponi's *Istorie*,[46] provides the same information.

Machiavelli writes that Sforza sent 1,000 cavalrymen followed by a further 500. According to della Tuccia, the Sforza troops numbered 2,000, whereas Aretino reduces the northern reinforcements to 700 cavalrymen.[47] Giovanni Simonetta, secretary to Francesco Sforza, states that the reinforcements were commanded by Bosio, Troilo, and Niccolò da Pisa. Benadducci,[48] by contrast, records that the captains were Niccolò da Pisa, Troilo, and Accattabriga, with 800 cavalrymen and 900 infantrymen.[49]

Capponi and Ammirato report that Troilo, while in Città di Castello, commanded 100 lances – that is, 300 cavalrymen. This figure is confirmed by Platina and by the poem *La Fuga del Capitano*. Biondo writes that Troilo and the Papal captain Paolo della Molara together had 300 cavalrymen, whereas della Tuccia assigns them 700 cavalrymen.[50]

Capponi alone mentions the strength of Niccolò da Pisa's cavalry when, after the victory at Anghiari, he accompanies him to Poppi and states that he had about 350 cavalrymen.[51]

Another Sforza captain who arrived with these reinforcements was Piero or Pietro Torelli, who appears only in the two poems and in Viviano's account of the Battle of Anghiari. Bartolomeo Litta, in his genealogy of the House of Torelli, identifies him as Pietro Guido Torelli of the Lords of

---

44 Also called Troilo da Muro da Rossano, one of Francesco Sforza's *famigli*. Cf Viviano, *Registri*. libro 3569, f. 62.

45 Between 1431 and 1434, Bosio or Buosio served in Micheletto Attendolo's company with 18 cavalrymen. Cf Viviano, *Registri*, libri: 3356 f. 20r, 3558 ff. 15r and 19r, 3592 f. 139v, 3572 f. 13r.

46 Capponi, 'Commentari', 1193; Ammirato, *Istorie Fiorentine*, vol. IV, p.260.

47 Machiavelli, *Istorie Fiorentine*, vol. 2, p.80; Tuccia, *Cronaca di Viterbo*, p.173; Aretini, 'Commentarius', col. 941.

48 Niccolò Gambacorti also known as 'da Pisa', companion of Sforza.

49 Johannis Simonetae, 'Vita Francisci Sfortiae,' *Muratori Rerum Italicarum Scripores* XXI, col. 288; Giovanni Benadducci, *Della Signoria di Francesco Sforza nella Marca* (Tolentino: Francesco Filelfo, 1892), p.178; Benadducci is the only one who mentions Accattabriga in Tuscany; Sanudo, 'Vite,' col. 1089, calls him Don Cattabriga and reports that he had 400 cavalrymen.

50 Capponi, 'Commentari', 1194; B. Platina, *Vita Nerii Capponii*, col. 500; *La Fuga del Capitano,* p.259; Biondo, *Historie*, p.127; Tuccia, *Cronaca di Viterbo*, p.175.

51 Capponi, 'Commentari', 1196.

Guastalla and notes that, in 1440, he followed Francesco Sforza in Venetian service with 200 cavalrymen – the same number reported by Sanudo.[52]

The final Sforza contingent was that of Micheletto Attendolo from the Marca (modern Marche), whose role would prove decisive in securing victory. Aretino states that he commanded 700 cavalrymen, Graziani 800, and Palmieri 1,000.[53] As usual, the chroniclers disagree. Fortunately, however, we possess the registers of Micheletto's own company, compiled by his accountant Francesco Viviano. In the volume entitled *Carte Varie* among these registers, preserved in Arezzo, an unnambered folio reads: '*A dì 15 di maggio 1439 gomincia lo soldo del conte Francesco Sforza in fra lui el S. Mess. Michele*' (On 15 May 1439, the contract between Count Francesco Sforza and Sir Michele began). The document specifies that the contract concerned the enlistment of 400 lances and 250 infantrymen for three months at six florins per lance and two florins per infantryman. It further records a renewal on 15 August, increasing the force to 450 lances and 300 infantrymen at eight florins per lance and two florins per infantryman.

This gives a total of 1,350 cavalrymen and 300 infantrymen – a figure that exceeds the 1,000 cavalrymen reported by Palmieri.

At this point, another register, numbered 3574, proves particularly valuable. It records outflows from 1439 to 1441, corresponding to Sforza's period of service. In this volume, all expenditures relating to soldiers under *condotta* – from captains down to simple muleteers, that is, all individuals receiving pay – are meticulously entered. What is especially significant are the names of the captains, the composition of their forces, the dates of their instalments, and the locations where payments were made. On the basis of pay and advances recorded on 25, 26, and 27 June in '*campo sotto Anchiarj*' (in the camp at Anghiari), it is therefore possible to verify the presence of captains and cavalrymen at the battle itself.

Table 1 below lists the captains who received payment, indicating on the left the folio number of register 3574 and on the right, indicated by 'c.', the number of horses under each captain.

52 *La Fuga del Capitano*, pp.251 and 265; *La rotta del Piccinino*, p.291; Viviano, *Registri*, book 3574, foglio di guardia; Pompeo Litta, *Famiglie celebri italiane*, Milan 1818 –1873, 7, tav. Sanudo, 'Vite,' col. 1088.

53 Aretini, 'Commentarius', col. 941; *Diario del Graziani*, p.450; Palmieri, *Annales*, p.148.

Table 1: Captains and the strength of their 'company'

84v	Giovanni da Dragura	c.6	112r	Agnolo di Tarsia di Calabria	c.10
96v	Moschino and Antonio	c.10	112v	Jacopo da Fraruffino	c.6
97r	Giorgio da Brescia	c.9	114r	Baron of Consoleto	c.18
97v	Cola Guercio	c.6	114v	Corrado d'Alviano	c.10
99v	s. Betuccio de Cortesi da Cotignola	c.159	115v	Franceschino da Siena	c.9
100r	Villano and Batista di Bambo	c.10	116v	Nardello di Francalancia	c.5
100v	Agnolo di Bambo	c.5	117r	Giovanni da Casale	c.12
101v	Antonello and Francesco Siguro	c.18	117v	Verdiramo di Giufreda from Naples	c.12
102r	Romanello da Subiaco	c.6	119r	Man-at-arms	c.7
102v	Antonello da Lucca	c.6	119v	Corrado Tedesco	c.5
103r	Fraruffino da S. Agata di Romagna	c.6	120r	Mattioccio da Terni	c.8
103v	Bagnacavallo da Bagnacavallo	c.10	121v	Stefano da Matera	c.5
104r	Donato and Roberto da Meglonaco	c.10	122v	Rinaldo Pudorico	c.12
104v	Arzimaldo da Benevento	c.6	123r	Marinino da Bologna	c.7
105r	s. Raffaello di Vramonte s. di Carpi	c.90	135r	Todero da Lecce	c.5
106r	Cola da Trani	c.9	135v	Bartolomeo da Siena	c.18
107r	s. Gabriello da Monte Aureo Foggia	c.45	144r	s. mess. Orso Orsino	c.36
107v	Paulino da Barbiano	c.6	146r	Niccolò da Bologna and Guaspari	c.6
108r	Romanello da Cingoli and Antonello	c.13	154r	Antonello di Donno and Arrigo	c.13
108v	Tartaglia d'Arezzo	c.18	155r	Martino Schiavo	c.9
111r	Carnecina and Ragazzino	c.10	158r	Marco degli Attendolo	c.111
111v	Antonello da Renda di Calabria	c.18	159r	Jacopo Rosso da Napoli	c.18

This gives a total of 818 cavalrymen, to which must be added the men-at-arms belonging to the 'household' of the lord – Micheletto himself. The precise size of his 'household' is difficult to determine, since the books of *condotta* do not include the relevant payment records. However, Mario Del Treppo found and published a list with the composition of the company's squadrons for its first *condotta* with Venice in 1441.[54] Although this document dates to a year after the events in question, it records that Micheletto had 89 lances – 267 cavalrymen.

We therefore reach a total of 1,085 cavalrymen, a figure that coincides with that reported by Palmieri.

To this number must be added the infantrymen recorded in register 3574 under the command of three constables: Colella da Castellaneta with 56 *paghe* (infantrymen) and 9 cavalrymen; Cristofano da Cremona with 120 *paghe* and 12 cavalrymen; Francesco da Bibiena with 74 *paghe* and 15 cavalrymen.[55] Finally, there was also a squadron of 12 handgunners under the command of Giovanni Colonna.[56]

To conclude this chapter by attempting to calculate the overall strength of the forces engaged in the battle (needless to say, any total must remain largely hypothetical). Before doing so, however, it is necessary to subtract the losses sustained in previous engagements and the soldiers left behind in garrisons. These earlier clashes occurred primarily to conquer the places crossed by the Milanese during their march in Tuscany. In these episodes, the Florentine side mainly deployed local garrison infantry rather than field troops.

On the Milanese side, apart from relatively minor losses, it is necessary to account for the soldiers detached to hold the conquered positions. The chronicler Giusto d'Anghiari provides useful evidence in this regard, mentioning 60 Milanese cavalrymen and 60 men from Bibbiena stationed in the garrison of Rassina, which surrendered to the Florentines in the first days of July.[57]

This information allows us to estimate the forces left by Piccinino in other occupied places, such as San Niccolò, Bibbiena, Romena, Chiusi, and many others. It is possible that the Perugian commander left several hundred infantrymen and cavalrymen to secure these locations, for a total possibly approaching 1,000 men.

54 M. Del Treppo, 'Sulla struttura della compagnia o condotta militare' in *Condottieri e uomini d'arme nell'Italia del rinascimento*, (Napoli: Liguori, 2001, p.439.

55 Viviano, *Registri*, libro 3574, ff. 22v, 74r ,91v, 92r, 161v.

56 Viviano, *Registri*, libro 3574, ff. 128r–133v, 137r.

57 d'Anghiari, 'Memorie', f. 39v.

Table 2: Summary of the opposing forces immediately prior to the battle

(NB as above 'c.' indicates the number of horses)

Milanese Army		League Army	
Niccolò Piccinino	2,200 c.	Pier Giovanpaolo Orsini	1,200 c.
Duke's familiars	600 c.	Angelo Pieri d'Anghiari	302 c.
Lance spezzate	600 c.	(Florentine) Infantrymen	1,300 p.
Count Carlo Fortebracci	200 c.	Simonetto da Castel Pietro	600 c.
Sacramoro Visconti	200 c.	Averso d'Anguillara	230 c.
Rinaldo da Monte Alboddo	100 c.	Molara, Roncone, Farnese	400 c.
Guidantonio Manfredi	500 c.	Pope's lance spezzate	1,000 c.
Francesco Piccinino	600 c.	Infantrymen of the Church	1,000 p.
Astorre Manfredi and other captains, about 600 c.		Micheletto Attendolo	1,120 c.
		Troilo da Muro	300 c.
Total	about 5,600 cavalrymen	Niccolò da Pisa	350 c.
Milanese infantry	about 2,200 *paghe*	Piero Torelli, Bosio Sforza	250 c.
Citizens of Borgo	about 1,500 infantrymen	Sforzeschi infantrymen	1,032 *paghe*
		Total	about 5,752 cavalrymen
			about 3,332 infantrymen

The Milanese forces also included the citizens of Borgo Sansepolcro, who had aligned themselves with Piccinino prior to the battle. Their role and contribution is examined in greater detail in a later chapter of this study.

The League forces similarly included the units of Troilo and Molara, which, although they did not take part directly in the battle, were stationed in Città di Castello at the time.

7

Non-Combatants in Micheletto Attendolo's Company

With reference to the non-combatants mentioned at the beginning of the previous chapter – namely the actual personnel of a company of fortune, which included numerous auxiliaries, members of the retinue, or *saccomanni* (that is, individuals who were not soldiers) – the following table lists all those recorded in the pay of Micheletto Attendolo's company in the years 1439–1441 in register 3574.[1]

These people represent only a part of those paid to follow their lord in the expedition to Tuscany, as documented by the payments entered with a date and location in or nearby Anghiari.

In the table below, the left column indicates the page number of register 3574, followed by the name of the person, their occupation, and any associated servant, family member, or relevant annotation. The abbreviation S. indicates that the person belonged to the lord's 'household', while M. indicates *Magistro.*

14r,	Anichino di S. Martino di Rapara di Basilicata, sutler, S. (of the lord).
16v,	Tomaso, baker: following the company in Arezzo, he receives 2 ducats to pay for lodging.
17r,	Piero, German baker and cook, S. In 1441, he enters the service of Betuccio
19r,	Lorenzo da Canpagna, muleteer, S.
19v,	Giovanni, German baker and muleteer: in June, he is at Anghiari
21r,	Sir Piero da Aquasparte: accompanied by his wife, son and daughters
23v,	M. Bernabo, saddler of S. In May, in Florence, he receives a large *giornea* bearing our device
24v,	Antonello, infantryman.

1 Viviano, *Registri della compagnia di Micheletto Attendolo*, in Fraternita dei Laici di Arezzo, libro 3574.

25r,	Bartolomeo da Campagna di Egoli, principality of Salerno. 'He was Colella da Castellaneta's companion on foot'
25v,	Marino da Frassina, secretary S. Accompanied by his wife and daughter.
26r,	Simone da S. Giovanni Valdarno di Sopra, trumpeter of S. His brother, Agnolo di Nanni, barber, is with him. On 8 June, the brother receives 3 lire in his name in Valdarno '(...) when he lay ill in bed with his woman.'
27r,	Giovanni da Benevento, muleteer of S. In April-May, he was in Tuscany
29v,	Giovanni Erin, German baker of S. In June, he was in Arezzo. He receives 1 florin per month.
30r,	Giovanni di Corrado, German trumpeter of S. On 11 June, he is in Arezzo; his wife accompanies him.
30v,	Naples, high-tenor piper of S.
34r,	M. Giovanni da Potenza, piper of S. He receives 2 florins per month.
34v,	M. Roberto d'Ansy, tenor piper of S. Messer Michele.
37v,	Lapo muleteer. On 20 May, he is in Anghiari. In May 1439, M. Speranza, Jewish, treats him for illness.
42r,	Antonio da Taranto, *spenditore* of S.
57r,	M. Luca da Castello, our physician and surgeon from Teresia. In April, he was in Arezzo; with him are his *famigli* Mariano da Pisa and Roberto, and his page Matteo.
57v,	Luca da Lancisa, muleteer S. On 30 April, he was in Arezzo
59v,	Domenico da Atella, muleteer S. On 30 April, he receives 2 ducats for lodging in Arezzo
60v,	Grigoro, muleteer. On April 30, he was in Arezzo.
65r,	Lorisgi da Monte Varchi, muleteer S. On 25 May, he is in Anghiari; with him are his brother-in-law, his brother, and Boldrino, page of S.
66v,	Piero di M. Antonio, bricklayer from Sartiano da Romagna. On 24 April, he is in Arezzo.
69r,	Tiraqua, our blacksmith.
69v,	Giorgio di Lianello, notary. On 12 June, he is in Arezzo.
71v,	Bartolomeo da Prato Vecchio, mule blacksmith of S.
99r,	M. Jacopo da Matera. On 21 April, he was in Arezzo.
109r,	Vangelista da Fagiolo, our butcher from Imola. On 24 April, he was in Arezzo with his colleague Niccolò, butcher, and other companions.
113r,	Messer Merlino da S. Gemini, our adviser. Accompanied by his wife.
124r,	Angelino di Larnano, our priest. 'To be given on the first day of April 1 ducat, which he had in Arezzo, as he wished to buy a couple of barrels of wine'.
124v,	Francesco da S. Gemini. On 30 April, he receives one ducat upon joining the lord in Arezzo
125r,	Giovanni da S. Gemini. On 30 April, he receives one ducat upon joining the lord in Arezzo
125v,	Scaramuccia da S. Gemini. On 30 April, he receives one ducat upon joining the lord in Arezzo

127r,	Matteo by Piero di Bartolo di Mugello, our mule driver, accompanied by his wife. He is paid 8 lire per month '... to drive mules'.
138r,	Agnolo di Marsico, our treasurer. On 26 June, he is at La Verna near Arezzo. With him are messer Lionardo, his brother, and Giovanni Novello, trumpeter.
159v,	Simone, muleteer. On 3 July, he is in the camp at Anghiari
213v,	Madonna Sovena, who is with *Madama* Isabella, Micheletto's wife: Sovena is *Madama* Isabella's lady-in-waiting.
217v,	Francesco da Viviano d'Arezzo, treasurer and administrator of the S. funds, here with his brother Niccolò

In total, the list records 40 people in service, in addition to approximately 21 others not directly in receipt of pay but connected through family ties (wives, brothers, sons or daughters) or as companions, assistants, servants, or boys.

Balestracci devotes a chapter to the structure of the company of fortune, using Micheletto's company as a case study.[2] He highlights the remarkable variety of trades present in the train of a company and the considerable number of people involved.

He first identifies the administrative and organisational roles – accountants, clerks, secretaries – who did not generally accompany the army on military campaigns but operated from fixed locations, such as cities. In the present list, four people belong to this category and likely did not follow the company into Tuscany: Piero da Aquasparte, the secretary Marino da Frassina, Agnolo di Marsico, and Madama Isabella.

On the other hand, certain administrators occasionally went to the military camp to deliver instalments or advances of pay, such as the treasurer Antonio da Taranto, the notary Giorgio di Lianello, Merlino da San Gemini, and Niccolò Viviano, Francesco's brother.

Balestracci then lists the other auxiliaries who travelled with the company, including servants, cooks, physicians, religious personnel, et cetera. This second and more numerous group occupies almost the entirety of the above register-based list.

An analysis of the professions recorded reveals several noteworthy aspects.

There are eight muleteers, two blacksmiths, one saddler, and one waggon driver responsible for transport and vehicles. Three trumpeters and three pipers are also listed, enrolled among the soldiers.

Those responsible for provisioning include two bakers, one baker and cook, one baker and muleteer, a butcher, and a sutler.

The list further includes a barber, a bricklayer, a priest, and a Jewish physician named Speranza. Another doctor, Luca da Castello, was also

2 Balestracci, *Le armi, i cavalli, l'oro*, pp.56–61.

a man-at-arms and commander of a lance. Finally, there are a couple of infantrymen and some people whose profession is not specified.

Salaries varied considerably. Some received notably high wages, such as a certain Antonio di Marsico, probably a treasurer, who was paid 50 florins per year. He does not appear in the list because he fled on 7 August 1439 '... with the aforementioned money of S.' Giovanni Alemanco, a baker, received 1 florin per month; Matteo di Piero, mule driver, earned even less, 8 *lire* per month, while a piper such as Giovanni da Potenza received the pay of an infantryman, 2 florins per month.

Almost all the people listed depended directly on Micheletto's 'household'. However, other important captains with a high number of cavalrymen also had their own servants and auxiliaries. The following examples are taken from register 3574:

> Betuccio de Cortesi had his own trumpeter Pietro, accompanied by his wife, madonna Santina.[3]
>
> Vramonte, Lord of Carpi, travelled with the chancellor Giovanni Porceno and a merchant named Xpofano da Todi.[4]
>
> Gabriello da Monte Aureo was with his chancellor Felipo, while Cola Scrima brought with him his servant boy Nardo Vechio.[5]
>
> Jacopo Rosso from Naples had with him a boy named Cola Gayrano as well as an unnamed slave.

At this time, the use of slaves was relatively widespread in Italian cities. This practice had expanded in the second half of the fourteenth century in response to the labour shortages caused by the Black Death of 1348. Slaves were bought and transported from the Eastern Mediterranean by Venetian and Genoese merchants and employed in heavy agricultural labour or transport.

Enslaved women were more numerous than men. Many were described as 'Tartar', who were considered to be physically robust, but others were Greek, Russian, Turkish, or Slavic. They cost between 50 and 60 florins, and they were employed as domestic servants or exploited sexually by their masters, their sons, or their clients.

Some masters appeared to have treated them with relative consideration. Jacopo Rosso, for instance, paid 7 florins and 30 bolognini for a skirt '... for his slave', a sum exceeding three months' pay for an infantryman. A year later, Viviano records that Rosso paid for a cloak: '... *per la schiava sua*

3 Viviano, *Registri*, lib. 3574, f. 115r.
4 Viviano, *Registri*, lib. 3574, f. 105r.
5 Viviano, *Registri*, lib. 3574, ff. 107r & 110r.

chera pregna del sopradetto Jacopo' (for his slave, who was carrying Jacopo's child).[6]

Balestracci also lists other interesting figures who commonly followed companies of fortune but do not appear in Viviano's registers, such as *ribaldi*, buffoons, and prostitutes. He recalls the Battle of Brentelle in 1386, during which 215 prostitutes were reportedly counted among the prisoners.[7]

6 Viviano, *Registri*, lib. 3574, ff. 121r & 182v.
7 Balestracci, *Le armi, i cavalli, l'oro*, p.59.

8

The Battle

On 29 June 1440, the feast of Saints Peter and Paul, Nicolò Picinino came to Borgo Sansepolcro with 6,000 cavalrymen. There he faced the Patriarch and Lord Michele, Pietro Giampauolo captain of Florence, Simonetto of Castello di Piero, Angnolo d'Anchiari, Nicolò da Pisa, Francesco Count of Matelica,[1] Piero Torello, and Troiolo and many other *condottieri*, Roman princes, numerous members of the Orsini family, and other lineages. They had taken position in the field below Anghiari, determined not to lose their standing of Florentines, Venetians, the Pope, Genoese, and the entire League.

Nicolò Piccinino controlled Borgo and showed open hostility towards the League's supporters. He sought to force them into battle and advanced arrogantly and proudly against them. On that very day, the assembled people and captains appointed the distinguished Messer Michele degli Attendolo da Cotignola as their commander. He defeated Nicolò Picinino on the battlefield and captured 2,500 horses, and there were many casualties on both sides. By the evening, at the 24th hour, each army returned to its quarters with considerable spoils and numerous prisoners. Among these were 1,457 prisoners held for ransom taken from Borcho Santo Sepolcro. Nicolò Piccinino stayed in Borgo for the night. The following morning, defeated, he fled first to Bologna and then to Milan. This outcome was thanks to the bravery of Messer Michele's men, to God, and to Saints Peter and Paul, who on that day granted victory and brought about the defeat of the duke's forces.[2]

---

1 Matelica belonged to the Ottoni family of the Marche and fought for the Sforzas. Among all the documents on the Battle of Anghiari, he is mentioned only in this one. Some information about this man can be found in: Antonio Gianandrea, *Della Signoria di Francesco Sforza nella Marca* (Milano: Tortolotti di Dal Bono, 1885), pp.33–35 and 102.

2 This text was adapted to facilitate its translation into English. In the document,

THE BATTLE OF ANGHIARI, 29 JUNE 1440

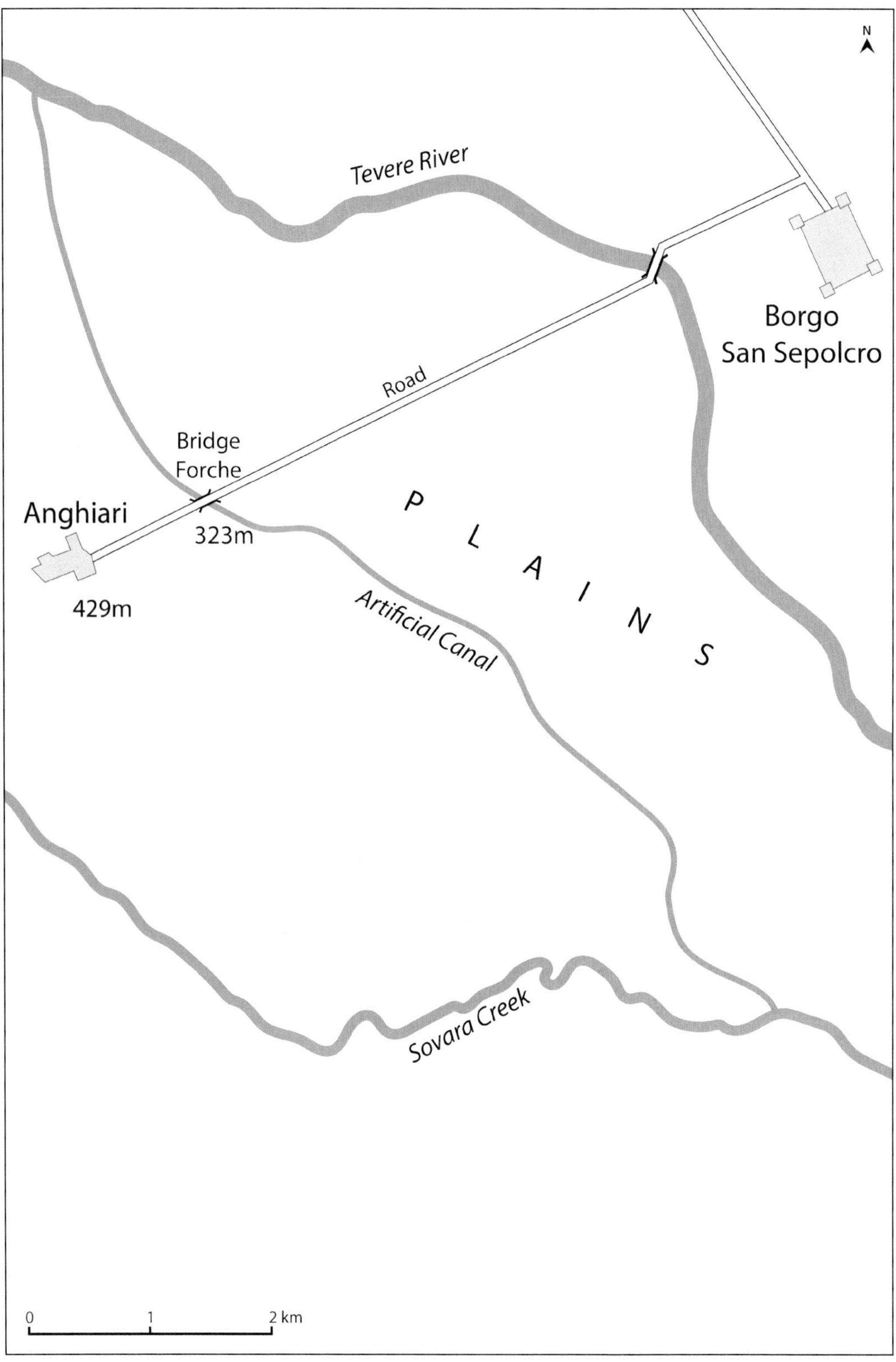

24. Plain of the Battle of Anghiari.

This brief account was written by Francesco Viviano concerning the Battle of Anghiari and is preserved in register 3574 relating to the movements of Micheletto Attendolo's company in the years 1439–1441.[3] The text appears on the front sheet – that is, on the inside of the volume's cover – and is severely damaged by weathering and wormholes, which have rendered several words incomplete and therefore difficult to decipher. Nevertheless, the text is noteworthy for its reports on the deployed forces, the names of the captains, and the losses suffered by the Milanese in the battle; contemporary chronicles confirm this information.

Unfortunately, the account does not dwell on the course of the battle, neither do several other chronicles, such as the *Istorie* by Cavalcanti, the *Storia di Parma*, the *Annales* by Palmieri, the *Vite dei Duchi* by Sanudo, as well as others.[4] These historians and chroniclers generally devote only a few lines to the fighting itself, while providing more detailed accounts of the Milanese losses or the considerable spoils captured by the Florentines.

Other writers, by contrast, dwell on the violence of the feats of arms – among them Simonetta, Poggio, Decembrio, Corio, and others – but the most expansive narratives are undoubtedly the two poems *La rotta del Piccinino* and *La Fuga del Capitano*. The latter recounts the clash at length and, in the manner of epic poetry, often lingers on individual duels between opposing captains. Yet, these poems are highly emphatic, and they frequently diverge from one another – one may describe an event or a character entirely omitted by the other, and vice versa.

But to turn to the sequence of events.

On the morning of 29 June, Piccinino had his troops prepared. From reconnaissance carried out towards the enemy camp, he had noted the lack of cohesion that often characterises coalition armies such as that of the League. He had also observed that, because of the intense heat of the days, the League's soldiers would send out the *saccomanni* in the morning while they themselves stood armed and ready until noon. In the following hours, however, they laid aside their arms and rested unarmed in the shade of their pavilions or nearby houses, since the camp was close to the city walls.[5]

On that feast day – the anniversary of Saints Peter and Paul – around midday, the Braccesco commander left his camp with all his baggage,

---

proper names are in lower case. In the transcription, I have put them in upper case for clarity.

3 F. Viviano, *Registri della compagnia di Micheletto Attendolo*, in Fraternita dei Laici di Arezzo, book 3574.

4 Other chronicles that do not describe the battle: the '*Commentarius*' by Leonardo Aretino; Buoninsegni, *Storia*; the '*Cronica*' by Benedetto Dei, the 'Memorie' of Giusto d'Anghiari, the 'Cronaca malatestiana' by Broglio, and the '*Diario del Graziani*'.

5 Ammirato, *Istorie*, vol. IV, p.262; Pier Candido Decembrio, 'Vita di Niccolò Piccinino' in *Muratori Rerum Italicarum Scriptores* XX, 1081; Lorenzo Taglieschi (Daniele Finzi & Matteo Parreschi eds), *Delle memorie istoriche e annali della terra di Anghiari* (Anghiari: Sansepolcro, 1991), p.254.

25. Anghiari plain with chapel commemorating the battle. (Photograph by the author)

feigning a retreat to Romagna.[6] He passed through Borgo Sansepolcro, where he left the baggage train, and persuaded a large number of citizens to join him by enticing them with the prospect of an easy victory and conspicuous plunder. He then advanced on the road to Anghiari.

Machiavelli and Ammirato recorded that 2,000 Biturgians joined Piccinino, whereas Marco Antonio Sabellico, the Venetian historian who wrote the *Istories* at the end of the fifteenth century, reports that they numbered 1,000.[7]

Anghiari lies at the foot of the Apennines upon a hill of moderate height, such that from the eastern side, facing the village, the ascent is relatively gentle. From that point to Borgo Sansepolcro the terrain stretches flat for about five miles, intersected by a small river that descends from the hill of Anghiari, bordered by steep banks and crossed by a small bridge. This bridge, known at the time as Ponte delle Forche,[8] stands about 300 paces from the hill; from there the road runs in a straight line towards Borgo Sansepolcro, crossing the Tiber shortly before reaching the town. It was along this route that the Milanese had to advance to attack the League forces.

As Piccinino had anticipated, the Florentines had only sent out their foragers, while the remainder of the army had stayed within their tents to escape the heat.

6 Johannis Simonetae, 'Vita Francisci Sfortiae', *Muratori R.I.S.* XXI, col. 292.

7 Niccolò Machiavelli, *Istorie Fiorentine* (Milan: Società Anonima Notari or Alpes, 1928), vol. 2, p.89; Ammirato, *Istorie*, vol. IV, p.262; M. A. Sabellico, *Degl'Istorici delle cose Veneziane* (Veneziane: 1747), vol. V, p.158.

8 Death sentences were probably carried out on it.

26. Anghiari with the steep climb on the right. (Photograph by the author)

The only one who remained under arms to maintain vigilance was Micheletto Attendolo, a veteran of a number of battles. From the hill of Monteloro where his camp was, he saw a dust cloud gradually rising across the plain. It was Piccinino and the army advancing from the village, 'at about the nineteenth hour and 20', as Capponi records in his 'Commentari'.[9]

In Italy at this time, the hours of the day were counted from the first hour after sunset, that is, from the first hour of the night; in common usage, the 24th hour corresponded to sunset. In June, the sunset is around 20:30, therefore the 'nineteenth hour and 20' would correspond to around 16:30 in modern reckoning. However, according to a study of the battle by Carlo Pellegrini, the 'nineteenth hour and 20' should instead correspond to 15:30.[10]

Once Attendolo recognised the approaching force as the enemy, he sounded the alarm and, with his company, hastened to secure the bridge. He was followed by Simonetto, captain of the Papal troops, Giovanpaolo Orsini, and gradually by the other captains, while the entire camp was in turmoil.

At the stream, the commanders conferred on their course of action, even as the enemy skirmishers had already come within crossbow range.

The League commanders deployed their forces in three groups. In the centre stood Micheletto with Sforza's men, who had already reached the bridge. On the left were Orsini and Agnolo Taglia with the cavalry and the Florentine commissars; on the right, Simonetto and the Papal troops. A part of the cavalry remained on the hill with the patriarch, together with the flags, while the infantry guarded the embankments flanking the bridge

9 N. Capponi, 'Commentari' in *Muratori Rerum Italicarum Scriptores* XVIII, col. 1195.

10 F.Carlo Pellegrini, *Un documento della battaglia di Anghiari* (Livorno: Tipografia di R. Giusti, 1901), p.7.

to block the advance of the Milanese infantry.[11] Pazzaglia Guasparini led the Florentine infantrymen, and Bernardo Duti commanded the Genoese crossbowmen. On the Milanese side, the names of the constables commanding the infantry are not recorded. Only Giusto d'Anghiari mentions a certain Piero Bernardo, described as constable of Niccolò Piccinino. However, this captain appears among the Milanese garrison during the Florentine recapture of Rassina on 6 July 1440 and therefore could not have been present at Anghiari.[12]

The soldiers were not yet in formation when the Milanese vanguard reached the bridge and collided with Micheletto's cavalrymen, who resisted the assault and forced the Milanese back.

At this point, Piccinino committed his son Francesco, Astorre Manfredi and Sacramoro Visconti, at the head of two selected companies. They charged Micheletto's men, seized the bridge, and drove him and his forces back towards the slope leading up to Anghiari.[13]

In describing this initial engagement, *La Fuga del Capitano* lingers on a series of duels between captains. It recounts the clash between Astorre and Micheletto, which ended inconclusively when both lances broke upon impact. Likewise, the encounter between Filippo Schiavo and Torelli produced no decisive result. Finally, the clash between Niccolò da Pisa and

27. The Forche Bridge today. (Photograph by the author)

11 Ammirato, *Istorie Fiorentine*, vol. IV, pp.262 – 263; Decembrio, 'Niccolò Piccinino' 1081; Taglieschi, *Delle memorie*, pp.171–172; Capponi, 'Commentari', 1195; Simonetae, 'Vita,' col. 293; Machiavelli, *Istorie Fiorentine*, vol. 2, pp.89–90.

12 G. d'Anghiari, 'Memorie dall'anno 1437 al 1481,' Bibl. Naz. Fir. Ms. II. II. 127, f. 40v.

13 Ammirato, *Istorie Fiorentine*, vol. IV, p.263; Decembrio, 'Niccolò Piccinino' 1081; Simonetae, 'Vita,' col. 293; Machiavelli, *Istorie Fiorentine*, vol. 2, p.90; Bernardino Corio, *Storia di Milano*, vol. II (Torino: Utet, 1978), p.1140; Poggio, *Vita di Piccinino*, p.255.

Roberto da Monte Alboddo culminated in a violent collision in which the latter was nearly unhorsed by Niccolò's spear.[14]

Perceiving the danger, Simonetto promptly rushed to help his companions. He drove the Milanese back to the bridge, where the fighting flared up anew; once Micheletto had regained control of the position, the *condottiero* of the Papal forces returned to the right wing.[15]

For nearly an hour, the battle surged back and forth: first, the League's men secured the bridge, then Piccinino's troops recovered it. Taglieschi wrote: 'they performed admirable feats, and both sides fought with valour. Among the common soldiers, Renzino di Menco della Valle [from Anghiari], who performed remarkable deeds with a spontoon, killing and wounding many enemies. From that day forward, he was known as Renzino dallo Spuntone [Renzino of the Spontoon].'[16]

The Milanese forces, however, suffered a tactical disadvantage, as they faced greater difficulty in bringing reinforcements to the front line. On the side towards Anghiari, the ground was open and level – Orsini had ordered it cleared – allowing the cavalry to move freely. Beyond the bridge, by contrast, the passage narrowed and was obstructed by ditches dug by local farmers to collect rainwater and to protect cultivated fields from livestock. Therefore, when the Florentines were driven back, they could readily receive support, whereas the Milanese were hindered by embankments and ditches, and their reinforcement struggled to reach them. Piccinino had noticed this obstacle during reconnaissance but had underestimated its significance, confident that he would catch the enemy unprepared and overcome them with ease.[17]

He therefore dispatched his son once more, together with Astorre, to renew the assault with their selected cavalry. According to *La Fuga del Capitano*, Lodovico da Parma, Iacopo d'Ariano, and Antonello da Santa Marta led this attack; Bernardino Corio, for his part, speaks of nine squadrons of Milanese cavalry.[18]

The Visconti soldiers pressed Micheletto so vigorously that they surrounded him, while on the left side of the bridge they captured Niccolò Gambacorti (known as 'da Pisa').

Simonetto and Orsini again descended from the hill with part of the cavalry and succeeded in rescuing Niccolò by pushing back the Bracceschi.[19]

14 *La Fuga del Capitano* in A. Fabretti, *Note e documenti da biografie dei Capitani Venturieri dell'Umbria,* vol. Unico (Montepulciano: Angiolo Tumi, 1842), pp.263 – 264.

15 Simonetae, 'Vita,' col. 293; Ammirato, *Istorie Fiorentine*, vol. IV, p.263.

16 Taglieschi, *Delle memorie*, p.172.

17 Ammirato, *Istorie Fiorentine*, vol. IV, p.263; Taglieschi, *Delle memorie*, p.172; Machiavelli, *Istorie Fiorentine*, vol. 2, p.91.

18 *La Fuga del Capitano*, p.265; Corio, *Storia*, vol. II, p.1140.

19 Simonetae, 'Vita,' col. 294; Ammirato, *Istorie Fiorentine*, vol. IV, p.263; Taglieschi, *Delle memorie*, p.172; *La Fuga del Capitano*, p.265.

At this point of the battle, *La Fuga del Capitano* relates other duels. Simonetto di Castel di Piero charged at Tartaglia della Guancia and, with a well-aimed thrust of his spear, unhorsed him. Meanwhile, Niccolò da Pisa engaged Antonello da Santa Marta in a sword fight; eventually, the Pisan grabbed the crest of his weakened opponent's helmet and dragged him to the ground. Both Milanese cavalrymen were taken prisoner and brought into Anghiari.[20]

However, the Bracceschi regained strength, intensified their attacks, and reinforced their hold on the bridge. The fighting between the bridge and the slope leading to the hill flared up again, with all the soldiers compressed into that narrow space.

Decembrio writes that the animosity of the struggle was such that:

> … once their spears and swords were broken, they struck one another with fists and iron gauntlets. It was a marvellous sight. No shout could be heard, nor any distinct voice be understood. Only the discharge of hand cannons and springalds resounded. Niccolò Piccinino's army had more hand cannons and springalds, while the enemy camp had heavier artillery, and when they directed it towards the bridge, they killed many soldiers.[21]

28. Anghiari, Church of Sant'Agostino. (Photograph by the author)

20 *La Fuga del Capitano* , pp.266 – 268.

21 Decembrio, 'Niccolò Piccinino,' col. 1081.

Plate A
1: Standard of Firenze
2: Standard of the Church
3: Commissioner Bernadetto de' Medici
4: Commissioner Neri Capponi
5: Patriarch Ludovico Scarampi Mezzarota
(Artwork by Massimo Predonzani © Helion & Company 2026)

Plate B: Milanese Knights
1: Standard of the Bracceschi
2: Standard of the *radia magna*
3: Niccolò Piccinino
(Artwork by Massimo Predonzani © Helion & Company 2026)

Plate C: Knights of Attendolo-Sforza
1: Standard of Attendolo-Sforza
2: Marco degli Attendolo
3: Bosio Sforza
4: Micheletto Attendolo
5: Standard of Micheletto Attendolo
6: Page Attendolo-Sforza
(Artwork by Massimo Predonzani © Helion & Company 2026)

Plate D
1: Standard of the Duchy of Milan
2: Man-at-arms of the Manfredi
3: Francesco Piccinino
4: Milanese infantryman
5: Milanese infantryman
(Artwork by Massimo Predonzani © Helion & Company 2026)

Plate E: Mercenaries in the pay of Florence
1: Agnolo Taglia
2: Pier Giovanpaolo Orsini
3: Orsini standard
4: Niccolò da Pisa
(Artwork by Massimo Predonzani © Helion & Company 2026)

Plate F
1: Milanese infantryman with a hand cannon
2: Guidantonio Manfredi
3: Astorre Manfredi's *lanciotto* (a type of lance)
4: Boy called *famiglio*
(Artwork by Massimo Predonzani © Helion & Company 2026)

Plate G: Army of the Church
1: Broglia mercenary
2: Church trumpeter
3: Simonetto da Castel di Piero
4: Shield Bearer of the Patriarch
5: Infantryman with long spear
(Artwork by Massimo Predonzani © Helion & Company 2026)

Plate H: Coats of Arms

1: *Radia magna* and *colombina* (dove)
2: Orsini coat of arms
3: Barbiano coat of arms
4: Manfredi coat of arms
5: Gambacorti coat of arms
6: Chevronelly and *radia magna*
7: Scaly and *radia magna* and *colombina* (dove)
8: Wavy and *raggiante*
(Artwork by Massimo Predonzani © Helion & Company 2026)

Plate I: Battle of Anghiari.
Reproduced with the permission of the National Gallery of Ireland.

Plate J: Battle of Anghiari.
Reproduced with the permission of the Archaeological Museum in Madrid

Plate K: Battle of Anghiari.
Lost painting, once in the Bryce Collection

Plate L: Battle of San Romano.
Reproduced with the permission of the Louvre

The combat continued for more than three hours with an uncertain outcome, until the Milanese began to falter. This reversal occurred both because they were targeted by missile troops positioned on higher ground and because of sheer exhaustion: the Milanese soldiers had endured a 12-mile march in oppressive heat, and their horses were spent.[22]

In *La Fuga del Capitano*, further clashes between captains and Milanese prisoners taken are described. Niccolò da Pisa wounded and captured Astorre Manfredi, shortly after, Sacramoro Visconti was wounded in the side and compelled to surrender. Filippo Schiavo and Roberto da Monte Alboddo were also taken prisoner. The tireless Niccolò da Pisa also captured Captain Iacopo d'Ariano, while Micheletto Attendolo disarmed Lodovico da Parma, and Torelli defeated Iacopo da San Gemini.[23]

In the companion poem *La rotta di Niccolò Piccinino*, the duels are fewer and differ in detail. At the beginning of the battle, Astorre Manfredi is said to have clashed with the 'Sire de Charpi',[24] without either gaining the upper hand. Later, Niccolò da Pisa defeated Danese della Torre, and Torelli captured his brother Antonello della Torre. Finally, as in *La Fuga del Capitano*', Niccolò da Pisa captured Astorre.[25]

This last episode – the capture of Astorre Manfredi by Niccolò Gambacorti da Pisa – is the only one among the many duels that was consistently recorded by historians, especially for its ruthless epilogue.[26]

The author of '*Fuga del Capitano*' continues his detailed narrative: Piccinino managed to dispatch yet another squadron, reinforced by crossbowmen and handgunners, in support, but to no avail. The Milanese lost control of the bridge and were forced back to the road, where they were also exposed to Florentine artillery fire. The poem describes this artillery as consisting of 40 springalds and even more falconets, capable of striking the Milanese even beyond the bridge.

At that point, the main clash shifted onto the road itself. Orsini, commander of the League forces, saw the struggle and sent fresh troops to support his men. At the same time, the Braccesco leader refused to yield, and committed additional reinforcements – handgunners, the *salariati* (salaried troops),[27] and the Biturgians – that is, the remaining troops.[28] According to *La Fuga del Capitano*, Piccinino even ordered 50 trumpets

22 Simonetae, 'Vita,' col. 294; Taglieschi, *Delle memorie*, p.173; Poggio, *Vita di Piccinino*, p.256.

23 *La Fuga del Capitano*, pp.268–271.

24 Raffaello di Vramonte, Lord of Carpi.

25 Angelo Ascani, *La rotta di Niccolò Piccinino* in Angelo Ascani, *Anghiari dalle origini all'anno 1440* (Città di Castello: Città di Castello, 1973), pp.290–292.

26 Simonetae, 'Vita,' col. 294; Corio, *Storia*, vol. II, p.1141.

27 They were the *familiari armigers*, see: Maria Nadia Covini, 'Per la storia delle milizie viscontee: I familari armigeri di Filippo Maria Visconti' in L. Chiappa Mauri & P. Mainoni (eds), *Il dominio di Milano fra XIII e XV secolo* (Milano: La Storia, 1993), p.41.

28 *La Fuga del Capitano* , pp.272 – 273.

to sound to rally his men for a renewed attack. This final and violent clash lasted half an hour.

Then, according to some chroniclers, an almost prodigious event occurred. Giovan Battista Poggio wrote 'In the evening, a wind arose from the mountains that blew thick dust into the faces of the Milanese, depriving them of sight and breath.'[29] The Florentines seized the opportunity and launched a massed assault with such ferocity that the Milanese were thrown into disorder and forced to flee.[30]

Biondo recounts that the rout of the Visconti troops was so complete that the confusion of the fleeing mass, combined with the onset of darkness, prevented the League forces from fully exploiting their victory.

Piccinino, together with his son, Guidantonio Manfredi, and Carlo Fortebracci managed to take refuge in Borgo Sansepolcro with 1,000 cavalry.

The Milanese infantry was almost entirely dispersed; many horses were captured, as nearly all the Biturgians who had joined Piccinino shortly before the battle.[31] All the flags were captured. Capponi recalls that the '*capitano nostro*' (our captain), Orsini, captured a banner, while *La rotta del Piccinino* mentions another flag – that of the leopard – seized by Tartaglia d'Arezzo, a captain in Micheletto's company.[32]

Many of the women tasked with carrying water were trampled to death by horses during the rout. (For a more detailed discussion of the casualties sustained in this battle, see the chapter below.)

Sometime later, Niccolò Piccinino would recount that, on that day, it had not been the enemy or adverse fortune that had brought about his downfall, but rather his own lack of devotion to God. Having chosen to attack on the Feast of the Apostles Peter and Paul – protectors of the Holy Roman Church – he attributed his defeat solely to their divine intervention.[33]

To support this belief, he frequently recounted that, during his march with the army from Borgo Sansepolcro to Anghiari, he had witnessed an event that foreshadowed his defeat. Shortly after leaving the town, he saw a large, elongated serpent coiled upon a tree, preparing to leap onto a neighbouring fig tree of the variety known as Fico San Pietro. When the reptile finally sprang, it struck a sharp branch that pierced its throat and

29 For Decembrio, 'Niccolò Piccinino,' col. 1082 and Flavio Biondo, *Historie* (Venezia 1547), p.128, as well as windy, there was also a lunar eclipse.

30 Poggio, *Vita di Piccinino*, p.256; Taglieschi, *Delle memorie*, p.173; Nicola della Tuccia, *Cronaca di Viterbo* (Firenze: G.P. Vieusseux, 1872),175.

31 Ammirato, *Istorie Fiorentine*, vol. IV, p.264; Taglieschi, *Delle memorie*, p.173; Machiavelli, *Istorie Fiorentine*, vol. 2, p.91; Biondo, *Historie*, p.128; Tuccia, *Cronaca di Viterbo*, p.175; Simonetae, 'Vita,' col. 294; Corio, *Storia*, vol. II, p.1141; Capponi, 'Commentari,' 1195; Lorenzo Spirito Gualtieri, *L'Altro Marte*, (Venezia: Leonardus Achates, 1489), cap. 59.

32 Capponi, 'Commentari,' 1195; *La rotta di Niccolò Piccinino*, p.292.

33 Popular imagination attributed the Florentine victory to the intervention of St Andrea Corsini, whose menacing presence in the sky would have frightened the Milanese, cf Chapter 4, The Battle of Anghiari in Art.

29. The plain with the road to San Sepolcro seen from Anghiari. (Photograph by the author)

it fell to the ground, lifeless. Neither Piccinino nor his men grasped the meaning of the omen at that time; only after the battle's outcome did its meaning become clear. The serpent symbolised the Visconti arms – that is, the ducal army – destined to be overcome by the Apostle Peter.[34]

Modern historians tend to regard this episode as a retrospective invention by Piccinino, devised to justify to Filippo Maria Visconti the failure of his attempted surprise attack. The *condottiero* was well aware of the duke's pronounced superstition and his susceptibility to ill omens.[35]

In conclusion, attention should be drawn to a study of the battle published in 1909 by Edmondo Solmi, then professor of History of Philosophy at the University of Pavia.[36]

In this essay, Solmi – a scholar of Leonardo da Vinci – sought to demonstrate the existence of a personal and intellectual relationship between Leonardo and Niccolò Machiavelli. He went so far as to suggest that certain writings of the Florentine Secretary had been confused among Leonardo's papers. He referred to folios 74r and 74v of the 'Codex Atlanticus', which he believed contained Machiavelli's notes describing the Battle of Anghiari – notes that Leonardo allegedly used as inspiration for his fresco of the battle, executed mainly in 1504 in the Palazzo della Signoria in Florence (now the Palazzho Veccio).

34 Ammirato, *Istorie Fiorentine*, vol. IV, p.264; Taglieschi, *Delle memorie*, p.173; Poggio, *Vita di Piccinino*, p.257.

35 Pier Candido Decembrio, *Vita di Filippo Maria Visconti* (Milano: Adelphi Edizioni, 1983), pp.121 – 125.

36 E. Solmi, *Pagine autografe di Niccolò Machiavelli nel 'Codice Atlantico' di Leonardo da Vinci*, in *Giornale storico della letteratura italiana*, vol. 54 1909, pp.90–102.

Solmi hypothesised that the two eminent Tuscans first met in Urbino in 1502, through the mediation of Duke Cesare Borgia, and that their relationship continued in other cities of Romagna subject to Valentino's rule. The duke employed Leonardo as an architect, while Machiavelli served him as commissioner of the Republic of Florence. Both men, acute observers and pragmatic thinkers, shared a keen interest in the art of war and in fortifications.

They returned to Florence at the beginning of 1503, and in April of that year, Leonardo accepted the commission to paint one wall of the main hall in the Palazzo della Signoria. According to Solmi, he sought Machiavelli's help in preparing what would become his renowned – but now lost – *Battle of Anghiari*.

Solmi further argued that the Florentine secretary had written, in his own hand, the narrative preserved in the 'Codex Atlanticus,' which Leonardo kept among his papers.

To substantiate this claim, Solmi consulted chronicles and contemporary accounts of the battle, comparing them with the text contained in the 'Codex'. He considered, among others, the chronicles of Cavalcanti, Capponi, and Giusto d'Anghiari; the poem *Serena patria illustra alma cittade;* the two short poems *La Fuga del Capitano* and *La rotta di Niccolò Piccinino;* and the *Tropheum anglaricum* by Leonardo Dati. He claimed that he found no direct correlation between these sources and the text in the 'Codex.'

However, upon re-reading Machiavelli's *Istorie Fiorentine*, he declared himself 'immediately struck' by the similarity of figures, reports, and movements to those found in the 'Codex Atlanticus'.

Thus, Solmi published in full the narrative attributed to Machiavelli and preserved in the 'Codex Atlanticus,' followed by the parallel account of the battle from the *Istorie Fiorentine,* in order to facilitate comparison between the two texts.

In his analysis, Solmi twice repeats – in identical wording – that 'the narrative published in the Florentine Stories is not very dissimilar from [Machiavelli's] autograph narrative.'

Yet his discussion focuses primarily on Leonardo's artistic interpretation allegedly derived from the autograph text – which, according to him, the artist followed faithfully – rather than on providing concrete evidence to support the analogies drawn between the two texts.

Solmi also inserts two documentary images: a photograph of a passage attributed to Machiavelli in the 'Codex' and, alongside it, a photograph of part of a handwritten letter by Machiavelli from 1502 to compare the handwriting – the script does indeed appear similar. However, this resemblance must be contextualised within the broader convention of Renaissance cursive writing, which relied on widely shared forms of letters or syllables, standardised abbreviations, and conventional graphic style.

While the hypothesis that Leonardo may have used a Machiavellian text as inspiration for his artwork is plausible, the assertion that the original text preserved in the 'Codex' was by Machiavelli himself is far more problematic.

In fact, Machiavelli composed a summary of Leonardo Dati's *Tropheum anglaricum*.[37]

A comparison between Dati's work and the text in the 'Codex' reveals that the characters and events correspond and appear in the same sequence. The patriarch (in reality, it was Micheletto) first sights the approaching Milanese Army, Micheletto repels the initial assault of Francesco Piccinino, the Manfredi brothers (actually, only Astorre) then renew the attack on the bridge, Simonetto confronts them with 600 cavalrymen, which is followed by the intervention of the patriarch, Niccolò da Pisa, and the young Napoleone Orsini – notably, the only account on the battle examined thus far that mentions Orsini. The narrative continues with the Florentine victory, achieved with *'grande strage di uomini'* (a great slaughter of men).

By contrast, Machiavelli's *Istorie Fiorentine* does not report in detail the same sequence of characters found in the 'Codex'. In the *Istorie*, it is Micheletto – not the patriarch – who sights the Milanese Army, which corresponds to the historical record. The narrative then continues with a punctual yet general account of the battle, without listing the principal characters: Guidantonio Manfredi, Niccolò da Pisa, or Napoleone Orsini are not mentioned.

Moreover, the well-known epilogue of the battle in the *Istorie* – the death of a single man, not from wounds but for falling from his horse – stands in stark contrast to the conclusion of the 'Codex', which speaks instead of a 'gran strage di nemici' (a great slaughter of the enemy).

This discrepancy alone would suffice to raise legitimate doubts regarding the attribution of the writing in the 'Codex' to Machiavelli. Nevertheless, Solmi omits consideration of the famous passage from the *Istorie Fiorentine* – 'only one man died there; not of wounds or other virtuous blow but having fallen from his horse' – which does not appear in the version of the battle he reproduces from the *Istorie* in his publication.

37 L. di Piero Dati, 'Dal Tropheum anglaricum,' in *Giornale Storico della Letteratura Italiana* (Torino: Ermanno Loescher, 1890), vol. XVI, pp.49-55, 101–104.

9

Casualties of the Battle

Calculating casualties in a fifteenth century – or, more broadly, medieval – battle is an inherently complex task. The same difficulty applies to estimating the strength of an army during a campaign or immediately prior to battle (see Chapter 6: The Opposing Armies), not least because contemporary chroniclers often diverge considerably in their accounts.

30. Fifteenth century sallet, Luigi Marzoli Museum, Brescia. (Photograph by the author)

The Battle of Anghiari offers a particularly striking example. Reported losses and wounded range from 900 dead among the Milanese ranks, according to the poem *La Fuga del Capitano*, to the paradoxical claim of a single fatality reported by Machiavelli – and that, a man who did not die in combat or from wounds, but from falling off his horse and being trampled.[1]

Machiavelli's well-known disdain for mercenary armies renders his assessment comprehensible within his broader political thought. He adopted a similar stance regarding the Battle of Riccardina in 1467, when he wrote that 'no one died there'. For the Florentine politician, Renaissance warfare often amounted to what he regarded as 'battles without blood'.

Fortunately, not all sources display such extreme divergence, and several versions broadly agree – particularly regarding the number of Milanese prisoners. Some chroniclers, such as Biondo, prove remarkably accurate in reporting casualties, including losses of horses.

1 *La Fuga del Capitano* in A. Fabretti, *Note e documenti da biografie dei Capitani Venturieri dell'Umbria*, vol. Unico (Montepulciano: Angiolo Tumi, 1842), p.274; Niccolò Machiavelli, *Istorie Fiorentine* (Milan: Società Anonima Notari or Alpes, 1928), vol. 2, p.92.

Chronicle Accounts of Casualties

Capponi reports that 22 Milanese squadron commanders out of 26 were captured, along with 400 men-at-arms, about 3,000 cavalrymen, and an additional 1,540 prisoners held for ransom. He adds that, according to the customary – though in his view foolish – practice of the time, the victors released the men-at-arms and the wealthiest gentlemen after collecting their ransom, allowing them to depart with nothing but their doublets. It was only with considerable effort that the Florentine commissioners Bernadetto de' Medici and Neri Capponi succeeded in retaining six captains: Astorre Manfredi, Lodovico (or Sagramoro) da Parma, Romano da Cremona, Sacramoro Visconti, and Danese and Antonello della Torre.[2]

Flavio Biondo – described by Ammirato as a '... writer of the time and secretary to the pope, who would fully know the facts' – wrote that the Visconti forces suffered 60 dead, more than 400 wounded, and 1,800 captured, including 28 captains and 1,300 men from Borgo Sansepolcro (Biturgians). Among the League forces, 200 were wounded and of these only 10 later died of their injuries. Biondo further records the loss of 600 horses on both sides. He adds that the following morning, without the knowledge of the Apostolic Legate Scarampi Mezzarota, all prisoners were released again except for six captains whom the legate managed to detain – but among them, were Astorre Manfredi, Sagramoro de Parma, and Romano da Cremona.[3]

Scipione Ammirato essentially reproduces the casualty figures reported by Capponi and Biondo.

Poggio Bracciolini records that 1,800 cavalrymen were captured, together with several captains – Astorre Manfredi, Lodovico da Parma, Romano da Cremona, Sacramoro Visconti, and Danese and Antonello della Torre – the same names listed by Capponi. He further reports approximately 40 casualties among Piccinino's soldiers, most of whom died of their wounds, as well as the capture of numerous Standards and Banners by the Florentines. Several citizens of Borgo Sansepolcro were also captured and subsequently ransomed.[4]

According to Simonetta, Piccinino barely managed to take refuge within Borgo Sansepolcro. His infantry was almost entirely dispersed, the insignia were captured and promptly brought to Florence, the military camp and equipment plundered, and only a small number of cavalrymen managed to escape. He further notes that Niccolò da Pisa captured Astorre and that 1,200 Biturgians were taken prisoner.[5]

The Venetian chronicler Sabellico writes that many were killed or wounded and that many more were captured. In addition to Astorre, the

2 N. Capponi, 'Commentari' in *Muratori R.I.S.* XVIII col. 1195.

3 F. Biondo, *Historie* (Venice: 1547), pp.128–129.

4 Poggio Bracciolini, *Historia Fiorentina* (Venice: 1715), p.349.

5 Johannis Simonetae, 'Vita Francisci Sfortiae,' in *Muratori R.I.S.* XXI, col. 294.

victors allegedly captured 32 condottieri, 1,800 cavalrymen, and all the citizens of Borgo Sansepolcro.[6]

In the *Vita di Piccinino*, Giovan Battista Poggio records that casualties were limited on both sides but confirms, in agreement with Sabellico, that 1,800 cavalrymen and 1,300 Biturgians were taken prisoner. He concludes:

> ... *e furono anco nella fuga calpestate e morte da' cavalli intorno a 60 donne, che Nicolò havea fatto stare da ogni banda della strada, con vasi grandi di legno pieni d'acqua, affinche così i cavalli, come gli huomini, affaticati dal viaggio e dal combattere, si potessero rinfrescare, e non si venisero meno dalla sete e dal caldo* (... during the retreat, around 60 women were trampled to death by horses. Piccinino had placed them along both sides of the road with large wooden vases filled with water, so that both horses and men, exhausted by marching and fighting, might refresh themselves and not succumb to thirst and heat.)[7]

In a Perugian chronicle known as the *Diario del Graziani*, it is reported that many died in the clash, and that Estorre, together with several men from Borgo Sansepolcro, were captured. The chronicle claims that 10,000 infantry were taken prisoner, excluding the men-at-arms, and that numerous men, women, and children were killed. The victors also captured two Milanese standards: one bearing the leopard insignia and another the Biscia insignia. Piccinino reportedly escaped with his son, Count Carlo, and 2,000 cavalrymen.

This chronicle is particularly noteworthy, as – aside from the two short poems – it is the only source describing the emblems displayed on the captured standards and explicitly mentioning the deaths of women and children. Nevertheless, it clearly exaggerates the number of captured infantry, since 10,000 would correspond to the entire strength of the Milanese Army.[8]

Della Tuccia likewise mentions the death of women: '... *e furon morti da una parte e dall'altra ben cento persone, tra quali femmine assai, che portavano rinfrescamento a quelli di Nicolò urtate tutte da' cavalli*' (... a hundred people were killed on both sides, and among them several women who were carrying water for Niccolò's men and were trampled by horses). He further reports that the League captured approximately 3,000 horses and took numerous prisoners, including the son of the Lord of Faenza, Tartaglia della Guancia, the Danese da Mugnano, Alberto da Carrara, and

6 M. A. Sabellico, *Degl'Istorici delle cose Veneziane*, Veneziane 1747, lib. V, p.159.

7 Giovan Battista Poggio, *Vita di Niccolò Piccinino*, (Perugia: 1619), p.256.

8 'Diario del Graziani,' *Arch. Stor. Ital.* XVI 1, 1850, pp.458 and p.461.

other *condottieri* of Piccinino – 10 in total – together with large numbers of men-at-arms.[9]

Domenico Buoninsegni recorded, '... our enemies captured more than 2,500 cavalrymen, many infantry, and many [important] prisoners held for ransom – most of them Biturgians. Antonio da Faenza[10] was captured and wounded, as were many other corporals and squadron commanders. Niccolò fled to Borgo Sansepolcro with about 800 cavalrymen. Two of the duke's captured main flags were hung upside down in Santa Maria del Fiore.'[11]

Giovanni Cambi, another Florentine citizen, recounts the event thus: 'Niccolò Piccinino was soundly defeated at Anghiari. Two of our commissioners, Neri di Gino Capponi and Bernadetto di Antonio de' Medici, were greatly honoured for their valour and carried the flags and weapons of the Duke of Milan and his captain.'[12]

The Milanese historian Bernardino Corio reports Simonetta's account almost verbatim: '[They took] the Milanese banners and brought them to Florence, along with the waggons and pavilions; only a few men-at-arms escaped. Niccolò da Pisa captured Astorre da Faenza, and more than 1,200 Biturgians were taken prisoners.'[13]

According to Marin Sanudo, the prisoners numbered 4,000 cavalrymen, including the men of Borgo Sansepolcro and several squadron commanders, among them Sagramoro, Lodovico da Parma, Iacopo da Camerino, Francesco di Santa Maria, Roberto da Monte Acuto, Filippo Schiavo, and Iacopo da Rimini, together with numerous waggons and bombards. A few lines later, he refers to a list drawn up by the Cardinal of Venice, who was in Florence and reported in a letter to the doge, written during the retreat, that '2,800 cavalrymen and 13 squadron commanders were taken, as well as 300 men-at-arms, plus flags and waggons; Niccolò Piccinino escaped, as did the Lord of Faenza, with no more than about 400 cavalrymen.'[14]

Giusto d'Anghiari, secretary to the *condottiero* Agnolo Taglia, recorded that 'about 3,000 cavalrymen were captured among the Milanese ranks, together with 16 squadron commanders and many other men-at-arms, as well as 1,456 Biturgians prisoners held for ransom and many other prisoners from other places; Piccinino's flags were captured as well. Niccolò Piccinino fled with about 1,500 cavalrymen to Borgo.'[15]

In Viviano's text (see the start of the chapter The Battle), it is reported that there were many deaths on both sides, substantial spoils for the League, and even the capture of 2,500 horses. Among the other prisoners, there

9 Nicola della Tuccia, *Cronaca di Viterbo* (Firenze: G.P. Vieusseux, 1872), pp.175 – 176.

10 Buoninsegni here means 'Astorre Manfredi'.

11 D. Buoninsegni, *Storia della città di Firenze*, (Florence: 1673), p.73.

12 G. Cambi, 'Istorie' in *Delizie degli Eruditi Toscani* (Firenze: 1785), vol. I, p.230.

13 Bernardino Corio, *Storia di Milano* (Torino: Utet, 1978), vol. II, pp.1140 – 1141.

14 M. Sanudo, 'Vite dé duchi di Venezia,' *Muratori R.I.S.*, XX col. 1099.

15 G. d'Anghiari, 'Memorie dall'anno 1437 al 1481,' Bibl. Naz. Fir. Ms. II. II. 127, f. 39v.

were 1,457 men from Borgo Sansepolcro – one more than the number recorded by Giusto![16]

Platina records that the Milanese lost 140 cavalrymen, that many of their men were wounded, that 1,500 were captured, and that they also lost their banners.[17]

According to Palmieri, the captured Milanese soldiers numbered 3,000 cavalrymen and more than 2,000 infantrymen, including many citizens of Borgo Sansepolcro and some from Perugia. Astorre da Faenza was wounded and taken prisoner.[18]

The poet and contemporary historian, Benedetto Dei, wrote that 'Filippo Maria's camp was defeated and the men put to flight; the horses and artillery were captured; and prisoners were taken for ransom, namely 1440 soldiers from Borgo Sansepolcro and 12,000 cavalrymen. Eight captains were imprisoned, among them Astorre of Faenza, who was detained for three years in the Stinche prison in Florence. They also captured the banners of the Duke of Milan, Filippo Maria – that of his *fazuolo* and the other of gold satin.'[19]

There are two inaccuracies to be noted. The first concerns the number of captured cavalrymen: the figure of 12,000 is clearly exaggerated and most likely corresponds to the total number of cavalry engaged by the two opposing armies. The second concerns the banner of the *fazuolo*, that is, the *capitergium cum gassa* or Knotted Veil, an impresa particularly dear to Filippo Maria Visconti, but one that was not sported in this battle.

The *Storia di Parma* briefly mentions the defeat at Anghiari only to recall that among the six captured *condottieri* of Piccinino there was also one of his fellow citizens, Lodovico da Parma.[20]

In the 'Cronaca Bolognese' a passage concerning the Milanese prisoners reports that '*... et multi condutieri fuon tomi de quili de Nicolò Pezenino, i cui nomi erano quisti, zoè: Estore di Manfredi da Fenza, Lodovigo da Parma, el Danexe, Ruberto da Monte Alboto, Antonelo da la Torre; e evenat il stindardi*' (... many *condottieri* of Niccolò Piccinino were captured, whose names were Estore Manfredi da Faenza, Lodovico da Parma, il Danese, Roberto da Monte Alboddo, and Antonello della Torre. They also lost the banners).[21]

According to Leonardo Aretino, all the enemy flags were captured, together with tents, waggons, and more than 1,200 Biturgians.[22]

---

16 F. Viviano, *Registri della compagnia di Micheletto Attendolo*, in Fraternita dei Laici di Arezzo, libro 3574, endpaper.

17 B. Platina, 'Hist. Mantuane,' *Muratori R.I.S.* XX col. 835.

18 M. Palmieri, 'Annales,' *Muratori R.I.S.* Bologna 1922, volume XXVI, appendix, p.149.

19 Benedetto Dei, *La Cronica dal anno 1400 alle anno 1500* (Firenze: Papafava, 1984), p.56.

20 Angelo Pezzana, *Storia di Parma* (Parma: Dalla Ducale Tipografia,1842), II, p.427.

21 Anon., 'Corpus Chronicorum Bononiensium' in *Muratori R.I.S.* (Bologna 1922), XVIII, part I, p.100.

22 L. Aretini,' Commentarius,' in *Muratori* XIX, col. 942.

Cristoforo da Soldo writes that '[they captured] 3,000 cavalrymen and the brother of da Faenza.'[23]

Leonardo Morelli recounts that '... the Florentines defeated Niccolò Piccinino at Anghiari and captured more than 4,000 cavalrymen. Ten of his principal corporals were taken prisoners, as well as the valiant men of Borgo Sansepolcro, Perugia, and Siena. Among them was Astore di Faenza, who was detained in the Stinche prison.'[24]

The 'Cronache Malatestiane' reports, 'Nicolò Picinino, captain of the Duke of Milan, fought against the forces of the League and was defeated, and many people and horses were killed. Most of the men of Borgo Sansepolcro were captured. 3,000 cavalrymen were lost, and nine squadron commanders were captured and Astorre da Faenza was among them.'[25]

In 'Cronaca Malatestiana' Broglio records that Piccinino lost 3,400 cavalrymen and approximately 300 men from Borgo Sansepolcro, all of whom were captured together with some of his banners and 12 squadron commanders, who remained prisoners. Broglio assigns an incorrect date to the battle, recording it as 29 June 1441, though he is not alone in this error. In the *Vita di Niccolò Piccinino*, Decembrio likewise provides an incorrect date, placing the battle on 5 August 1440.[26]

In the poem *La Fuga del Capitano*, it is stated that more than 900 Bracceschi were killed and wounded and that 1,800 of them were taken prisoner, including 32 squadron commanders and 1,300 Biturgians and civilians. The poem lists the captured captains as Filippo Schiavo, Astorre da Faenza, Sacromoro, Iacopo d'Ariano, Lodovico da Parma, Antonello da Santa Marta, Tartaglia della Guancia, Iacopo Fracassa, and Roberto dal Monte. It further reports that the victors seized the Milanese standards, while Piccinino, his son Francesco, and Guido Manfredi managed to find refuge in Borgo Sansepolcro. The poem concludes by stating that on the following day the army of the League ransomed the 1,300 Biturgians and released them together with the 1,800 Bracceschi.[27]

The painter and chronicler of Forlì, Giovanni Pedrino, writes that Astorre was taken to Florence, while his brother Guido Antonio was severely beaten. Many squadron commanders were captured, although some were subsequently ransomed. They victors seized the flags and numerous men from Borgo Sansepolcro, as well as many peasants from the surrounding *contrada*. Numerous women and individuals tasked with bringing wine

23 Cristiforo da Soldo, 'La cronaca,' in *Muratori R.I.S.* XX. col. 823.

24 *Croniche di Giovanni di Iacopo e di Lionardo di Lorenzo Morelli* (Florence: 1785), p.171.

25 'Cronache Malatestiane dei secoli XIV e XV,' in *Muratori R.I.S.* XV col. 938.

26 Gaspare Broglio Tartaglia (A. G. Lucani, ed.), *Cronaca Malatestiana del secolo XV* (Rimini: Bruno Ghigi, 1982), p.72; Decembrio, 'Niccolò Piccinino'.

27 A. Fabretti, 'La Fuga del Capitano' in *Note e documenti da biografie dei Capitani Venturieri dell'Umbria*, vol. Unico (Montepulciano: Angiolo Tumi, 1842), pp.274 – 275.

and water to refresh Piccinino's cavalrymen also lost their lives. Piccinino himself barely managed to escape the battlefield.

Pedrino further reports that the Florentines had deployed approximately 4,000 cavalrymen and an equal number of infantrymen, whereas the Milanese fielded 4,000 cavalrymen but fewer infantrymen, who were poorly positioned. Finally, he states the engagement lasted five hours.[28]

To conclude this survey of the statements in the chronicles, two letters published by Masetti-Bencini must be considered. These are two reports on the battle: one sent by the Commissioners Neri Capponi and Bernadetto de' Medici, and the other by Patriarch Scarampi to the *Dieci di Balìa*. Both are dated 29 June, immediately after the actual battle.

The Florentine commissioners report that the following captains were taken prisoner: Sagramoro and Lodovico da Parma, Tartaglia da Guancia, Antonello da Santa Marta, Iacomo da Ghaviano, Ruberto da Monte al Boddo, Filippo Sorano, Jacomo da Santo Gemini, and Astorre da Faenza – the same names cited in the poem *La Fuga del Capitano*. The list of captives continues with 500 Biturgians and some Perugians, together with the waggons, the banners, 300 men-at-arms, and more than 2,500 cavalrymen.

In the other report, the patriarch instead refers to 2,000 captured cavalrymen and lists the following captains: Astorre da Faenza, Opizo da Carrara, Tartaglia della Guancia, Lodovico da Parma, Antonello de la Torre, Roberto da Montalboddo, Boldrino da Pavia, and Romano da Cremona, as well as several men-at-arms and other individuals.[29]

Despite having been written at the same time, immediately after the battle, and not by subordinate captains but by the commanders of the League – who were the best informed about the events – these letters diverge on several points. They differ in the number of cavalrymen taken prisoner (2,500 versus 2,000) and, even more notably, in the captured captains: the commissioners mention nine captains, whereas Scarampi lists eight. Moreover, only four names appear in both letters: Astorre Manfredi, Sacramoro Visconti, Lodovico da Parma, and Antonello della Torre.

There is more. The report sent by Neri and Medici to the Dieci also differs from the account of casualties that Neri Capponi himself provides years later in his 'Commentari', where he records a different number of prisoners; regarding the captains, only Astorre, Scarampi, and Lodovico da Parma correspond to those named in the earlier letter.

What accounts for these inconsistencies? Several factors may have contributed to them.

With regard to the letters of the commissioners and of Scarampi, the primary explanation lies in their being written immediately after the end of the battle. In the general confusion that followed a victory of such

28 Giovanni di m. Pedrino Depintore, *Cronica del suo tempo* (Rome: Biblioteca Apostolica Vaticana, 1929), vol. I, pp.102–103.

29 I. Masetti-Bencini, 'La bataglia di Anghiari' in *Rivista delle biblioteche e degli archivi*, Luglio-Agosto 1907, pp.121–122.

magnitude, information was likely fragmentary. The Milanese suffered a crushing defeat, and a large number of soldiers were taken prisoner. Every cavalryman and soldier of the League was busy plundering and capturing prisoners – the wealthiest being the most valuable.

In this regard, Viviano records in his 'Registri' the case of the Baron of Consoleto, who received 30 florins, that is, 1/10 of a total of 300 florins paid as ransom by a certain Benedetto da Modigliano,[30] 'who was captured during the retreat of Nicolò Piccinino from Anghiari.'[31] Benedetto was evidently captured by 10 soldiers, who divided the ransom equally and subsequently released him.

Considering that at that time the average monthly wage of a cavalryman was approximately three florins, it is clear how important the capture of prisoners was following a victory.

By contract, all the members of a company of fortune were required to hand over prisoners taken in battle to the lord or lordship that had hired them; however, this rule was frequently disregarded. Indeed, as Capponi and Biondo report, after being ransomed, almost all the prisoners were released the day after the battle, and the commissioners struggled even to retain a few captains.

In this regard, it is also noteworthy that in register 3574 by Viviano, the record of payments to Tartaglia d'Arezzo, Micheletto's squadron commander, for the months of June and July 1440, includes, under the date 22 July, an entry of two heavy gold florins '... *per due salvicondottj delli prigionj quando fu la battaglia Anchiarj*' (... for two safe-conducts issued for prisoners taken at the Battle of Anghiari).[32]

Who were the Milanese captains taken prisoner?

From the accounts examined above, the captains or squadron commanders serving in the Milanese Army must have numbered around 30. As a result of the rout, more than 20 of them were captured and later released after paying a ransom, except for around six who were retained by the commissioners.

The most prominent among these captains was undoubtedly Astorre Manfredi, discussed in the chapter on historical figures and whose capture is unanimously reported by the chroniclers. In this regard, it is necessary to recall the unfortunate episode that followed his imprisonment. Manfredi had been wounded in the femur, and Niccolò Gambacorti captured him and delivered him to the Florentines for 3,000 florins, as per contract. Manfredi was confined in the infamous Florentine prison of the Stinche until the end of the hostilities. He was released on 21 November 1441,

30 Today Modigliana, province of Forlì. Benedetto was probably part of Astorre Manfredi's company.
31 Viviano, 'Registri della compagnia', libro 3574, f. 166v.
32 Viviano, 'Registri della compagnia', libro 3574, f. 136r.

filled with resentment and desire for revenge against Gambacorti, whom he accused of violating the rules of ransom by handing him over to Florence – it seems that Astorre had offered Gambacorti 4,000 florins. Sometime later, having learnt that the Pisan was in Bologna, he went there in disguise with some companions, discovered the house where Gambacorti was staying, captured him, and had him cut to pieces. On 6 February 1442, Bologna buried Niccolò with a solemn funeral in the church of San Petronio.[33]

The second most important captain among the prisoners was Sacramoro, or Sacromoro, Visconti – most contemporary chroniclers simply refer to him as Sacromoro. Flavio Biondo calls him Sagramoro da Parma, while Ammirato and Poggio record him as Sacromoro Visconti. In the list of cavalry captains of 1439, Sanudo refers to him as Don Sacramoro,[34] whereas Giorgio Giulini identifies him as the nephew of another Sacromoro, an illegitimate son of Barnabò Visconti, Lord of Milan from 1354 to 1385. Pompeo Litta calls him Sagromoro and includes him among the Visconti lords of Brignano. Litta provides an extensive account of his military exploits among the troops of Filippo Maria Visconti from 1436 to 1441 and mentions him in Anghiari, where he was taken prisoner.

In 1441, he was suspected of supporting Sforza and was declared a rebel. In 1447, he entered the service of the Milanese Republic and shortly afterwards that of Sforza, whom he served faithfully, eventually obtaining the office of ducal lieutenant of Genoa in 1466 and ducal councillor in 1468. In 1470, he was granted the Signoria of Brignano, and he seems to have died around 1472.[35]

Another captain frequently mentioned among the prisoners by the chroniclers is Lodovico da Parma. Piccinino reportedly referred to Lodovico as his companion, although little is known about him. He appears to have belonged to the Pastorani family and to have fought in the Milanese service from 1430; he died in 1448.[36]

Similarly, little information survives concerning Tartaglia della Guancia, although several historians include him in the list of Milanese prisoners after the defeat at Anghiari. In *Cortona nel medio evo*, Girolamo Mancini recalls him together with a certain Antonello Schiavo while making raids in the county of Cortona in April 1440.[37] Some modern historians identify him with, or confuse him with, Tartaglia da Massoro or Foligno. However,

---

33 Anon., 'Corpus Chronicorum Bononiensium' in *Muratori R.I.S.* (Bologna 1922), XVIII, part I, pp.103–104; Piero Zama, *I Manfredi signori di Faenza* (Faenza: Fratelli Lega, 1954), pp.185–186; Michael Mallett, *Signori e mercenari* (Bologna: Il Mulino, 1983), p.205.

34 See Chapter 6, The Opposing Armies.

35 G. Giulini, *Memorie spettanti alla storia della città e campagna di Milano*, VI, Milano 1857, p.366; Pompeo Litta, *Famiglie celebri italiane* (Milano: Luciano Basadonna, *c.*1869), 7, tav. VIII.

36 A Angelo Pezzana, *Storia di Parma* (Parma: Dalla Ducale Tipografia,1842), II, p.427.

37 G. Mancini, *Cortona nel medio evo* (Firenze: G. Carnesecchi e figli, 1897, p.350.

the latter was not a cavalry captain but a constable who appears in the registers of the *condotte* of the State of the Church in 1436 with 40 wages.[38] The chronicler Petruccio de Unctis refers to him as '*Tartaglia di Messero di Buonfante da Foligno*,' commander of 150 infantrymen for Vitelleschi in 1438. Fabretti and Graziani also mentioned Foligno and another Tartaglia, Tartaglia da Torsciano, the same individual previously noted among the Bracceschi in April 1440 in Perugian territory[39]

It should be remembered that, at the time, 'Tartaglia' was not a personal name but a widely used nickname.

Among the prisoners listed was also Antonello della Torre, mentioned in Capponi's 'Commentari', in Scarampi's letter to the Dieci, and in the poem *La Fuga del Capitano*. He is recorded in Bognetti's *Regesti Viscontei* as Antonello de Lature, a member of Niccolò Piccinino's squadron, in connection with concessions of property bestowed upon him by Duke Filippo Maria in 1441. Lorenzo Spirito mentions him at the Battle of Castel Bolognese in 1434 alongside Piccinino. He probably belonged to the Milanese family of Torre or Torriani; however, in Litta's *Famiglie celebri italiane*, this Antonello does not appear.[40]

Antonio Cristofani, in *Storia d'Assisi,* refers to him as Antonello della Torre, Lord of Sterpeto and captain under Piccinino. On 9 June 1444, Piccinino had Antonello arrested for treason and imprisoned in the fortress of Assisi – it seems that he intended to enter the service of Sforza – where he was hung by the feet from one of the towers and died after four days of agony.[41]

Danese della Torre is named together with Antonello by Capponi in the 'Commentari' and in *La Fuga del Capitano*. Della Tuccia refers to him as Danese da Mugnano, and in the *Bullettino senese di storia patria* he is mentioned as 'Danese Orsini, Lord of Magnano, who, after having fought under Niccolò Piccinino in the service of Filippo Maria Visconti, retired to Siena following the duke's death.'[42] Little is known about this captain, who

---

38 Archivio di stato di Roma, *Commissariato delle soldatesche e galere*, busta 80, libro 1436, f. 182r.

39 L. Muratori, *Antiquitates Italicae medii aevi*, 1741, vol. 4, p.161; A. Fabretti, *Note e documenti da biografie dei Capitani Venturieri dell'Umbria*, vol. Unico (Montepulciano: Angiolo Tumi, 1842), p.240; *Diario del Graziani*, pp.441, 444, 451, 483, 635. Also see Chapter 5, Background to the Battle.

40 Pompeo Litta, *Famiglie celebri italiane* (Milano: Luciano Basadonna, *c.*1869).

41 G. B. Bognetti, 'Per la storia dello stato visconteo' in *Archivio storico Lombardo* (Milano: Società storica Lombarda,1927), registers, pp.295 and 299; Lorenzo Spirito Gualtieri, *L'Altro Marte*, (Venezia: Leonardus Achates, 1489), cap. 49; A. Cristofani, *Delle storie d'Assisi* (Assisi: Dalla tipografia Sensi, 1866), p.301; A. Fabretti, *Note e documenti da biografie dei Capitani Venturieri dell'Umbria*, vol. Unico (Montepulciano: Angiolo Tumi, 1842) pp.277–278; *Diario del Graziani*, p.531.

42 *Bullettino senese di storia patria*, Assisi 1866, p.301

is also mentioned by Spirito alongside Piccinino shortly before the Battle of Castel Bolognese.[43] He died in Siena in 1449.

Roberto da Montalboddo[44] is mentioned among the prisoners in the letters sent by the commissioners and by Scarampi to the *Dieci di Balìa*, in *La Fuga del Capitano,* and in the 'Chronicorum Bononiensium'.[45] Sanudo also lists him among the prisoners of Anghiari, though under the name Roberto da Monte Acuto; in his list of Italian cavalry forces for 1439, he refers to him as Rinaldo di Monte Albotto.[46] Agostino Rossi states that he belonged to the Paganelli family. During his military career, Montalboddo frequently served in the Milanese Army, and Lorenzo Spirito records his presence in 1434 at Castel Bolognese together with Danese and Antonello della Torre.[47] In April 1442, Visconti rewarded his military merits by granting him the castle of Solero near Alexandria. In 1444, he married Bianciola, daughter of Nello Baglioni, and shortly thereafter entered the service of the Church, then later that of Venice. While serving Venice, he fought in the Battle of Caravaggio, where he was captured. He died in 1449.[48]

Less frequently mentioned, and less well known, are:

Filippo Schiavo had previously fought at the battle of L'Aquila with the Bracceschi and is later recorded in the chronicles as a captain under Francesco Piccinino.[49] In the letter from the commissioners to the *Dieci di Balìa* announcing the victory at Anghiari, he appears under the name Filippo Sorano. He died in Bologna in 1443.

Romano da Cremona is listed among the prisoners by four chroniclers: Capponi in the 'Commentari', in the letter from Scarampi to the *Dieci*, and by both Poggio and Biondo. Later, della Tuccia mentions him with Francesco Piccinino in 1444.[50]

Boldrino da Pavia is mentioned alongside the Bracceschi and Filippo Schiavo at the Battle of L'Aquila.[51]

For the other captains mentioned among the prisoners, the available information is unclear.

---

43 Gualtieri, *L'Altro Marte*, ch. 49.

44 Today Ostra in the Marche region.

45 Anon., 'Corpus Chronicorum Bononiensium' in *Muratori R.I.S.* (Bologna 1922), XVIII.

46 See Chapter 6, The Opposing Armies.

47 Agostini Rossi, *Notizie historiche di Mont'Alboddo* (Bologna: A Forni, 1980 reprint), p.118; Gualtieri, *L'Altro Marte*, ch. 49.

48 G. B. Bognetti, 'Per la storia dello stato visconteo' in *Archivio Storico Lombardo* (Milano: Società storica Lombarda,1927), pp.301E 323; *Bullettino della deputazione di storia patria per l'Umbria*, vol. 4, 1898, p.93; *Diario del Graziani*, pp.541, 545, 609, 619.

49 Bernardino Corio, *Storia di Milano*, vol. II (Torino: Utet, 1978), p.574; Deputazione toscana di storia patria, *Archivio Storico Italiano* (Firenze: M. Cellinni & C., 1872), vol.15, p.235.

50 *Giornale Arcadico di scienze, lettere e arti* (Roma: Tipografia delle Belle Arti, 1853), p.27.

51 Bernardino Corio, *Storia di Milano*, vol. II (Torino: Utet, 1978), p.574.

As for the total number of Milanese prisoners, the sources are at variance and at times ambiguous. Most chroniclers report the number of *cavalli presi* (captured cavalry) from 1,500 to 2,800 to 3,000. Some Italian historians, instead of using the expression *cavalli presi* refer to *prigioni* (prisoners), which in this context should be understood as equivalent. It should be recalled that in contemporary Italian registers and chronicles, cavalrymen or men-at-arms were recorded under the term *cavalli* (horses).

Two chroniclers provide more accurate figures in this regard. Capponi writes in the 'Commentari' that the prisoners amounted to '400 men-at-arms and about 3,000 cavalrymen', while Sanudo reports that '[they] captured 2,800 cavalrymen and 300 men-at-arms.' These two are the only chroniclers who clearly distinguish between men-at-arms and other cavalry.

Horses themselves, however, were also highly valued as booty. In the records compiled by Viviano, a Torre da Mare, a *famiglio* of Micheletto Attendolo, received eight gold florins '... *per la metà duno chavallo si guadangno al botino alla rotta di Nicolò Piccinino in fra Anchiari el Borcho.*' (...for half of a horse gained as loot in the rout of Niccolò Piccinino between Anghiari and Borgo).[52] Similarly, a captain of *condotta* named Antonello d'Alessandria received 110 florins for a horse obtained during the same rout of Piccinino – judging from its value, the horse must have been a well-bred stallion.[53]

Returning to the casualties, Palmieri is the only chronicler to also indicate the number of infantrymen among the prisoners: he reports 3,000 cavalrymen and 2,000 infantrymen. Other chroniclers limit themselves to mentioning 'many prisoners' or 'many infantrymen' after reporting the number of captured cavalrymen. Capponi calls them 'prisoners for ransom', which, according to him, numbered 1,540. These 'prisoners for ransom' should correspond to the citizens of Borgo Sansepolcro, who had joined the Milanese Army at the last moment, hoping for an easy victory and plunder. As noted earlier, many historians mention them among the prisoners, and it appears that all or almost all of them were captured. Their number varies in the sources from 1,200 to 1,400 men. In their accounts, Giusto d'Anghiari and Viviano provide precise figures – respectively 1,456 and 1,457 – although both define the prisoners as bourgeois citizens who, in addition to their weapons, could also pay for their ransom.

To conclude this view of Milanese casualties with the dead – the most debated figure since Machiavelli's claim that only a single man had died. How many casualties were there in reality?

Giovan Battista Poggio states that the dead were few, referring to both armies, while Poggio Bracciolini mentions only 40 deaths among Piccinino's soldiers. Platina, for his part, writes that 140 Milanese cavalrymen were killed. But which of these figures is more reliable? Della Tuccia places himself between these estimates, reporting 100 deaths on both sides – 30

52 Viviano, 'Registri della compagnia', libro 3593 f. 38v.

53 Viviano, 'Registri della compagnia', libro 3574 f. 184r.

31. Pope Eugene IV. Gravure n° 8 du recueil d'Onofrio Panvinio, *Onuphrii Panvinii Veronensis Fratris Eremitæ Augustiniani XXVII Pontificum maximorum Elogia et imagines accuratissime ad vivum æneis typis delineatæ*, Rome: 1568. (Public domain)

more than the total reported by Biondo, who counts 60 Milanese and 10 men of the League.

Could it instead be that the number of fallen was higher, as reported in the *Cronaca Malatestiana*, which states that 'many men and many horses were killed', or as reported by Graziani, who writes that '... many people died', a phrase closely resembling Sabellico's account: 'many died, many were wounded.' Viviano also seems to support this view, although he specifies only that there were 'several dead on both sides'.

Finally, the poem *La Fuga del Capitano* claims that the Bracceschi lost more than 900 men among the dead and wounded.

Nineteenth century historians such as Fabretti and Francesco lo Monaco generally tended to mention the limited number of casualties in this battle, reinforcing the widespread notion that Italian warfare at the time resembled a largely bloodless game.[54] However, at the beginning of the twentieth century, Willibald Block initiated a reassessment of this interpretation. By analysing the most well-known battles fought in the Italian peninsula during the fourteenth century, and particularly the Battle of Anghiari, he conducted a detailed study of the clash and argued for heavier losses.[55]

More recently, scholars such as Pieri and Mallett have further restored credibility to the military practices of Renaissance Italy, challenging the myth of bloodless battles.[56] With regard to the Battle of Anghiari, Mallett estimates that about 900 combatants died in total. He argues that, as in other fifteenth century battles, most casualties occurred among the lightly armed troops – infantrymen, *saccomanni*, and non-combatants – who were rarely included in casualty counts.

54 A. Fabretti, *Note e documenti da biografie dei Capitani Venturieri dell'Umbria*, vol. Unico (Montepulciano: Angiolo Tumi, 1842), pp.95–96; F. lo Monaco, *Condottieri*, Milan 1941, p.274.

55 Wilbald Block, *Die Condottieri: Studien uber die sogenannten 'unblutigen Schlachten'* (Berlin: Emil Ebering, 1919), pp.60–89.

56 P. Pieri, *Il rinascimento e la crisi militare italiana*, Turin, 1952; Michael Mallett *Signori e mercenari* (Bologna: Il Mulino, 1983).

All these people, except the infantry, usually supported the clash from afar, and the combat was fought primarily between heavy cavalrymen. For example, the page – the third member of the lance – remained in the rearguard, ready to assist the man-at-arms if necessary, by replacing a broken lance or a wounded horse, or helping the cavalryman if he were wounded. Likewise, the often numerous *saccomanni* and other non-combatants served as support personnel and did not participate directly in the fighting. Their duties usually consisted of managing supplies, carrying out raids, or assisting during sieges; in open battle, they stayed at a distance, prepared either to intervene in case of victory to plunder or to flee in case of defeat.

Another group consisted of the *famigli* or auxiliaries, who were attached to the infantry corporals and infantrymen equipped with the *targone*. They were also employed in combat as bearers of spears and shields.[57] These men assisted the infantrymen and like them – if not even more so, given their almost complete lack of protections – faced a significant risk of being wounded or killed.

All the others, such as bakers, muleteers, and the various trades listed in the table of the chapter Non-combatants in Micheletto Attendolo's Company, usually remained in the camp with the waggons. In this particular case, those attached to the Milanese Army stayed in Borgo Sansepolcro.

This analysis of the losses reported or estimated by both ancient and modern chroniclers and historians reveals considerable divergence in the figures provided. In conclusion, it is possible that both versions are correct. The Milanese likely suffered few losses among the men-at-arms – that is, among those considered worthy of note by contemporary chroniclers – probably around 60 to 80 cavalrymen. However, due to inadequate protection and, above all, the sudden retreat, many infantrymen, *saccomanni,* and auxiliaries must also have fallen. These men, who were not eligible for ransom and were therefore often ignored by chroniclers, could easily raise the actual number of casualties to 900, as reported by *La Fuga del Capitano* and by Mallett.

The following are the casualties among the victorious troops, that is, those of the League.

The vast majority of chroniclers do not mention losses in the pro-Florentine army. The few who do – such as Sabellico, Graziani, or the *Cronache Malatestiane* – report in generic terms that 'many people died', referring to both armies. Della Tuccia calculates a total of 100 deaths across the two sides, while Poggio speaks only of a small number of deaths.

Once again, the only chronicler to provide a precise figure is Flavio Biondo, who records 200 wounded and 10 dead 'from their wounds' among the League troops. It is likely that he too was counting only the cavalrymen among these losses – that is, those considered worthy of mention. Nevertheless, it is striking that a battle lasting three or four hours and fought

---

57 In this regard, see the beginning of the Chapter 6, The Opposing Armies.

in a confined space should have produced so few casualties, particularly given the considerable disparity between the number of dead and wounded, at a ratio of 20 to 1. The same proportion appears in the reported losses of the Milanese Army – 400 wounded and 60 dead. However, such figures become more plausible if they refer exclusively to the cavalrymen, who were protected by robust armour; indeed, the most efficient armour of the time were produced in Italy.

To verify, at least in part, the figures reported by Biondo – the only available source regarding Florentine losses – Viviano's records concerning Micheletto Attendolo's company proved particularly useful. During this battle, Attendolo's company constituted the spearhead of the League Army. Initially, it supported the first assault, then, it held the centre of the formation in front of the bridge and took part in nearly all of the engagements until the final victory.

The information contained in these registers, although intriguing, refers only to the captains of the *condotta*. Out of a total of approximately 1,120 cavalrymen, these captains numbered 45, including Micheletto himself and three constables. The documents primarily concern the administration and accounting of the company – including pay, supplies, and the purchase of horses or weapons – but they occasionally provide other information as well.

For example, they record that three captains were wounded at Anghiari.

The first was Raffaello di Vramonte, Lord of Carpi, the same individual mentioned in *La rotta di Niccolò Piccinino* for his duel with Astorre Manfredi. On 3 July 1440, Raffaello received 20 florins in Anghiari when he was described as '*feruto nella spalla*' (wounded in the shoulder). Payments made on his behalf continued in Arezzo – where he had been transferred – with the annotation that 'he was injured in Arezzo', and payments extended until mid-September, covering more than two and a half months of convalescence.[58]

Antonello da Lombardia, companion of Romanello da Cingoli, was wounded in the head and he too remained in Arezzo until July.[59]

The third was Todero da Lecce, '*feruto di lancia e restata nello petto dal lato diritto*' (wounded by a spear which remained in the chest on the right side). On 30 August, probably having recovered, he travelled to Florence '*per fare lo petto dela sua* coraza' (to commission the breastplate of his armour).[60]

There are no further references to others wounded in the Battle of Anghiari. However, Viviano's records generally concern the captains rather than the troops. At times, he mentions companions or *famigli* who collect money or other items on behalf of the captains. What he does record with precision, however, is the number of cavalrymen in each commander's

58 Viviano, 'Registri della compagnia', libro 3574 ff. 138v and 166r.
59 Viviano, 'Registri della compagnia', libro 3574 ff. 108r and 149v.
60 Viviano, 'Registri della compagnia', libro 3574 f. 135r.

condotta. From these records it is possible to see that Raphael di Vramonte – the same captain who was wounded at Anghiari – became a *casso* on 19 December 1440, meaning that he resigned from the company. In the final balance due to him, Viviano reports that during that year Vramonte had served at the rate of 8 florins per lance for one year: six months with 30 lances and another six months with 29 1/3 lances.[61] This means that from January until the end of June, Vramonte commanded 90 men, whereas from the beginning of July until December he had 88 men – two soldiers less. Since the Battle of Anghiari took place on 29 June, when the captain himself was wounded, it is possible that these two missing cavalrymen died there, or after from wounds sustained, as Biondo reports.

Unfortunately, this is the only indication of any losses within Micheletto's company at Anghiari. All the other *condotte* maintain the same total of cavalrymen until the end of 1440. Even the constables keep the number of infantrymen unchanged. This might suggest that they suffered no losses but does not necessarily mean that there were no wounded.

This data drawn from Viviano's records would therefore appear to confirm the limited Florentine losses reported by Biondo. However, as already noted, in register 3574 – which concerns the military campaign culminating with the Battle of Anghiari – there is no mention of Micheletto's '*casa*' (company), whose cavalry strength has been estimated at approximately 90 lances. Micheletto's account books have not survived, and consequently there is no way to determine the extent of any losses suffered by his company.

Micheletto himself was among the commanders most frequently mentioned by chroniclers for his valiant feats, along with the captain, Niccolò da Pisa. The latter was even captured at one point during the battle but was immediately freed and subsequently defeated more than one opposing captain. For these reasons, it is likely that the formations of these two captains bore the brunt of the Florentine losses. As a result, it becomes plausible that the number of deaths among the League troops was higher than the 10 reported by Flavio Biondo.

To conclude this complex chapter on casualties with a brief consideration.

Mortality among men-at-arms in Italian battles at the time was generally quite low, a view shared by several modern scholars. In his first study of the records of Micheletto Attendolo's company of adventure, historian Mario del Treppo observes that 'In the 25 years of its existence, Micheletto's company suffered, out of 521 men, 25 deaths – roughly one per year! In reality, however, only 15 of these died either in battle or from their wounds.'[62] The others, Treppo specifies, died from illness. As previously discussed, this was made possible by the effectiveness of contemporary armour and by the

61 Viviano, 'Registri della compagnia', libro 3574 f. 191v.

62 M. del Treppo, 'Gli aspetti organizzativi economici e sociali di una compagnia di ventura italiana' in *Nuova rivista storica*, 69, 1985, p.273.

widespread practice of the *taglia* (ransom), which in the event of defeat generally spared the life of the man-at-arms, though not his purse.

Ordinary soldiers, infantrymen, and *saccomanni* did not enjoy such privileges. They fought with far poorer protection and could usually offer only their weapons as ransom if captured. Even worse was the fate of the common people – peasants, citizens, women, and children – the defenceless for whom there was no '*buona guerra*' (good war), as Mallett called it, but only '*mala guerra*' (bad war).

During the Battle of Anghiari, 60 women from Milan were trampled by cavalrymen in the rout. This episode is recorded not only by Giovan Battista Poggio but also by della Tuccia and Graziani – the latter even mentions children among the casualties. These were probably the same children accompanying the women, who had been forced to stay in the rear with their mothers with buckets and jars to provide refreshment to the exhausted cavalrymen and their horses.

Flavio Biondo and the *Cronache Malatestiane* also include horses among the losses of that day. Biondo reports 600 horses were killed, while the *Cronache* refer more generally to many horses. The majority of these animals went into battle without protection: only captains or some heads of lances could afford caparisons made of leather or, more rarely, iron. All the other men-at-arms – as well as the pages – rode horses equipped only with basic harness, hence the high equine mortality in field battles.

Nevertheless, the '*mala guerra*' (bad war) waged against the defenceless manifested itself more often during sieges of castles and cities or in raids across the countryside rather than in open battle. In the Chapter 5, Background to the Battle, several episodes of looting and violence inflicted upon civilians in Tuscany by Milanese troops, and occasionally even by Florence's allies, have already been described. Among the most striking examples are the 37 people launched by catapult against the castle of San Niccolò and the 150 burnt alive at Raggiolo. In both cases, the armies made no distinction of sex or age.

10

The Heraldry of the Battle

Machiavelli described the outcome of the battle in the following terms: 'And it was a victory much more useful for Tuscany than harmful for the duke; because if the Florentines had lost, Tuscany would have been his, and by losing he forfeited nothing, except the arms and horses of his army, which could be replaced with much money.'

With this victory, Florence effectively freed itself from the Milanese threat that for more than 30 years had endangered the City of the Lily through wars and devastation. The battle was thus interpreted as the triumph of a democratic municipality over the authoritarian rule of a regime. Florence personified the freedom of Italy against Visconti imperialism as was reflected in the numerous celebratory literary and pictorial works produced after the battle. Thanks especially to the paintings, it is possible to attempt

32. Detail of the Battle of Anghiari on the Dublin Chest showing three Milanese standards. (Reproduced with permission from the National Gallery of Ireland, Dublin)

33. Milanese man-at-arms, detail of the Battle of Anghiari on the Dublin Chest. (Reproduced with permission from the National Gallery of Ireland, Dublin)

a reconstruction the heraldry – understood here as signs of recognition – of the two opposing armies involved.

Useful for this purpose are the three chest panels depicting the battle, described in Chapter 4, The Battle of Anghiari in Art. Among these, the most important for its historical reliability is the panel preserved at the National Gallery of Ireland in Dublin. This painting will serve as the principal point of reference for identifying the weapons and uniforms represented on banners, *giornee,* or hose worn by the soldiers. The so-called Dublin Chest will therefore be compared with the other two chests and with additional iconography related to the battle, as well as with literary texts and written historical sources, in an attempt to provide a realistic reconstruction of the heraldry adopted by the two opposing armies.

The Milanese Insignia

To begin by analysing the insignia reproduced on the Dublin Chest (see Plate I), all of which are displayed on swallow-tailed fly banners. This form was typical of cavalry standards, which usually had either a single or double tail. Square or rectangular insignia, by contrast, were typical of infantry units. These flags, commonly referred to as banners, were rarely used by Italian armies at the time of the Battle of Anghiari.

In the painting, three Milanese standards appear in four distinct groups or scenes: the first two are shown in front of San Sepolcro, one appears in the centre amid the heat of battle, and the last is in the parade of the victorious Florentine troops (image 32). The first insignia on the right bears the unmistakable coat of arms of the Visconti *biscione,* heraldically described as argent, a swaying serpent azure in pale, crowned or, swallowing a child gules, half-emerged, with arms extended (see Plate D, figure 1).[1]

The origin of this coat of arms remains uncertain. According to Litta, the earliest coat of arms of the Visconti were represented by seven garlands,[2]

1 It should be noted that on this chest the colour blue of the *biscione* has degraded to black.

2 Litta, *Famiglie, Visconti di Milano,* tav. 1. According to other sources the original coat of arms of the Visconti was seven gold crowns on a silver field.

other sources suggest seven crowns[3] or a silver-and-red chequy shield.[4] The *biscione*, also known as viper, is said to have appeared during the first crusade after the victory in a duel by Ottone Visconti over a Saracen nobleman named Voluce, who used a coiled serpent device. From that moment onward, Ottone supposedly adopted the same insignia as his coat of arms – an event dated 1090.

Another legend traces its origin back to 397 AD, when a certain Umberto, lieutenant of the count who ruled Milan, allegedly killed a dragon that had been terrorising the city. As a result, Umberto would have been called 'the Viscount' and would have adopted the dragon's head as a heritage.

A third version connects the symbol with the Battle of Altopascio in 1325. It is said that, during a pause in the fighting, the young Azzone Visconti, resting beneath the shade of a tree, did not notice a viper that had slipped into his helmet. When he later put it on, the snake slid out and brushed along his body from head to foot without biting him and then slithered away. From that moment onward, Azzone supposedly adopted the viper swallowing a child yet living him unharmed.

Finally, according to Emilio Galli, the origin of the Visconti *biscione* can be traced back to the first crusade, when it functioned as one of the insignia of the municipality of Milan. At that time, the Milanese carried two standards: one bearing a cross and another displaying a viper. The cross served as the insignia of the army, while the viper symbolised the camp commanded by Otto, deputy count of the Archbishop of Milan.

The viper supposedly derived from the bronze serpent preserved in the Basilica of Sant'Ambrogio which was believed to have healing powers and to offer protection to the Milanese on their journey to the Holy Land. The image of the Saracen being swallowed was later added to commemorate the victories achieved in the Holy Land. After the crusade, it was decided that this insignia should be granted to members of the Visconti family for their special merits, every time they needed to display it during battle. Over time, the Visconti adopted the *biscione* as their family badge and, once they had become lords of Milan, they imposed the emblem upon the city itself, replacing the red cross on a white field.[5]

The *biscione* appeared in numerous variations. The serpent was most commonly depicted in blue, although it was sometimes shown in green. In panel paintings, both colours tend to oxidise over time and appear today as black, as on the Dublin Chest. The field of the coat of arms was always silver (or white). In miniatures of the time, this colour was often created

---

3 G. Cambin, *Le rotelle milanesi Giornico, 1478* (Farvagny, Vétroz, and Bern: Società Svizzera di Araldica, 1987), p.100.

4 'Militaria, storie, battaglie, armate,' *Araldica* vol. 3 2006,p..574.

5 Other sources on the origin of the Visconti's coat of arms are: Cambin, *Le rotelle Milanesi*, pp.100–106; Carlo Maspoli (ed.), *Stemmario Trivulziano* (Milan: Edizioni Orsini De Marzo 2001), pp.27–28; E. Galli, 'Sulle origini araldiche della biscia viscontea' in *Archivio Storico Lombardo* (Milano: Fratelli Bocca, 1919), vol. III, pp.365–368.

with silver leaves, which frequently darken on paper and now appear as dark grey.

In 1336, the dukes Albert and Otto of Austria granted the Visconti the right to crown the *biscione*. Later, in 1395, when the Emperor Wenceslaus conferred the title of Duke of Milan upon Gian Galeazzo Visconti, the Visconti placed a ducal crown above their coat of arms.

According to the *Stemmario Trivulziano* compiled by Orsini De Marzo, Gian Galeazzo subsequently decreed that the *biscione* should be framed with the Imperial Eagle, thereby forming the official coat of arms of the Duchy of Milan. By contrast, Gastone Cambin argues that this quartered escutcheon had already appeared in the Visconti's arms as early as 1294, when Matteo I Visconti received the title of Imperial vicar.[6]

The eagle also appeared in the coat of arms of the county of Pavia, which consisted of three black crowned eagles arranged. This arms was often combined with the *biscione* in a shield divided vertically (parted per pale). Together with the associated title, it belonged to the firstborn of the Visconti family.

On the standards depicted on the Dublin Chest, the *biscione* is not crowned, and the same is true of the banners represented on the Madrid (Plate L) and Bryce Chests (Plate M). In these latter two paintings, the state insignia of Milan, Florence, and the Church have a stepped indentation at the fly end. Although this form of insignia was rare at the time, it appears in some painted chests, including the examples mentioned above.

The depiction of the second Milanese standard on the Dublin Chest (image 32), positioned in the middle and behind the other two, is heavily damaged and it is difficult to interpret in most of the scenes. It becomes clearly visible only in the parade depicted on the painting. The gold rays on a red field identify it as the *radia magna*, a military impresa of Duke Filippo Maria Visconti. The same insignia can also be recognised on the bardings and *giornee* of Milanese cavalry horses (image 33).

This impresa appears under several names – r*azza* (beaming sun), *raggera* (halo), *raggiante* (radiant), *fiammante* (flaming), *nimbo di sole* (sun halo) – all expressions intended to evoke splendour, grandeur and magnificence.

The *radia magna* first appeared as an impresa of Gian Galeazzo Visconti and was conceived by the poet Francesco Petrarca when Galeazzo was still young.[7] The impresa consisted of a gold radiant sun charged with a white dove and surmounted by a cartouche with the motto '*À Bon Droit*' (Well Deserved). The use of French for the motto honoured his wife Isabella de

6 Maspoli, *Stemmario Trivulziano*, p.28; G. Cambin, *Le rotelle Milanesi*, p.108.

7 P. Candido Decembrio, *Vita di Filippo Maria Visconti* (Milano: Adelphi Edizioni, 1983), p.70; L. Maini, *Le imprese dei Visconti e degli Sforza*, Tesi di laurea, Milan 1934–1935, pp.19–29.

Valois, the daughter of the King of France, whom he married when young in 1360.[8]

Within Visconti heraldry, the *radia magna* was accompanied by the dove or represented alone. One of its most monumental representations can be seen in the apsidal window of the Duomo di Milano, carved in 1402. After Gian Galeazzo Visconti, the impresa continued to be used by Filippo Maria Visconti.

In the *Stemmario Trivulziano*, among the emblems of Filippo, there is an arms displaying a gold radiant on a red field (see Plate H, figure 1 and figure 6)). The duke's secretary, Pier Candido Decembrio, devoted an entire chapter to the exploits of his lord and identifies 'the dove in a sun halo' as his common insignia in battle.[9]

Further evidence that the radiant insignia was indeed carried at the Battle of Anghiari is found in the poem *La Fuga del Capitano*, which mentions among the three Milanese standards one bearing the image of the sun.[10]

Among the other two chest panels depicting the battle, the radia magna appears only on the chest preserved in Madrid, and even there it is not clearly visible. This painting represents the battle immediately after its conclusion. The fleeing Milanese appear on the left side, while the victorious Florentine troops march towards Anghiari, dragging the large enemy standards they have captured along the ground (image 34).

The first standard from the left, entirely red, displays a dark and barely discernible emblem in the centre that resembles either a nebula, the coils of a snake, or even the knot of a handkerchief. Another red flag nearby is scattered with gold flames that recall the *radia magna*.

34. Milanese insignia dragged to the ground – detail. (Reproduced with permission from the Museo Arqueologico de Madrid)

8 Maspoli, *Stemmario Trivulziano*, p.33; Cambin, *Le rotelle Milanesi*, p.198.

9 Maspoli, *Stemmario Trivulziano*, pp.42 and 62; Decembrio, *Maria Visconti*, p.70; G. Giulini, *Memorie della città e campagna di Milano*, Milan 1857, vol. VI, p.206.

10 A, Fabretti, 'La Fuga del Capitano' in *Note e documenti da biografie dei Capitani Venturieri dell'Umbria,* vol. Unico (Montepulciano: Angiolo Tumi, 1842), p.251.

35. Standard of a leopard sejant. (Reproduced with permission of the National Gallery of Ireland, Dublin)

The third Milanese standard depicted on the Dublin Chest appears at the centre of the painting in the midst of the battle. It is the only one of the three that remains, at least momentarily, in Milanese hands (image 35). This banner has a gold field with a 'leopard sejant' placed within a circle. It is the standard of the Bracceschi, adopted by their most famous captain, Braccio Fortebraccio da Montone as a war emblem.

36. Galeazzo Visconti's Leopard Sejant. (Artwork by the author)

Campano recalls this insignia in the *Vita di Braccio,* adding that it had been presented to the Perugian captain by the Bentivoglio family of Bologna.[11] Graziani also mentions the leopard in his 'Chronicle' when describing in detail the funeral of the Perugian captain in 1432.[12] In his account he notes that 'among the many yellow and black flags bearing the ram' – the arms if Fortebraccio – there was also 'a white standard with the leopard' (see Plate B, figure 1).[13]

Another depiction of a 'leopard sejant' similar to the one on the banner can be seen on a fresco in the Sala dei Notari of Perugia, where it appears as the crest of the coat of arms of Braccio Fortebraccio.

When Braccio died in 1424, his captain, Niccolò Piccinino, inherited much of the remaining Bracceschi Army along with its company insignia, which he continued to lead in battle until his death. Three different texts on the Battle of Anghiari mention the leopard insignia: *La Fuga del Capitano, Diario del Graziani,* and *La*

11 G. A. Campano, *Vita di Braccio* (Perugia: 1621), p.212.
12 Eight years earlier, Pope Martin V had ordered the Perugian leader to be buried in deconsecrated ground.
13 'Diario del Graziani', *Arch. Stor. Ital.* XVI 1, 1850, p.361.

rotta.[14] The last of these recounts the capture of the Braccesco standard by Tartaglia d'Arezzo, one of the officers serving in the company of Micheletto Attendolo da Cotignola.

The leopard impresa was not unique to the Bracceschi and appears in the heraldry of several Italian noble families of the period. In his detailed study of the Rotelle of Giornico, Cambin notes that Gian Galeazzo Visconti himself sported a leopard, depicted in Lombard miniatures of the late fourteenth and early fifteenth century as a leopard sejant, with a collar, tied to a tree (image 36).[15]

Similarly, Mario Scalini mentions a leopard impresa belonging to the Florentine Miniati family. He reproduces a photograph of a *rotella* preserved in the Stibbert Museum in Florence, decorated with this impresa and the family livery together with the leopard sejant. He also mentions a fifteenth century chest preserved in the Bardini Museum of Florence, likewise painted with the Miniati's coat of arms with a leopard crest.[16]

Further discussion of this impresa is by Francesca Gado. In her analysis of the joust held in Florence in 1469, she examines the insignia and imprese sported by the participants and their men, belonging to the most prominent families of the city. Among them was Braccio di Carlo de' Medici, a member of a collateral branch of the Medici family, who carried a leopard tied to an oak on his standard and on the bardings of his horses. She observes that this impresa belonged to the House of Visconti and was later inherited by the Sforza family. She suggests that it may have been introduced into Florence by Gian Galeazzo Sforza during his stay in the city in 1459.[17] However, she also notes that Braccio de' Medici's mother, Caterina, was the daughter of the celebrated *condottiero* Braccio Fortebracci da Perugia, after whom his nephew was named. For this reason, it is perhaps more likely that the young Medici sported the leopard in memory of his grandfather's impresa.

37. Detail of Milanese standards from the lost Battle of Anghiari painting that was in the Bryce Collection. (Public domain)

The two remaining Milanese insignia appear on the chest formerly in the Bryce Collection in London. Unfortunately, as previously noted, this chest has been lost, and the painting survives only through a photographic reproduction published by Schubring.[18] Although the reproduction is

14 *La Fuga del Capitano*, p.250; 'Diario del Graziani', *Arch. Stor. Ital.* XVI 1, 1850, p.461; Angelo Ascani, 'La rotta di Niccolò Piccinino' in Angelo Ascani, *Anghiari dalle origini all'anno 1440* (Città di Castello: Città di Castello, 1973), p.292.

15 Cambin, *Le rotelle Milanesi*, pp.233–236.

16 M. Scalini, 'Divise e livree, araldica quotidiana' in 'Leoni vermigli e candidi liocorni, Comune di Prato' in *Quaderni* 1, 1992, pp.58–59 & 61.

17 F. Fumi Cambi Gado, *Emblemi a Firenze in epoca laurenziana*, Archivio Storico Italiano, 1992, pp.722–723 and 732–734.

18 Paul Schubring, *Cassoni*: *Truhen und Truhenbilder der italienischen Früh-*

of high quality – like the others included in his book – it is in black and white. Consequently, the original colours can only be hypothesised, and certain details, including the emblems displayed on these two insignia, are not clearly defined. Nevertheless, the available image still provides useful elements for analysis (image 37).

Both insignia are standards with forked fly ends and decorative edgings (fringes?) in two or more colours. The field is light grey, the same shade as the standard bearing the keys of the Church visible at the far right of the painting. This suggests that their original colour was most likely red. It is worth noting that a red field also appears on the two standards depicted on the Madrid Chest – those taken by the Florentines and dragged along the ground as a sign of contempt (see image 34).

Considering that the two chests share such similarities and may even have been painted in the same workshop, it is possible that these flags represent the same insignia depicted at different moments of the battle. In neither painting, however, are the standards are clearly visible.

The first Bryce standard is charged with an emblem depicting a winged creature in a rampant posture. At first glance, it resembles a griffin, similar to the emblem associated with Perugia shown by Pisanello in the medal crafted for Niccolò Piccinino.[19] Heraldically, the coat of arms of Perugia is gules, a griffin rampant argent crowned or.

The second standard presents an even greater interpretative challenge. Its field appears to be scattered with rays or small waves, with what seems to be a white animal placed at the centre – possibly a dove.

Renaissance. Ein Beitrag zur profanmalerei im Quattrocento (Leipzig: K.W. Hiersemann,1923), table n. 105.

19 L. Puppi (ed.), *Pisanello. Una poetica dell'inatteso* (Milano: Silvana Editoriale, 1996), pp.160–161.

11

The Insignia of the League

Thanks to the Dublin Chest, it is also possible to examine the standards of the army of the League, which appear clearly in two separate scenes: the initial deployment of the League forces (image 38) and the battle (image 39).

In image 38, two well-known symbols can be recognised: the lily of the city of Florence and the keys representing the State of the Church. (see Plate A, figure 1 and figure 2)

38. Three Standards of the League near Anghiari. (Reproduced with permission of the National Gallery of Ireland, Dublin)

The lily is associated with the Virgin Mary and, when used for Florence, functions as a canting arms because the name of the city evokes the image of a flower. As Passerini explains the emblem also refers to the *iris florentina* (*giaggiolo*), a plant that grows naturally around the walls of Florence. Passerini notes that this arms is ancient, dating to the eleventh century. Originally, it was described as gules, a fleur-de-lys argent. When the feud between the Guelf and Ghibelline factions ended in 1251, the victorious Guelfs expelled their rivals from the city and inverted the tinctures of the arms, adopting argent, a fleur-de-lys gules. From that moment onward, the Arms of Florence remained essentially unchanged, except for the occasional addition of a supporter – a lion sejant called *Marzocco*.[1]

1 Texts on the arms of Florence: Luigi Passerini, *Le armi dei municipi toscani* (Firenze: Tipografia di Eduardo Ducci, 1864), pp.100–102; G. di Crollalanza, Emblemi *Guelfi e Ghibellini*, *Emblemi* (Rocca S. Casciano: Stab. tip. di F. Cappelli, 1878), p.47; 'Militaria, storie, battaglie, armate', *Araldica*, vol. 2, p.358; *Araldica*,

39. Four League Standards in battle. (Reproduced with permission of the National Gallery of Ireland, Dublin)

The other standard, bearing the keys, is the emblem of the States of the Church. Heraldically, it is described as: gules, two keys in saltire or and argent, the wards upwards and the bows downward, tied with a cord. These keys refer to the Gospel passage granting authority to the Apostle Peter and symbolise the power given by Jesus Christ to bind and loose in heaven and on earth, as well as the leadership of the Church to Peter and his successors. The gold key represents spiritual authority, while the silver key symbolises temporal authority, and the ribbon indicates the inseparable relation between these two powers.

In ecclesiastical heraldry, the keys first appeared in the thirteenth century, in pale and addorsed (arranged vertically and back-to-back), with the wards pointing upward. Pope Boniface VIII (1294–1303) was the first pontiff to incorporate them into his coat of arms, after which they became the official insignia of the States of the Church. They are sometimes surmounted by the papal tiara, *triregnum*, symbolising the sovereign authority of the Pontiff of Rome.[2]

On both the Dublin Chest and the Bryce Collection Chest, however, the keys appear entirely in gold and without the tiara. The absence of the tiara likely served to distinguish the banners of the States of the Church from the Papal banners, which displayed it. Insignia with keys in gold and without the *triregnum* also appear in illustrations by Sercambi and in the chronicle of Villani – both fourteenth century sources.[3]

The third banner visible in the centre of the formation (image 38) belongs to the family of Attendolo-Sforza da Cotignola. Its heraldic composition is: quarterly, barry wavy argent and azure, and gules a quince or with the cross gules of the People of Florence in chief (see Plate C, figure 1).

---

origini, symboli e significato, Longanesi 1980, p.132.

2 *Militaria, storie, battaglie, armate, Araldica*, 3, p.436; www.araldicacivica.it, other States, Vatican; G. Aldrighetti, 'Araldica Ecclesiastica,' www.araldicavaticana.com.

3 Aldo Ziggioto, 'Le bandiere della cronaca del Sercambi' in *Armi antiche* (Torino: 1980), pp.68–69.

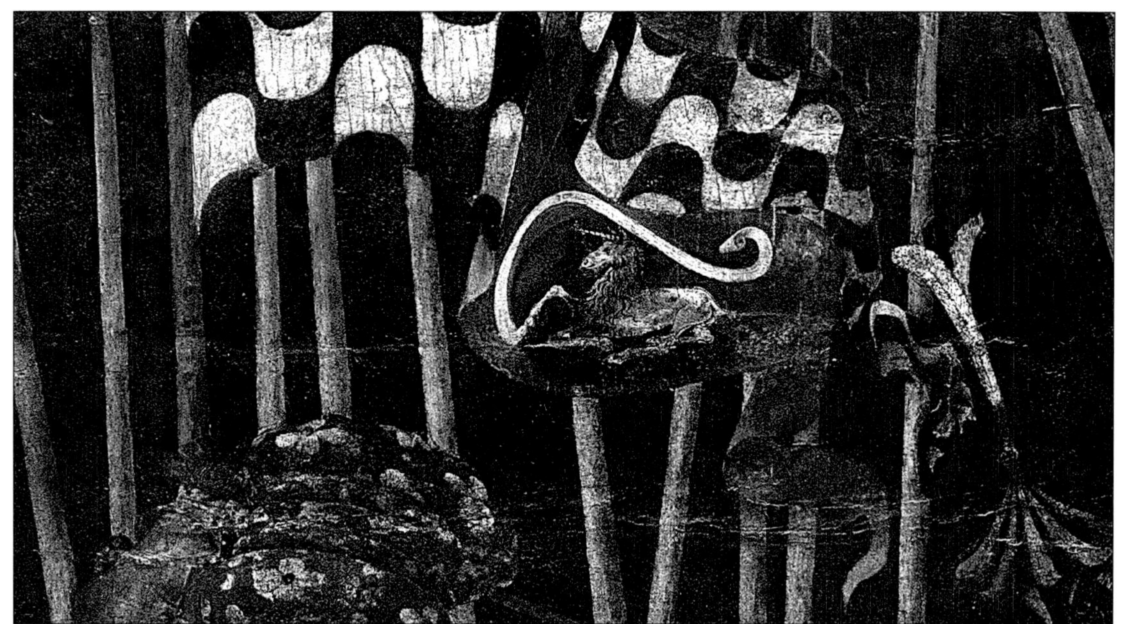

40. Standard of Micheletto Attendolo at San Romano. (Reproduced with the permission of the Louvre, Paris)

41. Count Francesco Sforza depicted in the church of San Sigismondo in Cremona. (Drawing by the author)

The impresa consisting of 'quarterly wavy and gules' dates back to Muzio Attendolo Sforza, during the period when he served under Alberico da Barbiano. Antonio Minuti, contemporary biographer of Muzio, recalls it: '*Sforza leva i quartieri che oggidì portano li Sforzeschi et fece le unde strette, et unite insiema dal canto mancho, el quartero rosso dal canto dirito, e la calza fessa dal canto dritto col bianco fora, al cilestro di dentro, e la rossa da la gamba mancha*' (Sforza sports the quartered escutcheon that the Sforzeschi still sport these days, and made the waves narrow and conjoined together on the left side and the red quarter on the right side; the right hose divided in two with white in the front and light blue behind, and the left hose red).[4] The same impresa or device is mentioned by sixteenth century chronicler Paolo Giovio as well as by Crollalanza and Ricotti in the nineteenth century.[5]

4 A. Minuti (G. Porro Lambertenghi ed.), 'Vita di Muzio Attendolo Sforza' in *Miscellanea di storia italiana*, VII (Torino: 1869), pp.116–117.

5 P. Giovio, *La vita di Sforza*, Florence 1549, p.7; G. Crollalanza, *Emblemi Guelfi e Ghibellini, Emblemi* (Rocca S. Casciano: Stab. tip. di F. Cappelli, 1878), pp.16–17; Ercole Ricotti, *Storia delle compagnie di ventura in Italia*, Torino: G. Pombar,

Several members of the Attendolo family served alongside Muzio under Barbiano – his three brothers Bartolo, Bosio, and Francesco, as well as their cousins Lorenzo and Micheletto. It was probably during this period that the Attendolos began to adopt the wavy as their emblem.

In his records, Viviano provides a detailed description of a taffeta standard bearing this same quartered device, made in April 1441 for the company of Micheletto Attendolo in the workshop of Master Luca Setaiolo in Florence.[6] The English translation of the document written in the fifteenth century Italian vernacular reads:

> On 14 April 1441 in Florence
>
> Matteo's expenses paid to master Luca Setaiolo for the standard according to one of his notes
>
> For one pound of grain taffeta for a banner, 7 *fiorini di suggello*.[7]
>
> For 4½ arms of blue taffeta for the fringes and waves of the same standard, weight 7 ounces, 13 *deniers*.
>
> For 3²/3 arms of white taffeta for said standard, for the waves and fringes, weight 11 ounces, 2 *deniers*, 6 florins. ½
>
> For one ounce of Florentine green taffeta for the meadows of said standard 10 *soldi*, 5 *deniers* per ounce.[8]
>
> For 3 arms of white *boccaccino* cloth for the bag of said standard 5 lire per ounce.[9]
>
> For the painting of said banner by Pesello and his fellow flag makers in Florence 19 *fiorini di suggello*.
>
> For the manufacture of said standard by Antonio, flag-maker, payment of 5 florins.

This standard corresponds to the one represented by Paolo Uccello in *The Battle of San Romano* in collection of the Louvre Museum in Paris, which depicts Micheletto's intervention in the battle (image 40). Its heraldic description is: quarterly, gules, a unicorn sejant on the countryside with a scroll argent at its right leg, and barry wavy azure and argent (see Plate C, figure 5). The Attendolo-Sforzas often placed their impresa in the red

---

1845), pp.272–273.

6 F. Viviano, *Registri della compagnia di Micheletto Attendolo*, in Fraternita dei Laici di Arezzo, libro 3593 'spese 1439–1446', f. 71v.

7 Grain taffeta: carmine red silk fabric. *Fiorini di suggello*: coins with a value guaranteed by careful checks.

8 Florentine green taffeta for the meadows: the green surfaces of the banner that represented the meadows where the unicorn sits.

9 *Boccaccino*: coarse cotton fabric.

quarters of this shield; for example, in the church of San Sigismondo in Cremona, Count Francesco Sforza is depicted together with his wife Bianca Maria Visconti wearing a tabard quartered with the wavy and the red field charged with a dog beneath a pine tree (image 41).

The unicorn – symbol of purity and faith – was one of Micheletto's impresas. In Viviano's records, it appears in references such as '*la giornea di liocornj dello Signore*' (the lord's *giornea* with unicorns) or '*due lancj a liocornj doro fine*' (two spears with gold unicorns).[10]

Chapter 4 above examines Paolo Uccello's painting and discusses the hypothesis that the scene may depict not the Battle of San Romano but rather the Battle of Anghiari. In addition to previously proposed arguments, this chapter lists further clues supporting this possibility.

On the Dublin Chest (image 38), Attendolo's standard has a red field with gold quinces – the canting arms of Cotignola, the birthplace of the Attendolo family. It likely represents all the forces of the Attendolo-Sforzas present at Anghiari under the command of Micheletto. The cross of the Florentine Republic may indicate that these forces were serving the city of Florence or, as suggested by Boccia, it may simply refer to the protection of St George.[11]

Another standard of the Attendolos family appears on both the chest preserved in Madrid and the one of the Bryce Collection. Its heraldic composition can be described as, quarterly gules, a dragon proper, and barry wavy azure and argent (see image 42 and image 43). In both panels, the colours of the insignia have deteriorated and in certain areas the pigment has darkened significantly. Nevertheless, the dragon remains visible, and on the Madrid Chest one of the quarters still shows the Attendolos' wavy.

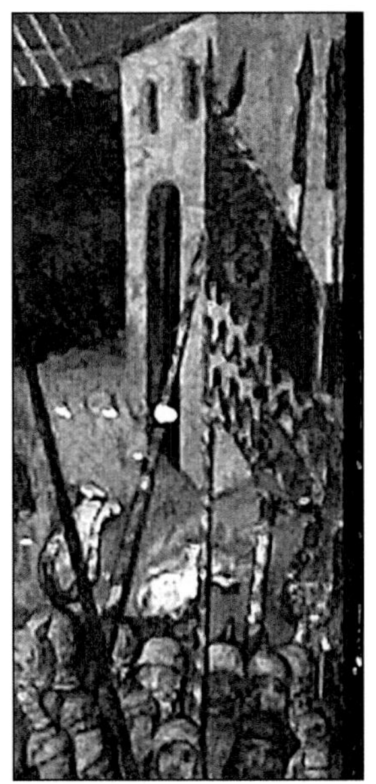

42. Attendolo-Sforza banner in the chest of Madrid. (Reproduced with permission of the Museo Arqueologico de Madrid)

43. Attendolo-Sforza banner on the Bryce Chest. (Public domain)

The impresa of a winged dragon with the face of an old, bearded man holding a diamond ring in its claws dates to a concession granted by Nicolò III d'Este, Marquess of Ferrara, to Muzio Attendolo. In 1409, Muzio served as the marquess' captain general. His son Francesco later sported this impresa as the crest to his coat of arms.[12]

10 Viviano, 'Registri della compagnia', book 3571 '*entrate* 1437–1449', f. 42v ; Viviano, 'Registri della compagnia', libro 3593 '*spese* 1439–1446', f. 31v.

11 L. G. Boccia, 'Le armature di Paolo Uccello' in *L'Arte*, III 1970, p.74.

12 Cambin, *Le rotelle Milanesi*, pp.122–123 and 431; Maspoli, *Stemmario Trivulziano*, pp.35 and 40.

44. Detail of the Orsini standards, from the 'Cavalcade of the Gentle Virginio Orsini' depicted on a fresco in the Orsini-Odescalchi Castle in Bracciano. (Drawing by the author)

However, Micheletto also sported the dragon impresa. It appears as a helmet crest in one of his company registers from 1432 to 1433 and again in a list of panaches and supplies for the *famigli* dated 1439.[13] One entry reads: '*al Signor Messer Michele per 15 penne di struzo e 7 penne di pavone per lalmetto dello dracho del Signore*' (to Messer Michele for 15 ostrich feathers and 7 peacock feathers for his dragon helmet).[14] In image 42 and image 43, the dragon lacks the old man's head and the ring, which suggests that it should be identified as Micheletto's impresa.

In image 39 of the Dublin Chest, another standard of the League appears. This standard has a completely red field with an animal in the centre positioned between two silver roses surrounded by a silver nebuly from which rays emerge, ending in shapes resembling stamens. This insignia corresponds to the one of Pier Giovanpaolo Orsini di Manupello, who had served as captain general of the Florentine militia since April 1440 (see Plate E, figure 3).[15]

The original coat of arms of the Orsini family was bendy gules and argent, in chief of the second charged with a rose gules, supported by a bar or (Plate H, figure 2). This arms was frequently shown with a bear crest – a canting arms referring to the family name – and after the acquisition of the fief of Anguillara, the bar was charged with an eel.[16]

13 Viviano, 'Registri della compagnia', book 3591 '*spese* 1432–1433', f. 61v.

14 Viviano, 'Registri della compagnia', book 3593 '*spese* 1439–1446', f. 3r.

15 I. Masetti-Bencini, 'La bataglia di Anghiari' in *Rivista delle biblioteche e degli archivi*, Luglio-Agosto 1907, p.107; Giovanni Cavalcanti, *Istorie Fiorentine* (Fiorenze: all'insegna di Dante, 1839), vol. II, Book XIV, Ch. XXIV; Capponi, 'Commentari', Muratori R.I.S. XVIII, coll. 1192, 1195; Francesco Guicciardini, *Le cose fiorentine*, vol. IV (Firenze: R. Ridolfi, 1945), p.269; Gustavo Brigante Colonna, *Gli Orsini* (Milano: Geschina, 1955), p.122.

16 Gustavo Brigante Colonna, *Gli Orsini* (Milano: Geschina, 1955), pp.26–30; F.

On the standard depicted on the chest, however, the colours of the emblem are inverted: the rose is silver while the field is red. In heraldic terminology, this chromatic variation of the original arms is known as a brisure.[17] Although such alterations were uncommon among noble families, they were sometimes used in Italy.

A comparable Orsini insignia appears in the *Cavalcata del Gentil Virginio Orsini* fresco in the Orsini-Odescalchi castle in Bracciano[18] The fresco commemorates the appointment of Virginio Orsini as captain general of the Aragonese troops in 1489. In the depicted procession of cavalrymen, several insignia display the inverted colours of the Orsini arms: red banners with the white rose, as well as trumpet banners quartered argent, a rose gules and gules, a rose argent (image 44).

Returning to the Dublin Chest, the central animal charge does not closely resemble a bear. This discrepancy may be due to a repainting or to the changing of the colours over time. Nevertheless, the Orsini insignia is mentioned in the accounts of the battle in the poem *La Fuga del Capitano,* where it is described as 'the banner with a bear.'[19]

As for the nebuly element, the Gamurri writes that the Orsini of Manupello – the branch to which Pier Giovanpaolo belonged – 'surrounded the Orsini arms with a fesse full of wheat', a motif that may recall the nebuly on this banner.[20]

A final insignia of the League appears on the other two chests: the one preserved in Madrid and in the Bryce Collection in London (image 45). In both artworks, this insignia is positioned in the background of the combat, among a group of cavalrymen. On the Bryce Chest, the insignia is difficult to identify, yet its field appears dark and scattered with leaves, recalling the bordure of the corresponding insignia on the Madrid Chest. On the latter artwork, the emblem is likewise indistinct, but it is sufficiently clear to establish that it represents an impresa rather than a coat of arms. The emblem shows a man surrounded by trees or leaves set on a red field. Both the figure and the vegetation are dark in colour, similar to the tone of the vegetation of the surrounding landscape, suggesting that the original colour was likely green and has darkened over time. Except for the face in a carnation colour, the rest of the man is covered with hair or leaves, evoking the medieval figure of the 'wild man'.

Gamurri, *Istoria genealogica delle famiglia nobili toscane e umbre* (Florence: 1668), vol. 1, pp.5–6.

17 H. Zug Tucci, 'Un linguaggio feudale l'araldica' in Karol et al, *Storia d'Italia* Annali I (Torino: Einaudi, 1978), pp.847–848; 'Militaria, storie, battaglie, armate' in *Araldica*, 3, p.575.

18 Clemente Vanenti, *Castelli in Italia*: *Le storie – le famiglie – le leggende* (**Köln:** Konemann, 2001), p.186.

19 *La Fuga del Capitano*, cit. p.258.

20 Gamurri, *Istoria genealogica*, p.19.

45. The wild man, a probable device of Pier Giovanpaolo Orsini. (Drawing by the author)

In medieval symbolism, the wild man embodied the contrast between man and nature, wisdom and ignorance, and more broadly the notion of man enslaved by natural impulses and desire. During the Middle Ages, he also represented strength, cunning, and gluttony. In pictorial representations from the fifteenth century onward, the wild man is shown covered with hair and with claws. In carnival celebrations at the end of February, the wild man is dressed as a reborn bear who emerges from hibernation at the approach of spring.

Since this is an impresa, it must have belonged to a *condottiero* serving with the League. Excluding Micheletto – whose banner appears on the far right in both paintings (see image 42 and image 43) –the most plausible attribution is to Orsini, commander-in-chief of the Florentine troops and therefore the most prominent captain of the League. On the Dublin Chest, the banner of Pier Giovanpaolo Orsini displays the bear and the rose. On the Madrid and Bryce Chests, however, there is no insignia bearing these emblems; instead, the 'wild man' appears, a figure that could also be symbolically interpreted as a bear – used by the Orsini family as both crest and impresa.

12

The Milanese Cavalrymen

Most Milanese cavalrymen sported the gold *radia magna* on a red field on their *giornee* and on the bardings of their horses (see image 33 and image 46). This device constituted one of the battle impresas of the duke and has already been discussed in the chapter devoted to insignia.

The right to bear the ducal insignia was granted to the *lance spezzate*, as reported by Biglia and Giulini.[1] The *lance spezzate* formed a special body of cavalrymen who, for various reasons, had left their original companies

46. Milanese knights. (Reproduced with permission of the National Gallery of Ireland, Dublin)

1 A. de Billiis, *Historia mediolanensis*, Muratori R.I.S. 1723–1751, XIX, col. 44–45; Giorgio Giulini, *Memorie spettanti alla storia della città e campagna di Milano* (Milano: Francesco Columbo, 1857), vol. VI, p.204.

or had remained without a commander. In the Milanese Army, this group consisted largely of Bracceschi and was placed under the direct command of Niccolò Piccinino (see Plate B).

Another elite Milanese cavalry contingent was that of the *Famigliari Armigieri,* or ducal soldiers. These were Lombard nobles and veterans who served as personal guards of the lord. They too were under the direct authority of Piccinino, and it is plausible that they likewise sported the ducal insignia.

Together, these two select contingents formed the most reliable elements of the Milanese forces and constituted the backbone of the army, serving to counterbalance and control the mercenary companies recruited by the duke through contractual agreements. These mercenary troops formed a third, and much more numerous, contingent referred to as the *conductitii.*[2]

47. Niccolò Piccinino. (Reproduced with permission of the National Gallery of Ireland, Dublin)

2 On the Visconti militias' organisation: Maria Nadia Covini, 'Per la storia delle milizie viscontee: I familari armigeri di Filippo Maria Visconti' in L. Chiappa Mauri & P. Mainoni (eds), *Il dominio di Milano fra XIII e XV secolo* (Milano: La Storia, 1993), pp.35–63.

48. Piccinino family coat of arms, from the State Archives of Perugia. (Drawing by the author)

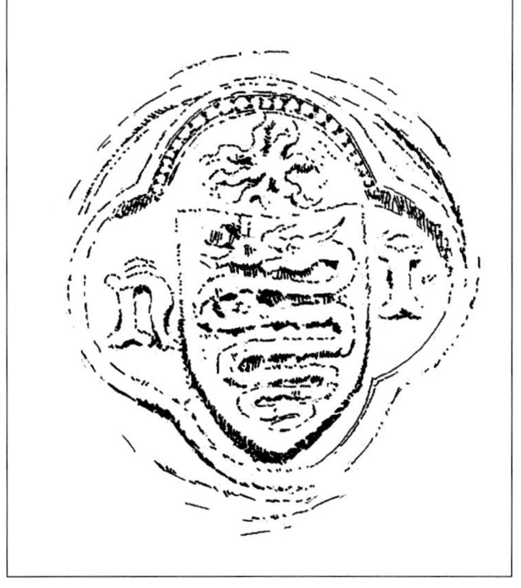

49. Seal with coat of arms of Niccolò Piccinino, from the State Archives of Lucca. (Drawing by the author)

Returning to the impresa of the *radia magna*, it is always shown quartered with a narrow wavy, arranged either vertically or horizontally, and rendered in three colours: red, white, and black. The black pigment, oxidised over time, was probably originally blue or green.

These three colours may refer to the Visconti device derived from the arms of the *biscione* – argent, a swaying serpent azure vorant a Saracen gules. Alternatively, they may depict the white, red and green livery of the city of Milan, worn by the servants of the municipality at the end of the fourteenth century.

In *Documenti diplomatici tratti dagli archivi Milanesi*, Luigi Osio records that on 19 October 1397 Duchess Caterina Visconti, wife of Gian Galeazzo, ordered that Antonio della Croce – the husband of the governess of Giovanni Maria Visconti – be admitted among the servants of the municipality who wore this white, red and green livery.[3]

The wavy motif most likely derives from the device used by the Bracceschi companies. Minuti recounts that Muzio Sforza and Braccio Fortebraccio originally served together under Alberico da Barbiano and initially wore the same uniform. The source translated reads:

> Thus, Sforza adopted the quartered device. At that time, Sforza and Braccio da Montone were still close companions and comrades-in-

3 Luigi Osio, *Documenti diplomatici tratti dagli archivi Milanesi* (Milano: G. Bernardoni di Giovanni, 1872), vol. I, p.317.

> arms. Sforza wore the quarters that the Sforzeschi still display today: narrow waves joined together on the left side and the red quarter on the right. The hose was cut on the right side, with the white portion facing outward and the light blue behind, while the left hose was entirely red. Braccio made his device symmetrical so that it would not be identical to Sforza's. In his version, he had the red quarters on the right side, the waves extended towards the left, and the hose cut on the left leg. In this way they sport their liveries today. Braccio would jokingly remark that 'You, Sforza, wear the narrow and proud wavy like the waves of a swollen sea, whereas I prefer them calm, flat and peaceful.' Sforza replied that Braccio preferred flat waves only because he lacked spirit. They exchanged such remarks in a spirit of laughter and playfulness.[4]

Paolo Giovio also records this tradition, noting

> They wore the same insignia and colours on their surcoats. Each man-at-arms had a surcoat quartered from the right shoulder to the left thigh: one half red, the other decorated with the white and light blue wavy. To create a distinction, Sforza graciously adopted sharp waves, while Braccio had round ones.[5]

Ricotti instead described Braccio's and Sforza's devices after the two *condottieri* had already parted ways:

> Up to now, the devices of Bracceschi and Sforzeschi had been the same, that is, a surcoat divided into quarters from the right shoulder to the left thigh of carnation colour [red], and the other side marked with a slightly sharp wave pattern. Braccio wanted to differentiate his device from that of his adversaries; he ordered that the garments of his men display more compact waves, due to the similarity of his consort's device.[6]

Both Giovio and Ricotti, although with some variations, refer to what had already been written in the fifteenth century by Minuti. The device in question consists of a red field quartered with the wavy, an emblem derived from the arms of Barbiano: argent, a cross gules; base parted gules, and chequy argent and gules (see Plate H, figure 3).[7]

---

4 A. Minuti (G. Porro Lambertenghi ed.), 'Vita di Muzio Attendolo Sforza' in *Miscellanea di storia italiana*, VII (Torino: 1869), pp.116–117.

5 P. Giovio, *La vita di Sforza* (Florence: 1549), p.7.

6 Ercole Ricotti, *Storia delle compagnie di ventura in Italia* (Torino: G. Pombar, 1845), vol. II, p.273; the coat of arms of Varano was vair, a wavy azure and argent.

7 Maspoli, *Stemmario Trivulziano*, pp.306 & 530.

50. Detail from the Dublin Chest. (Reproduced with permission from the National Gallery of Ireland, Dublin)

The Sforzesca uniform has already been discussed in the previous chapter dealing with the standard displaying the large wavy quartered with the red field bearing the quince emblem (image 38) as well as in the version featuring the dragon (image 42).

The Braccesca uniform, on the other hand, appears on the caparisons and *giornee* of the cavalrymen and is depicted as a narrow tricolour wavy quartered with a red field bearing the *radia magna*. Of the colours in this wavy, white is the only one that originally belonged to the Bracceschi device.

The red and green colours were added later and refer to the clothing of Piccinino, as recalled by Matarazzo in *Cronaca*, '*...li magnifici Baglione portavano la divisa che lo' donò el conte Iacomo quale fu de Nicolò Picinino, ciò è una calza verde, cioè la manca, e una roscia, cum lo schinire bianco de fora da man dritta*' (...the magnificent Baglioni [the Baglioni family of Perugia] wore the device donated to them by Count Giacomo [Giacomo Piccinino], which had belonged to Niccolò Piccinino; that is, a green left hose and a red one with the white greave on the right leg.)[8]

Near the centre of the painting, close to the bridge over the River Tiber, a cavalryman with a drawn sword and riding a rearing black horse is shown encouraging the Milanese troops forward. This figure represents Niccolò Piccinino (image 47). He wears a barbute helmet with a T-shaped opening and surmounted by a bat-winged crest. Over his armour he wears a gold half-*giornea*, and the harness of his horse is also gold. The barding displays the narrow wavy quartered with the *radia magna*. However, no additional arms or emblem appears that would clearly identify this figure as Piccinino.

8 'Cronaca del Matarazzo,' in *Archivio Storico Italiano* 1851, vol. XVI, part two, p.99.

51. Two Captains Fleeing across the Tiber. Detail from the Dublin Chest. (Reproduced with permission from the National Gallery of Ireland, Dublin)

52. Seal of Guidantonio Manfredi in the State Archives of Florence. (Drawing by the author)

Very little evidence of this Perugian captain's insignia survive because his bitter rival Francesco Sforza ordered the demolition of his funeral monument in 1455, deliberately erasing the memorials and insignia associated with him in the city of Milan.

A portrait of Piccinino appears on the reverse of a medal by Pisanello. On the opposite side, the artist depicted a griffin nursing two children – Braccio da Montone and Piccinino himself.[9] In this case, the griffin does not represent a personal coat of arms but rather the city of Perugia, the birthplace of both *condottieri*.

9 G. A. Pisanello, *L'opera completa di Pisanello, Classici dell'Arte*, 56, (Milano: Rizzoli 1972, tav. XLII-XLIII and pp.96–97.

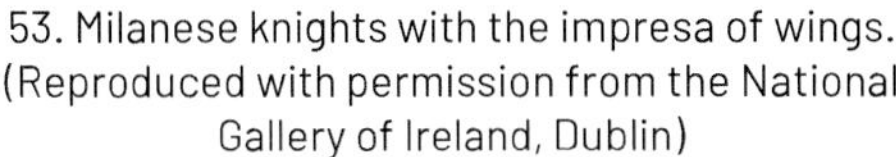
53. Milanese knights with the impresa of wings. (Reproduced with permission from the National Gallery of Ireland, Dublin)

54. Captured Milanese knights with the wings impresa. Detail from the Dublin Chest. (Reproduced with permission from the National Gallery of Ireland, Dublin)

The Visconti captain's arms appear in *Ritratti ed Elogi* by Totti, where a coat of arms bearing a rampant bull accompanies the section dedicated to Piccinino.[10] The same arms is preserved in the State Archives of Perugia, in the heading of the land register of Niccolò Piccinino and his sons Francesco and Giacomo, dated to 1446.[11] Although the document is in black and white, the notched shield with the rampant bull is clearly visible, surmounted by a helmet and accompanied by a leopard sejant (image 48).

Two further seals of Piccinino are preserved in the State Archives of Lucca.[12] These are attached to letters signed by the *condottiero* and addressed to the *Anziani* (Elders) of the municipality of Lucca. The first seal is indistinct but shows, between the letters 'N' and 'P', a shield bearing a rampant animal in the centre – possibly a bull.

---

10 P. Totti, *Ritratti ed elogi di capitani illustri* (Rome: 1635_.

11 In R. Rossi (ed.), *Storia illustrata delle città dell'Umbria* (Perugia: Elio Sellino Editore, 1993), p.416.

12 Archivio di Stato di Lucca, *Anziani al tempo della libertà*, book 442, *original letters 1430–1447.*

55. Coin of Astorre Manfredi with *salasso*. (Drawing by the author)

The second seal is far clearer and is on a letter written by Piccinino in 1438, also addressed to the *Anziani*. In this example, the Visconti *biscione* appears at the centre of the shield, flanked by two letters – 'N' and another character resembling either 'I' or 'P'. Remarkably, above the shield appears a sun, identifiable as the *radia magna* (image 49).

In March 1438, Duke Filippo Maria incorporated Piccinino into the Visconti lineage. At the same time, the duke confirmed him as captain general for life and granted him the coat of arms of the viper '*in ea propria forma qua nos ipsi ea deferimus ac habemus*' (in the same form in which we ourselves sport and possess it). Along with this honour, Piccinino was also appointed marquess and count of several territories.[13]

Another detail distinguishing Piccinino from other cavalrymen appears in the small, quartered shield placed at the centre of the horse's peytral. This escutcheon is quartered red and silver and accompanied on both sides by two round gold plates.[14] The same combination of quartering and gold plates can also be seen on the barding of Pier Giovanpaolo Orsini (image 74) commander of the troops of the League.

It is therefore plausible that both Piccinino and Orsini displayed these identification marks emphasising their status.

Another probable depiction of Piccinino appears in the background of the painting, among a group of Milanese cavalrymen. The *condottiero* is beneath the banners, rides a black horse and wears a red hat (image 50).

The Braccesca uniform also appears on the barding of the horse in image 51 on the right, though without a *raggiante*. In this scene, two horsemen are fleeing across the River Tiber. Their magnificent helmet panaches indicate that they are captains. The scene recalls the account of the only two captains of the Milanese troops who managed to escape the defeat together with Piccinino: his son Francesco and Guidantonio Manfredi, Lord of Faenza.[15]

---

13 Pier Candido.Decembrio, 'Vita di Niccolò Piccinino' in *Muratori Rerum Italicarum Scriptores* XX, col. 1070; L. Osio, cit. 1872, p.161.

14 In this regard, Scalini has suggested that these plates were probably nothing more than parts of the iron barding supplied to the captains – barding that was subsequently covered with cloth in heraldic colours.

15 For these two captains in Anghiari, see M. Sanudo, 'Vite dé duchi di Venezia,' *Muratori R.I.S.*, XX col. 1099; *La Fuga del Capitano*, p.274; Pier Candido Decembrio, 'Vita di Niccolò Piccinino' in *Muratori Rerum Italicarum Scriptores* XX 1082; Giulio Cesare Tonduzzi, *Historie di Faenza* (Bologna: Forni 1967), p.486; F. Biondo, *Historie* (Venice: 1547), p.128.

56. Detail of the funerary monument of Gian Galeazzo Visconti at the Certosa di Pavia. (Drawing by the author)

In reality, three captains or commanders succeeded in saving themselves. The third, rarely mentioned in the chronicles, was Carlo Fortebracci, son of Braccio da Montone. At the time, he was not yet 19 years old, yet he served in the Bracceschi ranks and commanded approximately 200 cavalrymen.[16]

Francesco Piccinino had already accompanied his father in a number of military campaigns since 1425, and, after Niccolò's death, he inherited the command of the Bracceschi and Visconti Army. Nevertheless, Francesco Piccinino's impresas or personal emblems remain unknown. During the Battle of Anghiari, he led the Milanese charge along with Astorre Manfredi and was constantly engaged in the fighting, unlike the other two captains mentioned above, whom neither chronicles nor poems record in the clashes.[17]

The captain depicted on the right in image 51 is likely Francesco Piccinino, as suggested by the Bracceschi device visible on his horse's barding. Over his armour he wears a crimson *giornea* adorned with white flames alternating with floral lines and motifs. Both horse and rider appear

16 See the personnel table in the chapter: The Opposing Armies.

17 Some texts on Francesco Piccinino in this battle: Johannis Simonetae, 'Vita Francisci Sfortiae,' *Muratori R.I.S.* XXI, col. 293; *La Fuga del Capitano*, cit. pp.262, 265; Lorenzo Spirito Gualtieri, *L'Altro Marte*, (Venezia: Leonardus Achates, 1489), cap. 58; Ammirato, *Istorie Fiorentine*, vol. IV, p.263.

57. Detail from the 'lost chest' from the Bryce Collection. (Public domain)

wounded: the Bracceschi captain has been struck in the left thigh by a crossbow bolt. Unfortunately, no surviving chronicle records this injury.

The captain on the left, however, is more difficult to identify. He wears a quartered *giornea* described as argent a vol gules, and gules a flaming or. For the following reasons, he may represent Guidantonio Manfredi.

The Lucchese chronicler Alessandro Boccella describes one of Manfredi's insignia during the Battle of Serchio in 1430, writing that 'He bore the arms of a falcon above leopards.'[18] In that battle, Manfredi fought for Florence and was defeated by the forces of Lucca and their Milanese allies. In his chronicle, Boccella refers to him as 'Astore, Lord of Faenza', confusing him with his brother Astorre, who, though younger than Guidantonio, became Lord of Faenza in 1448 after his brother's death.[19]

The falcon mentioned in the insignia is an impresa belonging to a broader tradition of bird emblems of the Manfredi family. Examples include the goshawk (*astore*) used by his brother Astorre and the rooster of his nephew Galeotto.

Another bird appears in a seal of Guidantonio preserved in the State Archives of Florence, more precisely in a file rediscovered in 1997 containing 28 original letters from various correspondents addressed to Cosimo the Elder between 1435 and 1457. Among these documents was a letter from Guidantonio dated 23 January 1439, in which the Lord of Faenza informed Medici of his arrival in Florence to meet the Signoria and expresses his hope of receiving favourable pay to recruit his *condotta*.[20] On the reverse of the letter, the imprint of Manfredi's seal remains visible, depicting an ibis on a branch (image 52).

18 A. Boccella, 'Historie Lucchesi,' in Biblioteca Statale di Lucca, ms. 892, f. 139r.

19 Biondo, *Historie*, p.50; Tonduzzi, *Historie*, p.480; B. Righi, *Annali della città di Faenza*, Faenza 1840, vol. I, p.197; Giovanni Cavalcanti, *Istorie Fiorentine* (Fiorenze: all'insegna di Dante, 1839), vol. I, p.401.

20 Archivio di Stato di Firenze, 'Acquisti e Doni,' 383, letter no. 5.

58. Detail from the Madrid Chest with a knight wearing a chevrony. (Drawing by the author)

The ibis was regarded as a sacred animal in ancient Egypt, associated with the God Thoth and symbolising intelligence and purity. It was also valued for its usefulness, since it fed on snakes, locusts, and carrion. In Greek culture this bird was linked to the God Hermes, while in Renaissance Europe it was hunted extensively because its delicate meat was served at banquets of the nobility.

Thus, the Lord of Faenza had two emblems – the falcon and the ibis – which may have been heraldically stylised in the form of wings. In heraldry, the vol does not refer exclusively to an eagle but may represent any bird, symbolising speed, ingenuity, and military prowess.

Four other cavalrymen bear the vol impresa. Two appear in the Milanese deployment at Borgo Sansepolcro, bearing a red vol on a silver field (image 53). Among the prisoners about to enter Anghiari, another cavalryman bears a gold vol on a red background (image 54). The fourth stands in the background among a group of Milanese at Borgo Sansepolcro and appears to carry a silver vol on a red field quartered with the Bracceschi wavy (image 50). These four cavalrymen thus carry the same impresa quartered with different emblems or colours.

Particularly interesting is the quartering carried by the first cavalryman on the right (image 53). Careful examination of the detailed photographic reproductions kindly provided by the National Gallery in Dublin, as well as direct observation during my visit to the museum, reveals traces of the underlying colour – blue/azure – beneath the two black fields with the wings

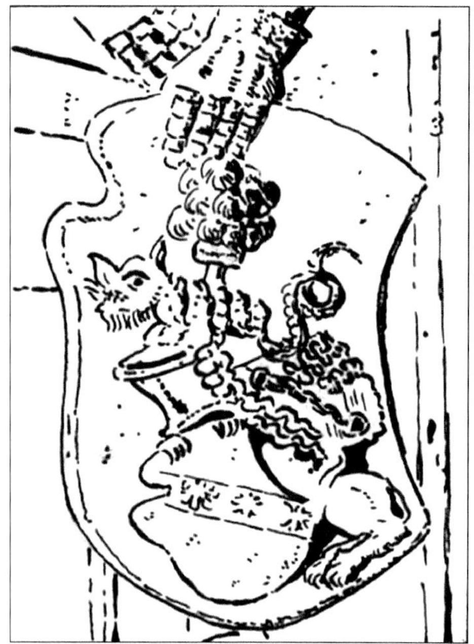

59. Coat of Arms on Antonello Arcimboldi's tomb. (Drawing by the author)

Consequently, this cavalryman likely bore a simple quarterly: argent a vol gules, and azure. Without the vol, it closely resembles the coat of arms of the House of Manfredi di Faenza. It is not identical, however, since the Manfredi arms was arranged in a specular quartering: quartered azure and argent. As already observed for the Orsini family, the inversion of the original colours was not uncommon at the time. The Manfredi family themselves employed such variations.

Evidence of this practice appears in the miniatures of the *Codici manfrediani*, where the family arms are depicted several times with the colours mirroring the original.[21] In addition, these arms is frequently represented combined with a chief of Anjou: azure, three fleurs-de-lys or, separated by a label of four points gules. Sometimes, the fleurs-de-lys appear in other colours, such as white or red. In the *Stemmario Trivulziano*, for instance, the Manfredi's arms is illustrated as quarterly, azure and argent, three fleurs-de-lys gules (Plate H, figure 4).

Returning to image 53, the second cavalryman with the vol – the one positioned further back – also displays on the rear barding of his horse arms described as party per fess argent, a vol gules and *fiammante* azure and argent. Taken together, these two men-at-arms carry emblems that share the same colours – the colours associated with the Manfredi's arms, as recorded in the *Stemmario Trivulziano*.

In conclusion, it is plausible to hypothesise that these cavalrymen bearing the emblem of the wings belonged to the company of Guidantonio. The prince himself may therefore be the captain depicted alongside Francesco Piccinino (image 51).

Let us now focus on a Manfredi whose identification is certain. In image 54, three Milanese cavalrymen are shown as prisoners. The first on the left sports on his *giornea* a quarterly with a blue or green field (now darkened to black) combined with the Bracceschi wavy. The other two cavalrymen sport a quarterly respectively on their horse bardings and the *giornee*: chevrony (or chevronelly) in bend (or in fesse) argent and gules, and azure, a salasso or. The *salasso* (bloodletting instrument) is an impresa of Manfredi and was also carried by Astorre, alongside his canting arms of the goshawk. This emblem can be observed on coins minted in Faenza during the Manfredi lordship (image 55),[22] where the *salasso* (also known as *temperino*, another surgical instrument used for bloodletting) appears clearly. Earlier chapters

21 Antonio Savioli & Carlo Moschini (eds), *Faenza nell'età dei Manfredi* (Faenza: Faenza Editrice, 1990), pp.117, 140, 143, 191.

22 Savioli & Moschini, *Faenza*, pp.71, 182, 184–186; Arturo Castiglioni, *Il salasso nell'arme gentilizia dei Manfredi, signori di Faenza* (Trieste: Stabilimento Artistico Tipografico G. Paoli, 1930), p.163.

60. Cavalryman wearing the Visconti *biscione* on the Dublin Chest. (Reproduced with permission of the National Gallery of Ireland, Dublin)

61. Detail of a Milanese cavalryman on the Madrid Chest. (Reproduced with permission of the Museo Arqueologico de Madrid)

of this book have already examined this prince in detail, and in the painting the artist represents him among the captured soldiers.

The question however remains: which of the two men is Manfredi?

The cavalrymen on the left displays the *salasso* on his horse's barding but not on his gold *giornea*. The captain on the right, by contrast, sports the *salasso* on his *giornea*, while his horse's barding presents four different emblems: the chevronelly, the wings, a sun and, on the peytral, another black and white chevronelly.

Two hypotheses are possible. Either the figures represent Astorre and one of his captains or – more plausibly – these riders were unhorsed during the battle and, after being captured by the Florentines, were forced to mount other available horses, perhaps even as an act of humiliation[23].

23 Regarding the owner of the horse bearing four emblems – the red and white chevronelly (a Visconti emblem), and the sun and wings (a Gonzaga impresa, also caried by Ludovico II) – see R. Signorini, 'Aenigmata Disegni d'arme e d'amore' in M. Rossi (ed.) *Monete e medaglie di Mantova e dei Gonzaga dal XII al XIX secolo*, vol. II (Milano/Roma: Electa 1996), pp.41–45 and 71–76. Graziani records that a young Ludovico was with the Milanese during a raid near Cortona in April 1440 (see Chapter *Historical Background to the Battle*). However, he is the only chronicler to mention the future marquess in Piccinino's army, and in any

The *salasso* is quartered with the red and silver chevrony, which is essentially a Visconti impresa frequently mentioned by Cambin in his writings.[24] In the *Stemmario Trivulziano*, there is a particularly fine arms showing the chevrony quartered with the *radia magna*, derived from the *Codice Trivulziano* 2168 (Plate H, image 6).

The same impresa appears in the relief of the funerary monument of Gian Galeazzo Visconti at the Charterhouse of Pavia, depicting a fight between Visconti and Florentine cavalry. This same relief was reproduced in an engraving by Litta in the work *Famiglie celebri italiane*.[25] Among banners and Milanese caparisons adorned with Visconti emblems, a cavalryman carries the chevrony in bend impresa (image 56).

In addition, in *Vita di Filippo Maria Visconti*, Pier Candido Decembrio records that purple red and white were the colours especially favoured by the duke, who had his subordinates wear them on their clothing.[26]

The chevronelly also appears in the chests of Madrid and of the Bryce Collection, where it decorates the caparisons of two Milanese men-at-arms. On the Bryce Chest, the cavalryman is shown charging his enemy just beyond the Ponte delle Forche, and the entire barding of his horse is decorated with the chevrony (image 57).

62. Detail of the Milanese knights in front of the gate of San Sepolcro. (Reproduced with permission from the Museo Arqueologico de Madrid)

On the Madrid Chest, another cavalryman has a barding decorated with a quartered escutcheon: azure, with a barely visible emblem in the centre, and chevronelly in bend gules and argent (image 58). Unfortunately, this portion of the painting is heavily damaged, and the colours of the emblem in the blue quarters have deteriorated. The central figure resembles three flowers with stems meeting at the base, though it could also represent three ears of grain or even a *salasso*. In fact, the quarter resembles that carried by the cavalrymen bearing the *salasso* in image 54.

On the Madrid Chest, yet another chevronelly appears, on a Milanese infantryman's *giornea*, which is discussed below the chapter devoted to infantry.

It is therefore possible that the Visconti family adopted the chevronelly or chevrony in bend red and silver primarily as a war impresa used by allied companies or contracted *condotte*. As

case no source lists him among the prisoners.

24 Cambin, *Le rotelle Milanesi*, pp.141,154, 247 & 284; Maspoli, *Stemmario Trivulziano*, p.43.

25 Litta, *Famigli, Visconti di Milano, tav.*

26 Pier Candido Decembrio, *Vita di Filippo Maria Visconti* (Milano: Adelphi Edizioni, 1983) , p.95.

discussed above, the *radia magna* and the wavy were reserved for the duke's *lance spezzate* and the *famigli*.

At the centre of image 53 is a cavalryman who, judging from the plumes on his helmet, may be a captain or squadron commander. He displays three different emblems: the Bracceschi wavy, the black (perhaps the colour has changed) and gold scaly, and a coat of arms described as argent, a bend azure charged with three stars with five silver rays. This design recalls the arms of the Arcimboldi family of Milan, originally from Parma, who moved to Milan in the first half of the fifteenth century.

Pezzana mentions two members of this family, who served as captains of the ducal men-at-arms.[27] The first was Antonello Arcimboldi, who distinguished himself in this role; after Antonello death in 1439, command of the men-at-arms passed to his brother Niccolò Arcimboldi. Niccolò, however, was more experienced in legal and financial matters than in warfare and appears to have remained in Parma during the campaign conducted by Piccinino.[28]

63. Milanese cavalrymen depicted on the side panel of the Bryce Collection chest. (Drawing by the author)

27 Angelo Pezzana, *Storia di Parma* (Parma: Dalla Ducale Tipografia,1842), II, pp.414 & 428; M. N. Covini, 'Per la Storia', p.56.

28 Pezzana, *Storia di Parma*, II, p.428.

Several variants of the Arcimboldi coat of arms are known. Among them are or, a bend azure charged with three stars or, and or, a bend gules charged with three stars or.[29] Particularly relevant for this research is the coat of arms carved on the tombstone of Antonello Arcimboldi, made after 1439 (image 59). On this monument, the arms displaying a bend charged with stars and is supported by a helmeted lion with the Visconti dragon as a crest, surmounted by a tree. The mantle displays a quartered escutcheon with the *morso* (bit) and the wavy.

This image also appears in the book by Cambin, who attributes all these impresas outside the coat of arms to the Sforza family. However, this attribution overlooks the fact that the helmeted lion, the tree, and the bit were already sported by the Visconti family early as the fourteenth.[30] These impresas later passed to the Sforza family when Francesco became duke. Only the wave is properly a Sforza impresa; however, in this case it likely refers to the Bracceschi impresa, since Antonello Arcimboldi died well before the Sforzas and the Visconti merged.

64. Milanese cavalrymen depicted on the side panel of the Madrid Chest. (Drawing by the author)

It may therefore be suggested that the cavalryman depicted here is a squadron commander from the company of ducal men-at-arms commanded by the Arcimboldi.

In image 60, another cavalryman appears bearing the Visconti *biscione*. He is shown among the prisoners, positioned in front of the cavalrymen depicted in image 54. Both his *giornea* and the barding of his horse

29 See Cambin, *Le rotelle Milanesi*, pp.248–255.

30 *Stemmario Trivulziano*, cit. pp.3–4; *Seta, oro, cremisi*, exhibition catalogue edited by Chiara Buss, Silvana Editoriale 2009, pp.178–179.

display the narrow wavy and the *radia magna*, together with the quartered escutcheon bearing broken spears. On the horse's barding, the Visconti *biscione* is displayed prominently. Since he is the only figure clearly sporting the Visconti's arms, he might represent Sacromoro or Sagramoro Visconti, mentioned in the chapter above devoted to the casualties of the battle.

Two other Milanese cavalrymen with noteworthy emblems appear on the Madrid Chest. One of them, armed with a spear, rides a horse with a decorated dark barding (image 61). Originally the colour could have been blue, while the decorative elements are nothing more than mantling – ribbon-like bands bearing mottos – which enclosed knotted veils similar to the *capitergium cum gassa* impresa. In his study, Gastone Cambin notes that both Gian Galeazzo Visconti and Filippo Maria sported the *capitergium*.[31] In this regard, the chronicler Benedetto Dei writes in his account of the Battle of Anghiari: 'And the banners of the Duke of Milan, Filippo Maria – the one with the Veil and the one of gold satin – were captured.' However, Dei is the only chronicler who explicitly mentions the Visconti veil or *capitergium* among the Milanese insignia.[32]

65. Detail of the Milanese shield in the panel depicting the Battle of San Romano, preserved in London. (Author's drawing)

31 Cambin, *Le rotelle Milanesi*, pp.220–225.

32 Benedetto Dei, *La Cronica dal anno 1400 alle anno 1500* (Firenze: Papafava, 1984), p.56.

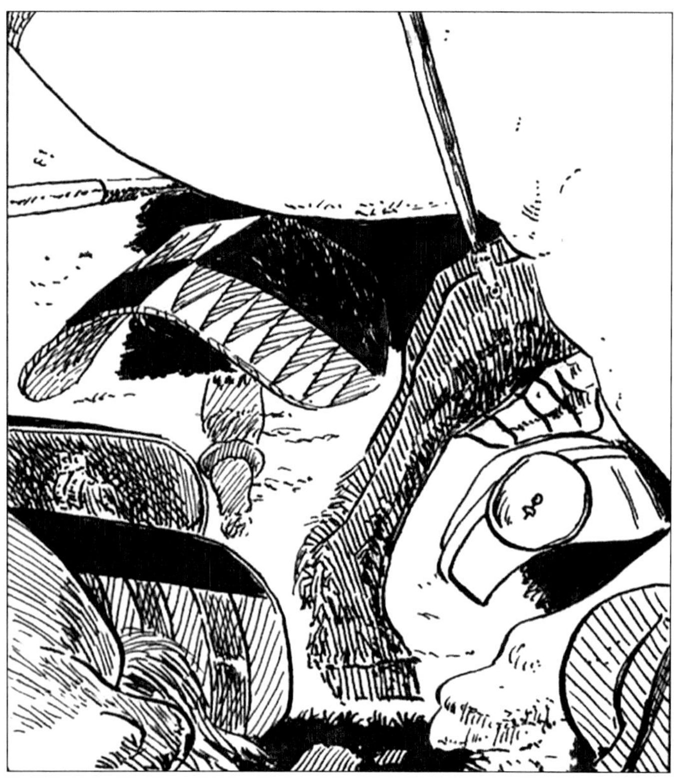

66. Detail of the Milanese shield in the panel depicting the Battle of San Romano, preserved in Florence. (Drawing by the author)

Finally, in front of the gate of Borgo Sansepolcro, some Milanese cavalrymen are depicted attempting to take refuge in the city (image 62). The horse of the rider on the left has a red barding scattered with gold flames, an emblem that alludes to the *radia magna* impresa. Behind them stands a captain, most likely Niccolò Piccinino, raising his right hand as if to halt the retreat of his troops guarding the gate.

Unfortunately, the painter of the Madrid Chest appears to have been poorly acquainted with contemporary armour. Many are depicted with cuisses and the back of greaves formed of lames perhaps an attempt to represent mail. The right or left spaulders are drawn as a single piece that often awkwardly covers the arm. Most striking of all are the helmets topped with spikes, reminiscent of the helmets worn by German soldiers during the First World War.

Let us now examine the last Milanese cavalrymen depicted on the side panels of the Bryce Collection chest, published by Schubring, and the Madrid Chest (see image 63 and image 64).

In image 63, the Milanese troops are shown entering Borgo Sansepolcro before the battle. The first man-at-arms on the right displays on his horse's caparison flames reminiscent of the halo (*radia magna*). The second cavalryman on the left sports on the rear of his caparison a quartered coat: sable (perhaps originally another colour), and the gules and argent.

His same quartering appears again on the left panel of the Madrid Chest. In that scene, the Milanese are represented fleeing from Borgo Sansepolcro. Among the armoured cavalrymen – who carry no visible insignia or impresa – there are also two infantrymen equipped with shield and spear (see image 64). The soldier on the right carries a shield party argent and gules, while the other bears the same quartered escutcheon as image 63. This repetition constitutes yet another point of similarity between the two paintings.

Paolo Uccello depicts this same quartered escutcheon – though with a red and silver indented in place of the *fiammante* – three times in his works. On a shield lying on the ground in the London panel, beneath the white horse of a Sienese fighter on the right (image 65); on a shield beneath the unhorsed cavalryman (called Bernardino della Carda) in the painting preserved in Florence (image 66); and on the trumpet banner of a retreating trumpeter in the upper right part of the background (image 67).

Boccia writes of this emblem in his study of the armour depicted in Paolo Uccello's works,[33] but the subject is examined more thoroughly by Roccasecca in the *Battaglie*.[34] Analysing the heraldry in the paintings of San Romano, he hypothesises that the quartered escutcheon belonged to the Sienese family of Petrucci, noting that Antonio Petrucci served as a Sienese commissioner at San Romano.

67. Detail of the trumpet banner on the panel depicting the Battle of San Romano, preserved in Florence. (Author's drawing).

Pertici shares this interpretation but also points out the differences between the shield shown in the painting and the coat of arms of Petrucci – tranché indented or and azure – which differs both in colour and in the fact that it is not quartered.[35]

My hypothesis is that these shields in the San Romano painting actually belong to Milanese soldiers, more specifically to those of the Bracceschi faction, whose livery used the colours red, silver, and green.[36] During that conflict, the Sienese forces received help from the Milanese troops commanded by Alberigo di Lugo, together with the companies of Francesco Piccinino, son of Niccolò and Bernardino della Carda.[37]

33 L. G. Boccia, 'Le armature di Paolo Uccello' in *L'Arte*, III 1970, p.77.

34 P. Roccasecca, *Paolo Uccello e le battaglie* (Milano: Electa, 1997), pp.12, 17, 22, 32, 68.

35 P. Pertici, 'Condottieri senesi e la rotta di San Romano di Paolo Uccello' in *Arch. Stor. Ital.* 1999, issue 581, pp.542–548. www.archiviodistato.firenze.it, *I blasoni delle famiglia Toscane nella Raccolta Ceramelli Papiani*, fam. Petrucci; Michel Popoff, *Toscane, hors Florence* (Paris: Le Léopard d'Or, 2009), p.128.

36 In the text by P. Roccasecca, *Paolo Uccello*, p.22, there is the shield of the painting of San Romano preserved in London with the quartered field of a beautiful dark green, perhaps repainted during a restoration.

37 Cf Giovan Battista Poggio, *Vita di Niccolò Piccinino* (Perugia: 1619), p.219; Boccia, 'Le armature,' p.71; Pertici, 'Condottieri senesi,' p.545.

13

The Milanese Infantrymen

In the painting on the Dublin Chest, three categories of Milanese infantrymen can be identified: *lanciotti*, crossbowmen, and handgunners. The latter two appear in the centre of the composition, grouped into two distinct companies supporting the cavalry.

Among the troops commanded by Piccinino, there were numerous handgunners (image 68), who were widely deployed during the battle.[1] According to be poem written by Leonardo Dati, there were 300 of them (see Plate F, figure 1).[2]

68. Detail of the Milanese handgunners on the Dublin Chest. (Reproduced with permission from the National Gallery of Ireland, Dublin)

1 Pier Candido Decembrio, 'Vita di Niccolò Piccinino' in *Muratori Rerum Italicarum Scriptores* XX, 1082; *La Fuga del Capitano*, p.272.

2 L. di Piero Dati, 'Dal Tropheum anglaricum' in *Giornale Storico della Literatura Italiana* (Torino: Ermanno Loescher, 1890), vol. XVI, p.52.

69. Detail of the Milanese crossbowmen on the Dublin Chest. (Reproduced with permission from the National Gallery of Ireland, Dublin)

In the painting, these soldiers wear barbutes or other helmets and doublets of various styles and colours. Their legwear consists of tight-fitting trouser leg arranged as a livery: the right leg is entirely pink, while the left is of three colours – red, white and black. The same appears on the hose of the crossbowmen (image 69), who have the right leg in red and the left leg in three colours. These colours correspond to those of the narrow wavy quartered with the *radia magna* sported by the Milanese cavalrymen – red, white, and green.

Among the infantrymen armed with spears, one figure appears on the far left of the painting moving away from the scene (image 70). He wears a helmet with a *mazzocchio* (*bourlet*)[3] and carries an oval shield decorated with the narrow tricolour wavy quartered with a red field, closely resembling the Bracceschi device displayed by the cavalryman on the right in image 51.

The first infantryman to the right in image 71 carries an identical shield, is wearing armour, holds a sword, and is wearing greaves. This figure is most likely a captain, and is followed by a line of infantrymen armed with spears. Their hose displays a variety of colours: some entirely red, others with the left leg blue and the right half blue and half white, and yet others black and red.

These soldiers are probably Bracceschi infantrymen mixed with the citizens of Borgo Sansepolcro, who had joined the army of Piccinino before the battle. Most of them were subsequently captured by the Florentine forces.

To the left of the Bracceschi captain in image 71, is shown an infantryman carrying a rectangular red shield bearing a white animal rampant, resembling a lion. In the background of the painting, to the right of a group

3 This was a man's hat formed by a pad (cloth wrapped in a circle) made of a wool, a little larger than the circumference of the head or military helmet. The *bourlet* was covered in cloth or velvet sometimes in the colours of the livery.

of Milanese cavalrymen, the same white 'lion' on a red field appears on round shields carried by two infantrymen. Apart from the red and white colours associated with Duke Visconti, the owner of this device has not yet been identified (see image 50).

On the Madrid Chest, beginning from the left side of the composition, a group of Milanese infantrymen can be seen fleeing beneath the walls of Borgo Sansepolcro (image 11). Most of them carry long spears, although some crossbowmen are also present among them.

The first infantryman on the left wears a *giornea* displaying two quartered emblems: 1 and 4, an ochre field; 2 and 3, a chevronelly per fess gules and argent, a Visconti impresa already observed on the Dublin Chest (image 54).

The infantryman standing behind the first soldier wears a dark impresa, and both men are equipped with greaves. Above them, a captain can be recognised by the red hat he wears. To the right, appears another infantryman carrying a shield over his shoulder and wearing a sallet fitted with a tip or nail at the top. His shield bears the following arms: tranché per bend or; gules a serpent or; and barry wavy or and gules. Among these emblems, the only clearly recognisable figure is the serpent alluding to the Visconti's *biscione*.

70. Detail of a Milanese infantryman armed with spear and shield, on the Dublin Chest. (Reproduced with permission from the National Gallery of Ireland, Dublin)

Four crossbowmen are also present, and are probably wearing padded doublets. Curiously, the last of them wears a sparrow's beak helmet, a type normally associated with cavalry – perhaps taken as a battlefield trophy. The infantryman behind wears the same type of helmet and carries a shield that can heraldically be described as: 1 and 4, barry or (or argent) and sable (perhaps altered in colour); 2 and 3, sable (again possibly altered).

Because this emblem is badly damaged, it is difficult to identify with certainty. However, enlarged images reveal traces of red on the black bands. This detail recalls – although this remains only my hypothesis – the coat of arms of the city of Cremona: divided; 1, barry gules and argent; 2 azure, a ball or held by an arm. Some chroniclers report that, among the Milanese captains taken prisoners, there was also a certain Romano da Cremona.[4]

Another infantryman in this painting sports an interesting emblem. This soldier is fleeing behind the walls of Borgo Sansepolcro and carries a shield

4 F. Biondo, *Historie* (Venezia: 1547), p.129; Ammirato, *Istorie Fiorentine*, vol. IV, p.264.

71. Detail of the Bracceschi infantry and the citizens of San Sepolcro on the Dublin Chest. (Reproduced with permission from the National Gallery of Ireland, Dublin)

decorated or, bars gemel in bend sable (possibly originally azure or vert) accompanied by two pellets sable (see image 72).

On the Bryce Chest, there are also Milanese infantrymen gathered near the river (image 73), most of them crossbowmen. One soldier, armed with a long spear and about to cross the bridge, carries a shield bearing the *fiammante* quartered with a dark field similar to the quartered escutcheon seen in image 63 and image 64.

This chapter on the heraldry of the Milanese infantry would not be complete without mentioning the illustrations of the 'Semideus', written around 1438 by the Milanese humanist Catone Sacco.[5] The third part of this work, entitled 'Dell'arte della guerra,' was dedicated to Filippo Maria Visconti and describes military techniques intended to expand the duke's territories through a hypothetical crusade in the Holy Land.

The illustrations depict battles, sieges, and naval clashes between Milanese soldiers and the enemies of Christianity – the Saracens. The weapons illustrated correspond to those typical of the first half of the fifteenth century in Italy. Infantrymen are shown armed with long spears, polearms, and crossbows, while protecting their heads with open sallets or war hats. They carry large, convex shields decorated with the principal arms of the Visconti: the blue *biscione* on a white field and the black eagle on a gold field.

Some shields are divided per fess (divided horizontally) with the blue *biscione* in the upper half and a red and white barry below (see Plate D, figure 4). These colours recall both the chevronelly and the two colours associated

5 The 'Semideus' is preserved in St Petersburg, Publicnaja Biblioteka, Lat. Q. v. XVII. 2.

72. Detail of a Milanese infantryman fleeing on the Madrid Chest. (Reproduced with permission of the Museo Arqueologico de Madrid)

73. Detail of the Milanese infantry on the Bryce Chest. (Public domain)

with Duke Visconti. Soldiers' clothing appears in many different colours, and their particoloured hose often includes soles. Groups of infantrymen wear hose in blue, white, and red, others in combinations such as white and red, white and green, or red and green; while some wear entirely white hose. Many soldiers protected their legs with *armisias*, iron rerebraces similar to those worn by the infantrymen depicted at the Battle of San Romano.

In these illustrations, the cavalry also carry weapons typical of the time. Their armour includes sparrow's beak helmets, sallets, and war hats, augmented by camails or mail on the arms and abdomen. Instead of a *giornea,* they wear a short particoloured coat or doublet.

The horses are fully harnessed and fitted with shaffrons, while caparisons and shaffrons are likewise particoloured and frequently display the man's coat of arms. Unfortunately, the emblems are difficult to see clearly.[6]

The most clearly visible coats of arms on the harnesses are again the *biscione* and the eagle. A large group of cavalrymen also have the white handkerchief, or *capitergium cum gassa*, on a blue or sometimes green, field. The standards likewise display the Visconti *biscione*, also often shown in the form of pennons or trumpet banners. One trumpeter has a banner bearing the *Ducale*, that is, a quartered escutcheon with the eagle and the *biscione*.

6 I contacted the Saint Petersburg museum to request higher-resolution photographs of the illustrations, but the staff kindly explained that they could not provide them due to the embargo resulting from the Russo-Ukrainian war.

14

The Cavalrymen of the League

Once again, the following description is based primarily on the painting of the Dublin Chest.

At the lower right of the painting appears the initial deployment of the League Army. At the centre of this formation, the commanders stand beneath the flags (image 74).

At the centre of this group is Lodovico Scarampi Mezzarota, Patriarch of Aquileia, the only figure dressed in ecclesiastical garments. (see Plate A, figure 5). Scarampi took command of papal forces in April 1440,

74. Detail of the League commanders on the Dublin Chest. (Reproduced with permission of the National Gallery of Ireland, Dublin)

75. Detail of the infantryman with the shield bearing the Scarampi Mezzarota Coat of Arms. (Reproduced with permission of the National Gallery of Ireland, Dublin)

76. Detail of the League commanders on the Madrid Chest. (Reproduced with permission from the Museo Arqueologico de Madrid)

succeeding Cardinal Giovanni Vitelleschi. Following the Battle of Anghiari, on 1 July 1440, Scarampi was elevated to the rank of cardinal.[1]

In this depiction, however, he still wears the vestments of a patriarch. On his head is a wide-brimmed green hat (the colour now darkened to black), rather than the more commonly seen red hat of a cardinal. He holds a baton, while his horse is equipped with a shaffron and gold harness.

His coat of arms appears in image 75, on the shield resting on the ground beside an infantryman on the left. The blue field has darkened with time, while the gold band is charged with three stars. Beneath the band, at the base of the shield, there is a gold half-wheel.[2]

1 See Capponi, 'Commentari', *Muratori R.I.S.* XVIII col. 1196; Flavio Biondo, *Historie* (Venice: 1547), p.129; *Diario del Graziani*, Arch. Stor. Ital. XVI 1, 1850, p.451.

2 For Scarampi's arms see V. Capobianchi, 'Immagini simboliche e stemmi di Roma' in *Archivio della Società Romana di storia Patria*, XIX 1896, p.405.

In the corresponding detail on the Madrid Chest, the patriarch is not shown. Instead, the group of cavalrymen includes commanders in armour together with two Florentine commissioners dressed in civilian attire (image 76).

Returning to the Dublin Chest, the Florentine commissioners Bernadetto de' Medici and Neri Capponi stand to the right of the patriarch, identifiable by their red hats (see Plate A, figures 3 and 4). To the patriarch's left likely stands Micheletto Attendolo da Cotignola, also wearing a red hat and holding a baton.

Neri Capponi is the only figure depicted in profile, a pose reminiscent of the effigy on his funeral monument in the church of Santo Spirito in Florence. Litta reproduced this portrait in *Famiglie celebri italiane*, 'I Capponi' (image 77).

Prominently positioned in the foreground is the Florentine Captain General Pier Giovanpaolo Orsini (image 74).[3] He is wearing a red hat and has a crimson surcoat over his armour, holds a baton, and rides a horse with gold harness (see Plate E, figure 2). The horse barding is decorated with several emblems. At the rear appears a black flame, an impresa frequently sported by Florentine cavalrymen. On the peytral is a quartered escutcheon in red and silver between two gold plates, similar to that seen on Niccolò Piccinino (image 47). The only difference is that here red flames appear on the white quarters.

Beneath the gold plates on the sides of the escutcheon is an emblem reminiscent of the coat of arms of the Capponi family. It is tranché, sable and argent, comparable to the first quarter of the shield carried by the second infantryman in image 75.

77. Neri Capponi on his funeral monument in the church of S. Spirito in Florence. (Drawing by the author)

3 For Orsini's standard see the chapter *The Insignia of the League*.

78. Milanese standard-bearer on the left is relieved of his Standard by a Florentine knight as portrayed on the Dublin Chest. (Reproduced with permission of the National Gallery of Ireland, Dublin)

79. Detail of the Capponi tent in the Capture of Pisa. Collection of the National Gallery of Ireland, Dublin. (Drawing by the author)

At first glance, this might suggest that the cavalryman depicted is Capponi himself. However, Caponi served as commissioner of the Florentine Republic and therefore could not have carried a baton. Two possible hypotheses may therefore be considered. The first is that the emblem does not represent the Capponi tranché but rather a company impresa, either Florentine or belonging to the Orsini, whose dark colour may have originally been blue. The second hypothesis is that the emblem indeed represents the Capponi tranché but was inserted by the painter as a tribute to the patron. The commissioner of the chest has been identified with the Capponi family.[4]

With regard to Orsini, contemporary sources consistently describe him as a brave captain who

4 Cf F. Polcri, 'La battaglia di Anghiari dipinta sui pannelli di tre cassoni preleonardeschi' in *Pagine Altotiberine* 13, pp.128–129; M. Scalini, 'Divise e livree, araldica quotidiana' in 'Leoni vermigli e candidi liocorni, Comune di Prato' in *Quaderni* 1, 1992, p.61; L. Tongiorgi Tomasi, *Osservazioni su una tavola poco nota raffigurante 'La presa di Pisa'* in *Antichità pisane*, 1975/2, p.12.

always fought in the thick of battle. In the 'Commentari' of Capponi, he records that '*il Capitano nostro*' (our captain) charged the enemy with his cavalry and succeeded in capturing the enemy standard.[5]

The central section of the panel illustrates precisely this episode. In image 78, a Milanese standard-bearer of the *lance spezzate* is on the point of being overcome by a Florentine cavalryman and losing the standard. The standard itself is largely indecipherable except for its red field, which is nevertheless sufficient to identify it as the *radia magna*.

The Florentine cavalryman, on the other hand, can be associated with the company of Orsini, based on the emblems displayed on his half-*giornea* and on his horse's barding. These include a *fiammante* or *fiammato* sable and argent quartered with a rose gules, rayonné and leaved vert on a field sable.

These symbols require careful analysis, especially considering that the black fields are probably altered or oxidised. As already noted in the chapter on the League's insignia, the red rose is an element of the arms of the Orsini family, generally depicted as red on a silver field or silver on a red field. In this case, however, the field differs – it may have originally been blue – suggesting a brisure of the Orsini coat of arms, probably

80. Detail from the Madrid Chest of a Knight of the League pressing the Milanese. (Reproduced with permission of the Museo Arqueologico de Madrid)

5 Capponi, 'Commentari', 1195.

81. Knight with the rope knot emblem. (Reproduced with permission from the National Gallery of Ireland, Dublin)

indicating recruitment or service under the Florentine army.

Turning to the *fiammante*, it appears on the rear of Orsini's horse barding (image 74), likely originally blue, although now altered to black, and silver. This impresa recurs frequently in painted chests, often quartered or accompanied by other arms or impresas of Florentine.[6]

A notable example appears in a frontal panel of the chest preserved at the National Gallery of Ireland in Dublin, depicting *The Taking of Pisa* (cat. N. 780).[7] This work, attributed to the workshop of Apollonio, represents the conquest of Pisa by Florentine forces in 1406.

Among the countless arms and impresas sported by Florentine soldiers, the *fiammante* frequently appears quartered with other emblems, such as the large Sforza wavy. Particularly significant is the decoration of certain tents, especially one whose upper section bears the Capponi tranché and whose lower part is covered with the *fiammante*. It is the tent of Gino Capponi, father of Neri and commissioner of the Florentine Republic (image 79). In this case, the flames are rendered in black, recalling Capponi's coat of arms.

On the Dublin Chest, however, the *fiammante* is also borne by local Milanese cavalry (see image 51 and image 53), suggesting that at the time it had become a widely adopted military impresa.

In Plate E, Commander Pier Giovanpaolo Orsini is shown bearing both of these emblems – the *fiammante* and the rose.

A comparable case appears on the Madrid Chest, where a man-at-arms displays similar emblems. Positioned at the centre of the composition, the cavalryman is shown on the bridge pressing forward against the cavalry of the Visconti. He wears a type of sallet with an elongated front, reminiscent of the burgonet of the sixteenth century, and pursues the fleeing enemy sword in hand (image 80).

On his horse's barding is a quartered escutcheon: *fiammante* gules and argent, and sable. The black field is certainly oxidised and is so deteriorated

---

6 Cf Graham Hughes, *Renaissance Cassoni* (London: Art Books International, 1997), pp.22, 64 & 107.

7 Tomasi, *Osservazioni*, pp.11–18; Scalini, 'Divise e livree', pp.61–65; M. Predonzani, 'La Presa di Pisa,' in *Archivum Heraldicum* I 2013, pp.22–35.

that the central emblem is no longer recognisable.

As for the battle depicted in the Dublin Chest, to the right of the Florentine cavalryman in image 78, there is another man-at-arms bearing a rope knot emblem (image 81).

A similar impresa appears on the cavalryman of image 82, who is escorting the prisoners towards Anghiari with his sword in hand. Both he and the figure in image 81 display on their *giornea* and horse barding a silver knot on a (certainly altered) black field. Only the first cavalryman's horse barding displays an additional 'pink' field quartered with the knot.

82. A second knight with the rope knot emblem. (Reproduced with permission from the National Gallery of Ireland, Dublin)

The knot is an impresa or arms first associated with the fourteenth century *condottiero* Ceccolo. or Cecchino, Broglia. The Tridinum Associazione of Trino, his birthplace, has published a beautiful study of this captain, including two illustrations drawn from the chronicles of Sercambi.[8] In these images, Broglia'a standards appear either entirely light blue or blue with a red knot.[9]

After Broglia's death, this emblem passed to his adopted son, Angelo Broglio da Lavello, known as Tartaglia. He inherited not only the surname but also command of the company of fortune and its standard. Tartaglia's emblem – gules, a knot argent – can be seen in the centre of the composition of *The Taking of Pisa*, where it appears on the barding of a cavalryman carrying the Marzocco standard (image 83).

Another pupil of Broglia, Erasmo da Narni, known as Gattamelata, was a captain of the Venetian forces and showed three knots on his arms. Captains such as Antonio Bocarini-Brunori, Pietro Brunoro, and Brandolo Brandolini similarly showed three knots on their arms. A different version, using four rope knots instead of cloth knots, appeared on the arms of the Florentine, Giovanni d'Andrea Minerbetti.

However, none of these figures seem to have been present at the Battle of Anghiari. Broglia, Tartaglia, and Antonio Bocarini-Brunori were already dead; Gattamelata and Brandolini were engaged in Northern Italy against Visconti; and no chronicle records Minerbetti during the battle. Although

---

8 L. Parodi and F. Ranalli (eds), *Ceccolo Broglia da Trino* (Trino: Tridinum Associazione per l'Archaeologia la Storia e le Belle arti, 2009).

9 G. Sercambi, 'Le croniche di Giovanni Sercambi lucchese,' Archivio di Stato di Lucca, Fondo Bibl. Mss. 107, vignette CCCLXXVIII and DXCIII.

83. Knight wearing the Tartaglia knot, depicted in the *Capture of Pisa*. Collection of the National Gallery of Ireland, Dublin. (Drawing by the author)

Pietro Brunoro is mentioned by Benedetto Dei's chronicle, this is probably an error, as other sources place him in the capture of Riva and Garda during May-June 1440.[10]

The question then arises: who are these cavalrymen bearing the knot impresa? A plausible answer emerges from the *Cronaca Malatestiana* by Gaspare Broglio Tartaglia, the son of Tartaglia.[11]

As a young man, Gaspare embarked on a military career and entered military service under Cardinal Vitelleschi, commander of the Papal forces. After Tartaglia's death in 1421, Vitelleschi welcomed part of the Tartagliesca company into his own army (while another portion joined the Bracceschi).

Gaspare Broglio recounts that shortly before his death, Vitelleschi intended to entrust him with his father's troops and insignia: '*La Signoria sua aviva adunati più di mille cavalli, fra condottieri e uomini d'arme, tucti stati discendenti Tartaglieschi, li quali aviva deliberato darmeli a me e voliva cu'io rilevasse lo stendardo di mio padre e più che me rediva una cittade chiamata Toscanella.*' (The lord [Vitelleschi] had gathered more than 1,000 cavalrymen, between *condottieri* and men-at-arms, all of whom were Tartaglieschi soldiers, who had decided to give them to me together with my father's standard and also the city of Toscanella).[12]

Vitelleschi's death in April 1440, however, prevented this, and all of his troops instead passed under the command of the Patriarch Scarampi Mezzarota, who led them to assist the Florentines in Tuscany in May and subsequently at Anghiari.

On this basis, it is reasonable to hypothesise that the cavalrymen bearing the knot represent these Tartaglieschi troops, incorporated into the army of the Church as *lance spezzate*, first under Vitelleschi and then under Scarampi. This would also explain their colours: the blue and silver of Pope Eugene IV, a silver knot on a blue field, perhaps altered to black.[13]

Nevertheless, documents of the Archives of Rome – particularly the 'Soldatesche e galere' – indicate that an heir of Tartaglia was still in

10 Benedetto Dei, *La Cronica dal anno 1400 alle anno 1500* (Firenze: Papafava, 1984), p.56; Biondo, *Historie*, p.126; Angelo Pezzana, *Storia di Parma* (Parma: Dalla Ducale Tipografia,1842), II, p.427; M. Sanuto, 'Vite dé duchi di Venezia,' in *Muratori R.I.S.*, XX col. 1094.

11 Gaspare Broglio Tartaglia (A. G. Lucani, ed.), *Cronaca Malatestiana del secolo XV* (Rimini: Bruno Ghigi, 1982).

12 Gaspare Broglio Tartaglia (A. G. Lucani, ed.), *Cronaca Malatestiana del secolo XV* (Rimini: Bruno Ghigi, 1982), p.69.

13 B. Vespasiano, 'Commentario della vita di Papa Eugenio IV,' *Muratori R.I.S.* XXV, col. 259.

84. Knight with a half-wheel quartered with the letter 'P'. Detail from the Dublin Chest. (Reproduced with permission of the National Gallery of Ireland, Dublin)

papal pay in 1439:[14] a certain Carlo di Tartaglia da Lavello, a man-at-arms commanding 12 lances, approximately 36 men.

Continuing the analysis of the artwork, to the right appears a cavalryman (image 84) whose *giornea* bears a half-wheel quartered with the letter 'P'.

The half-wheel is the emblem of the Patriarch Scarampi seen in image 75. The meaning of the letter 'P', however, is more uncertain. According to Polcri, it could represent the initial of the presumed author of the chest panels Apollonio or Pollonio,[15] though it may also stand for 'patriarch'. Since Scarampi himself did not take part directly in the fight but observed from Anghiari, this cavalryman may represent one of his captains. A possible identification could be Simonetto da Castel di Piero, a member of the Baglioni family of Castel di Piero or Piero.

However, this identification appears unlikely. Thanks to the research of Claudio Mancini, a scholar of the Baglioni family of Teverina, a seal of Simonetto dated 5 November 1441 has been identified on a letter.[16] Although not perfectly clear, it shows an escutcheon with the three-tiered tower, emblem of the Baglioni family, surmounted by a crest with a nascent dog (image 85).

Mancini also uncovered, in the State Archives of Rome, another identical seal dated 1434 belonging to Francesco Baglioni (known as Cecco), Simonetto's uncle, who had been appointed Count of Castel di Piero by

14 'Commissariato delle soldatesche e galere,' Archivio di stato di Roma, busta 80, libro 1439, f. 6.

15 F. Polcri, 'La battaglia di Anghiari dipinta sui pannelli di tre cassoni preleonardeschi' in *Pagine Altotiberine* 13, pp.134 & 141.

16 Archivio Storico di Orvieto, Letters, 676/2/41/2.

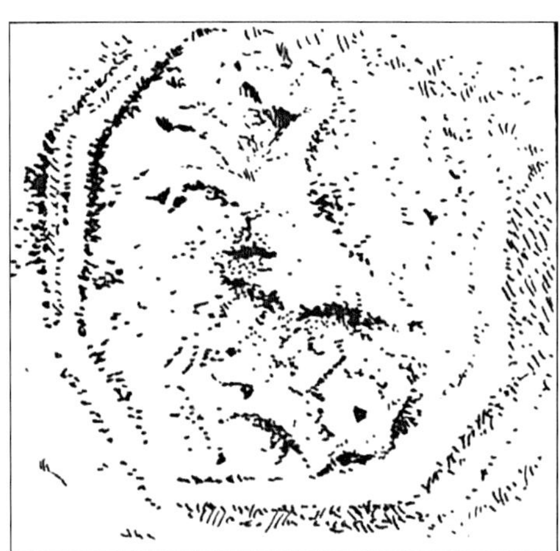

85. Seal of Simonetto da Castel di Piero. (Drawing by the author)

86. Detail from the Dublin Chest. Probably Simonetto da Castel Piero. (Reproduced with permission of the National Gallery of Ireland, Dublin)

Pope Eugene IV in 1431.[17] This seal likewise displays a three-storey tower or castle.

A similar castle appears on the horse barding of the cavalryman to the right of image 86, among the troops escorting prisoners into the city. This figure, holding in his right hand a rope tied to a captive, wears a *giornea* depicted as: per bend or and gules, in each division a three-storey castle counterchanged.

Although there are no colours on the seals, useful evidence comes from Sipicciano, which belonged to the Baglioni domains of Castel di Piero. In the Church of Santa Maria Assunta in Cielo, the Baglioni chapel has a sixteenth century fresco of the family coat of arms. The tower appears on a red field, rendered in white with gold outlines and openings. This closely matches the tower depicted on the figure on the Dublin Chest. While the *giornea* may include two mirrored towers, also in the colours as used at the time, the essential symbol remains a single three-storey tower, characteristic of the Baglioni della Teverina. See Plate G, figure 3 Simonetto da Castel di Piero.

Also in image 86, on the left, another cavalryman bears on his shoulder an emblem that recalls the knot of the Tartaglieschi, here black (likely changed) on a silver field. At the same time, this figure recalls the arms of the Anguillara family of Rome: argent, two eels in saltire azure. A member of this family, Count Everso d'Anguillara, served as a man-at-arms for the

17 The seal is published in Claudio Mancini, *Sipicciano* (Roma: Senza indicazione editoriale, 1994), p.119.

pope under Vitelleschi and later under Scarampi Mezzarota.[18] Della Tuccia records his presence among Scarampi's troops at Anghiari, making it plausible that this depicted *giornea* could represent him.[19]

Returning to image 84, just behind the cavalryman with the half-wheel, appears another cavalryman bearing the anchor impresa. This impresa is displayed both on the horse barding and painted on the shaffron. At that time, shaffrons could be made not only of iron but also of painted, hardened leather.[20]

The same anchor appears again in image 87 on the first cavalryman to the right. Here too, the scene shows prisoners being led towards Anghiari, and the cavalryman holds a rope attached to a Milanese captive. It is likely that this is the same man-at-arms depicted at two different moments, though in image 87 his emblems are more clearly visible.

His horse barding shows a gold anchor on an altered black field quartered with the blue and silver barry wavy of the Attendolo-Sforza.

A similar quartered escutcheon was noted by Pietro Roccasecca.[21] In his study, Roccasecca analyses the theme, composition and heraldry of the three paintings of the *Rotta di San Romano*. In the panel preserved at the National Gallery in London, he focuses on a cavalryman to the right of Niccolò da Tolentino, who wears a *giornea* decorated with this quartered escutcheon identifying him with Micheletto Attendolo (image 88). This *condottiero*, already discussed for his unicorn and dragon impresa in the chapter 'The Insignia of the League' (image 40 and image 42), may therefore be associated with the anchor, either as an impresa of Micheletto or as that of other Sforza captains who were at Anghiari and San Romano eight years before.

The most renowned Sforza captains at Anghiari were Pier Torelli and Niccolò da Pisa, though at San Romano they served under Niccolò da Tolentino and thus would not have sported the wavy design there.[22] A third captain, Bosio or Buoso Sforza, was in Micheletto's in San Romano, but he was 20 years old and commanded only 18 cavalrymen. Moreover, no chronicler records his presence at Anghiari.

---

18 Cf Andrea da Mosto, 'Ordinamenti militari delle soldatesche dello Stato Romano dal 1430 al 1470' in *Quellen und Forschungen aus italienischen Archiven und Bibliotheken*, V 1902, p.30; V. Sora, *I conti di Anguillara, Arch. della Soc. Rom. di* Sto. Patr. XXX 1907, p.66; Nicola della Tuccia, *Cronaca di Viterbo* (Firenze: G.P. Vieusseux, 1872), pp.169–170.

19 Tuccia, *Cronaca di Viterbo*, p.175.

20 See P. Ventrone (ed.), *Le tems revient 'l tempo si rinuova'* (Florence: Silvana Editoriale, 1992), p.176.

21 P. Roccasecca, *Paolo Uccello e le battaglie* (Milano: Electa, 1997), pp.22–23.

22 The two captains are mentioned at San Romano in L. G. Boccia, 'Le armature di Paolo Uccello' in *L'Arte*, III 1970, p.71; P. Pertici, 'Condottieri senesi e la rotta di San Romano di Paolo Uccello' in *Arch. Stor. Ital.* 1999, issue 581, pp.553–554, 556–557, 560–561.

It is therefore reasonable to identify this figure as Micheletto Attendolo. Although, unlike the unicorn and the dragon – both documented in Viviano's registers – no direct record of the anchor impresa has yet been found in those same sources, this absence does not preclude its attribution to him.

The cavalryman of image 87 also wears a *giornea* decorated: quarterly per saltire: 1 and 4 argent, 4 a *fiammante* gules; 2 and 3 azure (now changed to sable).

At the castle of Porta Giovia in Milan, within a pergola supported by columns whose capitals are carved with emblems and Sforza impresas, there is a quartered coat of arms with the *fiammante* and a three-pointed anchor (image 89). This anchor differs slightly from the one previously discussed as is not quartered with the wavy but with the *fiammante*.

This impresa does not belong to Micheletto but to Sacromoro Visconti, as identified by the heraldist Gianfranco Rocculi. Rocculi discovered the same coat of arms – with the addition of the Visconti *biscione* – in a chapel of the church of Santa Maria del Carmine in Milan. During recent restorations, some noble coats of arms dating to the second half of the fifteenth century were uncovered in the vaults, including the anchor.

87. Detail from the Dublin Chest: Knight with an anchor device. (Drawing by the author)

In heraldic description it is: quarterly, 1 argent, a *biscione* azure; 2 and 3, a *fiammante* gules and argent; 4 sable (changed), an anchor or. This coat belonged to the Visconti of Saliceto and Brignano – Sacromoro originated from this branch of the family.[23]

Sacromoro or Sagramoro Visconti has already been discussed in the chapter devoted to the heraldry of the Milanese cavalry in relation to the man-at-arms of image 60, although there he does not carry the anchor among his emblems. According to Rocculi, it is possible that Visconti adopted the anchor impresa only after the Battle of Anghiari, perhaps inspired by the deeds of Micheletto.

23 G. Rocculi, *Reperti heraldici nella 'chiesa nobile' di Santa Maria del Carmine a Milano*, in *Atti della Società Italiana di Studi Heraldici*, 32° Convivio, Turin 11 October 2014, pp.228–230 and 252–253.

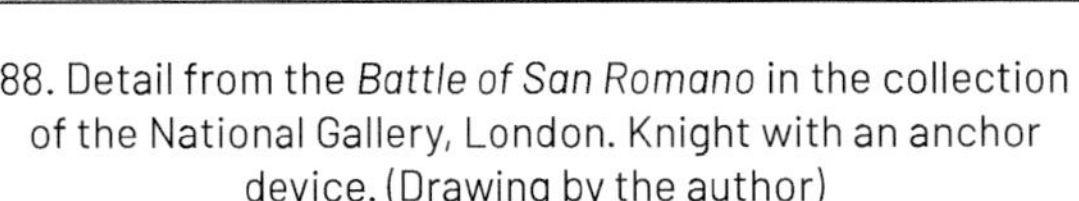

88. Detail from the *Battle of San Romano* in the collection of the National Gallery, London. Knight with an anchor device. (Drawing by the author)

89. Coat of arms with an anchor on the Porta Giovia Castle in Milan. (Photograph by the author)

Also in image 87, on the left, is a cavalryman wearing a *giornea* with an inverted chevrony, while his horse barding bears a quartered escutcheon: a *fiammante*, a narrow wavy, and a red field. This combination suggests that he may be a Milanese prisoner, since both the narrow wavy and the red field were carried by Milanese cavalrymen.

Although difficult to identify, the inverted chevrony recalls the arms of Baldaccio d'Anghiari, a captain in the pay of Florence. As reported by Luigi Passerini, his coat of arms consisted of: 'An inverted chevrony with the inscription below S. Baldacci de Angario.'[24] However, despite being mentioned by Passerini at the Battle of Anghiari, at the time, Baldaccio was with his troops in the Lordship of Piombino, devastating and plundering the territory. He was not in the service of Florence but of Guidantonio da Montefeltro, Count of Urbino, an ally of Visconti.[25]

24 L. Passerini, 'Baldaccio d'Anghiari,' *Arch. Stor. Ital.* IIIs. 1866 pp.146–147.

25 Romualdo Cardarelli, *Baldaccio d'Anghiari e la Signoria di Piombino nel 1440 e 1441* (Roma: Stabilimento Tipografico Leonardo da Vinci, 1922), vol. V, pp.438–440.

For this reason, the comparison remains only a similarity in the chevrony.

Completing image 87, there is one last coat of arms on the horseman's *giornea* located at the top right above 'Micheletto'. It is: quarterly per saltire: 1 and 4 sable (possibly originally blue or green if the colour has changed);[26] 2 and 3, or (covered with several small red spots).

This coat of arms recalls that of the Counts of the Guidi family, although with a different partition in the spaces: 1 and 4 or; 2 and 3 azure.[27] In earlier periods, these Tuscan nobles sported red in place of blue and silver instead of gold, and they often accompanied the quartering with a lion[28].

According to Passerini, it seems that the coat of arms of Francesco Guidi di Battifolle, Count of Poppi and last Lord of the Casentino fief in Tuscany, consisted of two lions affronty gules on a field argent. Litta, however, records that the Count of Poppi sported two lions affronty but quartered argent.[29]

90. Knight with small shield emblems, detail from the Dublin Chest. (Reproduced with permission of the National Gallery of Ireland, Dublin)

26 In the 1st quarter, there are also two thin silver bands.

27 For the arms of Guidi see Pompeo Litta, *Famiglie celebri italiane* (Milano: Luciano Basadonna, *c.*1869); I Guidi, vol. 17, tav. IV; V. Spreti, *Enciclopedia storico-nobiliare Italiana*, vol. III, pp.638–641; Luigi Passerini, *Le armi dei Municipi Toscani* (Firenze: Tipografia di Eduardo Ducci, 1864), pp.89, 192.

28 Passerini, *Le armi..*, pp.26, 192, 232, 291.

29 Passerini, *Le armi..*, p.227; Litta, *Famiglie*. I Guidi, tav. XIV.

91. A second knight and similar to image 90, detail from the Dublin Chest. (Reproduced with permission of the National Gallery of Ireland, Dublin)

In 1440, with the arrival of Piccinino's troops, this count abandoned the Florentine alliance and joined the Bracceschi leader. This decision proved disastrous: after the Florentine victory at Anghiari, he and his entire family were expelled from Tuscany, and all his possessions were confiscated. The Count of Poppi took refuge in Bologna, where he died a few years later.

Although contemporary chronicles speak of the deeds of Guidi during the war of 1440, none mention him at the Battle of Anghiari. It seems more likely that he remained to lead raids in the upper Valdarno rather than following Piccinino into Val Tiberina.[30] For this reason, it is safest to limit the conclusion to noting a resemblance between this arms and that of the Guidi family.

The horsemen depicted in image 90 and image 91 bear a peculiar emblem, shown respectively on the horse barding in one case, and on both the horse barding and the *giornea* in the other. It may be described heraldically: gules, a saltire argent charged with escutcheons argent bearing a cross with the vertical arm gules and the horizontal arm sable (with azure or vert replacing sable where the colour has altered).

In fact, the first cavalryman displays a cross formed by escutcheons arranged in the form of a Latin cross extending both horizontally and vertically across the horse barding. These escutcheons recall the cross of the Florentine stat and, on the rear of the horse barding in image 90, they are accompanied by three flowers resembling poppies.

The first reference to this coat of arms appears in the study by Boccia mentioned above.[31] In his analysis of the armour in the works of Paolo Uccello, he also examines the insignia and heraldic emblems in the *Battles of San Romano*. In particular, he notes that the red trumpet banners are marked by honourable ordinaries in various colours,[32] used to distinguish different formations within the army (image 92). In the Paris panel, these red draperies bear a saltire argent charged with escutcheons azure bearing a cross gules, alternating with small shields gules bearing a cross azure.

The red field, the St Andrew's Cross, and the shields resemble the emblems depicted on the cavalrymen of image 90 and image 91. In my opinion, this similarity suggests a connection between the two liveries.

As already noted, these shields refer to the arms of the Florentine people (argent, a cross gules). In the fifteenth century, the Republic of Florence granted this arms or insignia to citizens who had been knighted

30 Giovanni Cavalcanti, *Istorie Fiorentine* (Fiorenze: all'insegna di Dante, 1838), vol. I, pp.407–410; *Dizionario Biografico degli Italiani*, tomo 61, p.226.

31 Boccia, 'Le armature,' pp.74–75.

32 Honourable ordinaries: charges placed upon the field.

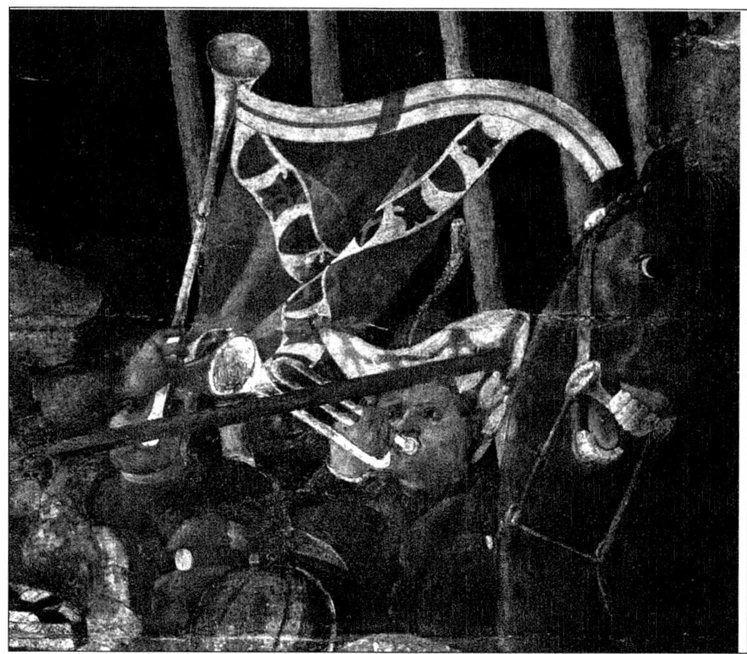

92. Detail of the red trumpet banners at the *Battle of San Romano* in the collection of Louvre, Paris. (Reproduced with the permission of the Louvre)

or had distinguished themselves in feats of arms. The colours of the shields, moreover, evoke those of the Florentine Guelph faction (argent, an eagle gules grasping a dragon vert).[33] Unfortunately, no further evidence has been found in either the republican or Guelph heraldic sources.

The poppies, by contrast, likely refer to the Sienese Salimbeni family, who moved to Florence in the fourteenth century and became known as Bartolini Salimbeni. They adopted withered poppies as an impresa in their coat of arms. In November 1440, Gherardo di Salimbeni was dispatched by the *Dieci di Balìa* with 150 soldiers to guard the castle of Marradi;[34] however, he does is not mentioned in any chronicle of the Battle of Anghiari.

On the other hand, a member of the Sienese branch of the family is recorded in the *condotta* of Miceletto Attendolo. This captain, called 'Bambo Salimbeni da Siena', appears in the records of the company from 1430 with 16 horsemen.[35] He died around 1436 and his company was divided among his family, who remained under Micheletto's command for a number of years and took part in the Battle of Anghiari. In the registers, they are listed as 'Villano and Batista [who] were under Bambo' with 10 horsemen, and 'Agnolo from Bambo' with 5 cavalrymen.[36]

33 See G. Salvemini, *La dignità cavalleresca nel comune di Firenze,* Feltrinelli editore, 1972. Pp. 148, 159–160, 182–186, 188–189, 197.

34 See *Delizie degli Eruditi toscani*, appendix of tomo XXIII, 1786, p.242.

35 F. Viviano, *Registri della compagnia di Micheletto Attendolo*, in Fraternita dei Laici di Arezzo, libro 3568 voci 1430–1431, f. 29r and libro 3573 uscite 1433–1434, f. 10r.

36 Viviano, 'Registri della compagnia', libro 3574 uscite 1439–1441, ff. 100r and 100v.

Further instances of poppies appear in the *Battle of San Romano* in Paris, on the hat of a trumpeter at the centre of the composition (image 92), identified by Pietro Roccasecca as an impresa of Salimbeni.[37] He is also associated with the family the 'halved almonds' bordering two shields carried by infantrymen (image 93), which recall the gold lozenges in the original red arms of the Salimbeni family (image 94).

(NB Pietro Roccasecca's hypothesis – that the Paris panel represents not the Battle of San Romano but the Battle of Anghiari – has already been discussed in Chapter 4 The Battle of Anghiari in Art.)

The scene depicts Micheletto and his entire company. Consequently, all the emblems represented – trumpet banners, poppies, related colours, et cetera – should, in my view, be attributed to the Attendolo-Sforza forces. Indeed, the trumpet banners bear the Attendolo device on the field, St Andrew's Cross and escutcheons in red, white, and blue (now tending to black). The same applies to the two cavalrymen depicted on the Dublin Chest, who display a St Andrew's Cross with silver shields bearing a cross with a vertical red arm and a horizontal blue arm.

As for documentary evidence, Viviano's registers provide little assistance this time. They only mention captains wearing red and white livery, and others with white bands on a red field. The sole noteworthy reference appears in register 3591, dated 18 June 1432, shortly after the Battle of San Romano, which records: '4 florins for 6 *braccia* of linen cloth to make crosses for the Lord's coverings.'[38] Since the linen cloth is white, these would have been white crosses intended to be sewn onto Micheletto's horse barding. At that time, however, the *condottiero* was fighting for Florence, whose emblem was the red cross rather than the white. Moreover, white crosses do not appear in the Attendolo-Sforza heraldry. The document does not indicate whether these crosses were subsequently painted in another colour. Nevertheless, their Latin form recalls the crosses displayed by the cavalrymen in image 90.

To turn to image 95 and image 96. In both scenes, the same cavalryman appears at two different moments: in image 95, he is about to charge the enemy, while in image 96, he is shown escorting prisoners towards Anghiari, sword in hand.

93. Detail of an infantryman with a shield decorated with halved almonds at the Battle of San Romano. In the Louvre collection. (Reproduced with the permission of the Louvre, Paris)

94. Salimbeni coat of arms. (Artwork by the author)

37 P. Roccasecca, 'La rotta di San Romano e la rotta di Niccolò Piccinino,' *Bulletin de L'Ahai* 2005, p.13.

38 In the original source, the word 'crosses' is represented with the + sign.

95. Knight with barry scaly, also see Image below.

96. The knight with barry scaly, see Image above.

The man wears a *giornea* displaying a quarterly escutcheon: 1 and 4, gules, a lamp argent; 2 and 3, barry scaly or and sable (the latter perhaps originally azure).

Beginning with the lamp, a similar – if not identical – motif appears alternating with the Medici 'balls' on the barding of the mule of Cosimo the Elder in the frescoes by Benozzo Gozzoli in the chapel of the Magi at the Medici-Riccardi Palace in Florence. In her studies, Acidini Luchinat hypothesises that this lamp may represent a personal insignia of Cosimo, describing it as 'a motif alternating with the 'balls' on the barding of Cosimo's mule, that is, a kind of cylindrical cage rendered in perspective and surmounted by a radiating crown, in which I believe one may recognise a stylised version of a lamp.'[39]

The scaly, on the other hand, is defined by Gastone Cambin as '... probably a stylisation of the Sforza barry wavy.' Indeed, the 'Codice Trivulziano' 2168 preserves a fine example of a blue and silver scaly quartered with the *colombina* (Plate H, figure 7).[40] This seventeenth century codex contains 69 painted imprese of the Trivulzio family but in its first 39 folios also includes

39 Cristina Acidini Luchinat, *L'immagine Medicea in Lorenzo il Magnifico e gli spazi dell'arte* (Firenze: Giunti, 1991), p.140; Cristina Acidini Luchinat, *Il palazzo Medici-Riccardi* (Firenze: Giunti 1990), p.86.

40 G. Cambin, G., *Le rotelle Milanesi Giornico, 1478* (Farvagny, Vétroz, and Bern: Società Svizzera di Araldica, 1987), pp.213–219.

earlier Visconti and Sforza imprese dating to the Sforza ducal period and thus preceding those of Trivulzio. These largely represent Sforza family imprese, together with Visconti imprese inherited after the conquest of the Duchy of Milan. A comparison between Plate H, figure 7 and Plate H, figure 8 clearly demonstrates how the scaly derives from the wavy. The same scaly appears in Paolo Uccello's *Battle of San Romano* preserved at the Louvre, where a cavalryman on the right – recognisable by his black horse with gold discs on its forehead (image 97) – bears a small shield on his shoulder decorated with a scaly closely resembling that of the Dublin Chest cavalryman.[41]

97. Knight with a shield decorated with a scaly. Detail from the *Battle of San Romano*, collection of the Louvre, Paris. (Drawing by the author)

In both image 95 and image 96, the horse barding repeats the same quartering of the *giornea*, with the addition of a five-petalled rose. In image 95 it appears on the peytral, silver on a red field, in image 96, it is placed beneath the horse's tail, red with a green stem on a silver field.

A comparable rose appears in the previously mentioned chest depicting *The Taking of Pisa*, where it decorates several *giornee* and horse bardings of Florentine cavalrymen. These likely represent men-at-arms of the *Compagnia della Rosa*, a company once in Florentine service but dissolved in 1410.[42] One should also note the five-petalled rose identified by Franco Cardini in *Le tems revient* carved on the facade of the Medici-Riccardi palace in Via Cavour and interpreted as a Medici impresa, particularly

41 P. Roccasecca, *Paolo Uccello e le battaglie* (Milano: Electa, 1997), pp.102, 116–119.

42 Ercole Ricotti, *Storia delle compagnie di ventura in Italia*, (Torino: G. Pombar, 1845), pp.206–207.

associated with Piero the Gouty, son of Cosimo. In the same work, Mario Scalini mentions another rose used as a *punzone* on the skull of an Italian sallet with a T-shaped opening dated to *c.* 1450–1460, associating it to the Medici imprese.[43] The rose, however, was also a symbol of the Orsini family, a member of which, Pier Giovanpaolo, served as captain general of the Florentine Army at Anghiari.

Among the three emblems borne by this cavalryman, the rose is the least prominent and may indicate his service under the Medici or the Orsini. The lamp, by contrast, is a heraldic symbol of reason and intelligence and was likely his personal impresa. The barry scaly – clearly derived from the Sforza barry wavy – signals his affiliation with contingent sent by Francesco Sforza.

The repeated depiction of this cavalryman on the chest suggests that he was a captain of some importance. In image 96, he follows the prisoners towards Anghiari immediately behind Astorre Manfredi, which might suggest his identification as Niccolò da Pisa. However, the coat of arms of the Gambacorti family, to which Niccolò belonged – or, a bendy lion barry argent and sable, with a chief of Pisa (Plate H, figure 5) – does not correspond to any of the elements displayed by this cavalryman, although the colours are indeed the same

A note regarding the Gambacorti arms. The version just described appears with these colours in the Ceramelli Papiani collection and in a manuscript of Pisan coats of arms preserved in the Bibliothèque Nationale de France in Paris.[44] By contrast, both Crollalanza and Ginanni record the same arms but differently; as a blue field instead of gold and without the chief of Pisa.[45]

Also in image 95, on the left, there is a cavalryman who bears the blue and silver barry wavy of the Attendolo-Sforza, quartered with a lamp topped by only three rays on black field (probably changed from blue).

This impresa can be identified in the aforementioned records of the company of Micheletto Attendolo, preserved at the Fraternita dei Laici di Arezzo – specifically in register 3574, which documents expenditures between 1439 and 1441. On folio 160v, among the payments made to Marco degli Attendolo of the Counts of Cotignola, the following entry appears at the centre of the page: '... 37 florins to be given on 10 September for a *giornea* of Alexandrian [blue] velvet with embroidered lanterns'.

---

43 M. Scalini (P. Ventrone (ed.), *Le tems revient – l tempo si rinuova. Feste e spettacoli nella Firenze di Lorenzo il Magnifico* (Milano: Silvana Editoriale, 1992), pp.63–64, 73 & 179–180.

44 www.archiviodistato.firenze.it , *I blasoni delle famiglia Toscane nella Raccolta Ceramelli Papiani*, fam. Gambacorti; Bibliothèque nationale de France (ms ita 1520) *Insigna Gentilia Pisanorum*, f 56, 219, in Michel Popoff, *Toscane, hors Florence* (Paris: Le Léopard d'Or, 2009), p.89.

45 G. B. Crollalanza, *Dizionario Storico Blasonico delle famiglie nobili italiane* (Pisa: Giornale Araldico, 1886), fam. M. Ginanni, *L'arte del blasone dichiarata per alfabeto* (Venice: 1756), p.200.

Marco degli Attendolo was a cousin of Micheletto and married his daughter Francesca in 1439. He commanded one of the largest contingents of the Attendolo company, with a *condotta* of 37 lances – equivalent to 111 horsemen – and he too was present at Anghiari.

Another folio of the same register records a further, curious device belonging to him, this time on a crimson velvet *giornea*, described as bearing '... mousetraps surrounded by mice ...' A third *giornea* is described as having '... 3 *braccia* of grain rose and 3 *braccia* of white and *cilostrum* for a *giornea* in his device ...'[46] This latter combination, in red, white, and blue, corresponds to the Attendolo-Sforza livery already noted several times in the registers, appearing also on the *giornee* and hose of other captains in the company.

Thus, the blue and silver wavy quartered with lanterns or lamps on a blue field suggests that this cavalryman is Marco degli Attendolo.

A similar lamp, comparable to that in image 95 with three rays at the top, also appears on a painted chest by Pesellino depicting David and Goliath, in the collection of the National Gallery in London, There, the lamp is visible on the *giornee* of David's pages (image 98).[47] In this instance, the lamp – on a black (originally blue) field – is quartered not with the wavy, but with a red and silver *fiammante,* reminiscent of that seen on the cavalryman's *giornea* with the anchor in image 87.[48]

Up to this point, the Sforza device has appeared quartered combining the large barry wavy in blue and silver with a red field, upon which a personal impresa was painted or embroidered (as in the unicorn, image 40, or the quinces, image 38). However, the Sforza device could also take the form of quartered in which the waves are paired with a blue field bearing the impresa itself (as in image 88 or the lantern in image 95). It is plausible that this second type of quartering was prerogative of the Attendolo da Cotignola branch rather than the Attendolo-Sforza line.

Indeed, in Viviano's records, the unicorn appears both on blue taffeta *giornee* and on those of crimson velvet.[49] We have also observed the use of emblems derived from the wavy, such as the scales (image 95). There is also a further variation of the Sforza or Attendolo device, in which the blue and silver wavy are replaced by a red and silver *fiammante*, quartered with a blue field charged with the impresa. Red, white, and blue are, in fact, the colours of the Attendolo, as can also be observed in Pesellino's painting, on the hose of the pages in the foreground and of the infantrymen in the background. Additionally, King Saul, depicted on horseback with a baton

46 Viviano, 'Registri della compagnia', libro 3574 uscite 1439–1441, ff. 77r & 118r.

47 Graham Hughes, *Renaissance Cassoni* (London: Art Books International, 1997), pp.108–109.

48 In registers Viviano, 'Registri della compagnia', libro 3558 debitori 1432–1433, f. 138r, there is a *giornea* for Marco degli Attendolo displaying four silver rays that should represent the *fiammante*.

49 Viviano, 'Registri della compagnia', libro 3593 spese 1439–1446, ff. 55v & 68r.

98. Detail from the David and Goliath chest by Pesellino. Collection of the National Gallery, London. (Drawing by the author)

99. Detail pf King Saul from the David and Goliath chest by Pesellino, Collection of the National Gallery in London. (Drawing by the author)

to the left of David (image 99), wears a dragon crest, an impresa that, as previously noted, is that of Micheletto.

With regard to Pesellino, an interesting detail emerges in Viviano's register 3593 (*spese grosse e minute,* 1439–1446). On folio 71v, dated April 1441, there is a record of an Attendolo-Sforza standard with a red field quartered with silver and blue waves, painted by '... Pesello *banderaro* and his fellow companions in Florence ...' Giuliano Ginocchi, known as Pesello, was the grandfather of Francesco di Stefano, called Pesellino; both were Florentine painters working in the same workshop until 1446, the year of Pesello's death.

All this means it is probably that, in executing *David and Goliath,* Pesellino drew directly on the devices and imprese of Micheletto's company.

To turn to the heraldry of other captains of the League who are not represented in the iconographies discussed so far but are documented in written sources.

Among the most prominent figures is Bosio Sforza, Count of Santa Fiora, born in 1411, the son of Muzio Sforza and Antonia Salimbeni. A life-long man-at-arms, this captain served first under Micheletto Attendolo and later under his brother Francesco Sforza, contributing to the latter's conquest of Milan.

His livery corresponded to that of the Sforza: wavy azure and argent, quartered with a field gules. A unique reference to his heraldry is provided by the scholar Andrea Baiardo, who describes a joust held in Parma in 1467 in which Bosio took part. On that occasion, he and his cavalrymen bore as their impresa a shield charged with a cross within a diamond and a fine quince as a crest (see Plate C, image. 3).[50]

Another figure is Troilo da Muro da Rossano – referred to by some chroniclers as Troilo Orsino – who was a companion of Francesco Sforza and had married Sforza's sister. He did not participate in the Battle of Anghiari, as he was with Paolo della Molara in Città di Castello.

The arms of the de Muro family are described as blue with two gold spears arranged in the shape of St Andrew's Cross and surmounted by three gold stars. In Viviano's register 3604, catalogued as *Carte Varie,* the seal of Troilo survives on a letter dated 5 July 1440. Although the seal is badly damaged, the trace of an X remains visible at its centre.[51]

A further important captain is Agnolo d'Anghiari, known as Taglia, one of the Florentine commanders who took part in the Battle of Anghiari. A native of the same town of Valtiberina, at the time he commanded approximately 300 cavalrymen and distinguished himself especially in the engagements preceding the famous battle.

Giusto Giusti discusses him extensively in 'Giornali',[52] having served as his legal representative in the *condotta* between 1437 and 1442. More recently, Nerida Newbigin, who transcribed and published these *Giornali,* identifies him as belonging to the Anghiarese family of Mazzoni, based on a reference within the text.[53] By contrast, in the *Dieci di Balìa* and in the *Dizionario Bibliografico degli Italiani,* Agnolo appears as Angelo Pieri d'Anghiari.[54]

The early seventeenth century Anghiarese historian Lorenzo Taglieschi refers to him Agnolo di Piero del Vecchietto called Taglia.[55] The latter

50 N. Ratti, *Della famiglia Sforza* (Rome: Presso il Salomoni, 1794), parte I, pp.175–179; A. Baiardo, *Libro d'arme e d'amore nomato Philogine* (Venice: 1520), p.24.

51 Anon. *Della nobiltà della famiglia Muro,* 1700, pp.23–28; *L'Araldo almanacco nobiliare del napoletano* (Naples: Libreria Detken & Rocholi, 1895), XVIII, pp.176–177; Viviano, *Registri,* register Carte Varie, not unnumbered: Sigillo Troilo.

52 G. d'Anghiari, 'Memorie dall'anno 1437 al 1481,' Bibl. Naz. Firenze, ms. II. II. 127.

53 N. Newbigin, 'I Giornali di Ser Giusto Giusti d'Anghiari (1437–1482)' in *Literatura Italiana Antica,* anno III- 2002, p.45.

54 Archivio di Stato di Firenze, X di Balìa, 'Deliberazioni e Condotte', ff. 16r, 18c, 24r. *Dizionario Bibliografico degli Italiani,* entry: Baldaccio d'Anghiari, p.438.

55 Lorenzo Taglieschi (Daniele Finzi & Matteo Parreschi eds), *Delle memorie istoriche e annali della terra di Anghiari* (Anghiari: Sansepolcro, 1991), p.164.

designation derives from his ancestor Bartolomeo, known as *Vecchietto* (Old Man), who settled in Anghiari in 1345 and gave rise to numerous descendants with families Taglieschi, Diani, Marcheschi, and Mazzoni. Taglieschi explains that the nickname 'Taglia' originated from the impresa borne on Vecchietto's Arms: the '*taglia*',[56] represented by a sceptre or baton placed palewise and wrapped in a handkerchief.

The Anghiarese families mentioned all sported this emblem, typically quartered with fields of wavy; only the colours and partitions varied among them.

Agnolo himself also bore the *taglia*, as documented in Giusti's 'Giornali', where it is recorded: 'Tuesday 16 December (1438), I took four *braccia* of green cloth from the stock of Benintendi and Antonio Pucci to make the *taglie* for Agnolo's devices.'[57]

It is therefore likely that the arms used by Agnolo were those of the Mazzoni family, as identified by Nerida Newbigin. According to the description of the Mazzoni Arms preserved in the 'Raccolta Ceramelli Papiani',[58] the blazon reads: quarterly: 1 and 4 vert, a sceptre palewise argent encircled by a ribbon gules; 2 and 3 vert, three barrulets wavy argent and gules (cf the horse barding in Plate E, figure 1).

56 Taglieschi, *Delle memorie*, p.164.

57 d'Anghiari, 'Memorie', ms. II. 127, f. 36r. Newbigin, 'I Giornali', p.56.

58 State Archives of Florence and available on its website.

15

The Infantrymen of the League

In the Dublin panel, the infantrymen of the League are armed with spears, crossbows, and shields, and almost all wear a barbute with a T-shaped opening, embellished, in only two cases, with the *mazzocchio*. Like the Milanese infantry, they wear their hose in livery colours, displaying colours and patterns to distinguish the various companies.

In images 75, 100, and 101, the infantrymen wear a red stocking on the right leg and a blue and white and on the left – here again, the black colour should probably be understood as an altered pigmentation which was originally blue. This scheme corresponds to the previously noted Attendolo-Sforza livery. Francesco Sforza himself wore similar hose in 1441 on the occasion of his marriage to Bianca Maria Visconti,[1] and Sforza infantrymen displayed the same on their hose in the *Rout of San Romano* panel now in the Louvre, discussed above.[2]

100. Detail of the Dublin Chest. Florentine infantryman with a bombard. (Drawing by the author)

1 P. Levi Pisetzky, *Storia del costume in Italia* (Milano: Istituto Editoriale Italiano, 1964), vol. II, p.430.

2 Roccasecca, *Paolo Uccello*, pp.103–104, 108, 116.

101. Detail of the Dublin Chest. Infantrymen of the League. (Reproduced with permission of the National Gallery of Ireland, Dublin)

The infantrymen among the prisoners (image 60), by contrast, wear black right hose – again, originally blue – with a white greave, while the left is parti-coloured red and white. The infantrymen depicted in front of Giovanpaolo Orsini (image 102), instead, wear a dark blue right hose and an entirely white left hose decorated with small black (blue) lozenges and red flames.

The identification of these two groups remains uncertain. They may belong to Florentine companies, perhaps the *condotte* led by Anghiarese captains such as Gregorio Vanni, Leale di Cristoforo, and Piero d'Anghiari, or alternatively to the forces of Orsini.[3] The red flames, *fiammante*, recall those worn by the cavalryman in image 87.

It should be noted that, at the time, soldiers frequently wore hose with soles, as attested to in the works of Paolo Uccello, Piero della Francesca, and numerous Florentine wedding chests. Viviano's registers likewise make frequent mentions to such hose.[4]

Turning to the shields, in image 102, behind the crossbowman, an infantryman wearing a bourlet (*mazzocchio*) and carrying a spear carries a partially hidden shield that may be decorated with the silver and black division by bend of the Capponi family.

---

3 See *Dizionario Biografico degli Italiani*, tomo V, p.438; Romualdo Cardarelli, *Baldaccio d'Anghiari e la Signoria di Piombino nel 1440 e 1441* (Roma: Stabilimento Tipografico Leonardo da Vinci, 1922), pp.36 & 37; Lorenzo Taglieschi (Daniele Finzi & Matteo Parreschi eds), *Delle memorie istoriche e annali della terra di Anghiari* (Anghiari: Sansepolcro, 1991), pp.164–172.

4 F. Viviano, *Registri della compagnia di Micheletto Attendolo*, in Fraternita dei Laici di Arezzo, libro 3574, ff. 86v, 181v, libro 3591 ff. 32v, 71v, 72r, libro 3593, ff. 5v, 9r, 25r, 43v.

In image 75, the same design appears on the shield of the infantryman on the right, where it forms part of a quartering consisting of four emblems: in the 1st quarter, the black and silver division by bend of the Capponi; in the 2nd, a gold rampant lion holding a twig in its right paw on a silver field; in the 3rd, the barry wavy of the Attendolo-Sforza; in the 4th, a silver and black *fiammante*.

The lion in the 2nd quarter recalls the Attendolo-Sforza arms granted by Emperor Ruprecht of the Palatinate in 1401 to Muzio Sforza and his family, though in that case it reads: blue, a lion or holding between its paws a quince or, leaved and stemmed vert.

As noted by Litta, the Capponi frequently used a lion sejant as a supporter for their coat of arms. He further observes that other Florentine families commonly used the lion as an impresa, in imitation of the Marzocco of Florence.[5]

In front of this infantryman stands another who bears on his shield the coat of arms of Patriarch Scarampi, described earlier.

Additional noteworthy shields were examined in connection with the Salimbeni emblems depicted in the Paris panel of the *Battle of San Romano* (image 93). These include two shields with gold lozenges on a red field,

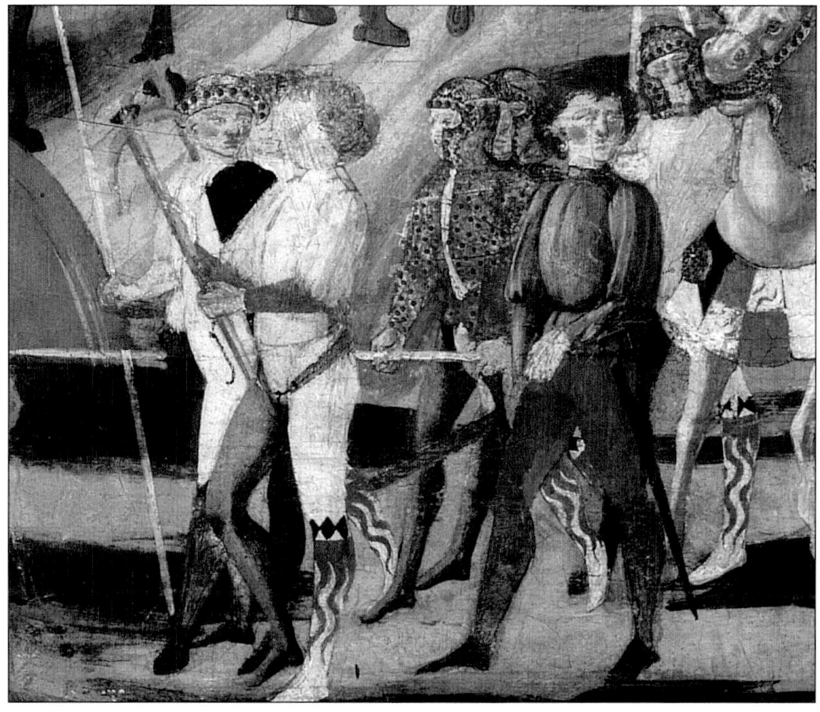

102. Detail of the Dublin Chest. League infantry with constable. (Reproduced with permission of the National Gallery of Ireland, Dublin)

5 Pompeo Litta, *Famiglie celebri italiane* (Milano: Luciano Basadonna, *c.*1869): I Capponi di Firenze, tav. 1.

closely resembling the Salimbeni arms. One of these also displays black triangles (likely altered in colour) interspersed among the lozenges.

In Viviano's registers, there are frequent references to the purchase of shields and their decoration; these are referred to in the texts as *taragoni*.[6] The same records also mention infantry armour or individual pieces of equipment. In book 3572, under January 1433, three companions of the Constable Cristofano da Cremona – Stefano da Prato, Antonio d'Arezzo, and Filippo di Calabria, certainly corporals – are recorded as receiving greaves, cuisses, vambraces, gauntlets, and spaulders.[7] This evidence further confirms both the use of armour among infantry and the accuracy of the battle scenes painted by Paolo Uccello.

In image 102, you can tentatively identify an infantry constable. He wears a blue doublet, red hose, greaves, and is bareheaded. He holds a sword; however, he lacks any clear identifying element.

Additional infantrymen of the League appear on the Madrid Chest, not on the frontal panel but on the right side (image 103). The scene depicts Florentine infantry armed with long spears, accompanied by trumpeters, entering Anghiari after the victory. These infantrymen have the legs of their hose in Sforza colours: a red right leg and a blue and white left leg.

103. Infantrymen of the League on the chest of Madrid. (Drawing by the author)

To conclude it is worth considering a detail that does not directly concern heraldry yet nevertheless highlights the historical reliability of the scenes represented on the Dublin Chest. In the upper right of the painting, near the city of Anghiari, women are depicted carrying vases and jars filled with water (image 104). Because of the intense heat of the day, both armies had stationed women to the rear with jars of water to refresh men and horses exhausted by combat. Given their placement in the painting – near a fountain beneath Anghiari – these women must be Florentines. They correspond to those mentioned in the poem *La Fuga del Capitano*, which, in several aspects, closely parallels the scenes on this chest.[8]

Further evidence of the historical accuracy of this painting lies in its

6 Some shield references: Viviano, 'Registri della compagnia', libro 3569 f. 66, lib. 3574 f. 22v, lib. 3560, f. 7v.

7 Viviano, *Registri*, libro 3572 f. 70v.

8 *La Fuga del Capitano* in A. Fabretti, *Note e documenti da biografie dei Capitani Venturieri dell'Umbria*, vol. Unico (Montepulciano: Angiolo Tumi, 1842), p.264.

precise rendering of the landscape, particularly the two bridges between San Sepolcro and Anghiari. Between these – that is, the bridge over River Tiber and over the so-called *delle Forche* – the painter depicts the final decisive clash, culminating in the defeat of the Milanese forces and the capture of their insignia by the Florentine troops.

Finally, one must note the careful depiction of standards and identifying emblems of the opposing armies, which this study has sought to accurately describe.

104. Detail of the Dublin Chest. Women with pots of water. (Reproduced with permission of the National Gallery of Ireland, Dublin)

16

The Aftermath of the Battle of Anghiari

On the morning following the Battle of Anghiari, the Milanese prisoners, with the exception of six or seven captains, among them Astorre Manfredi and Sacramoro, were released, still wearing their doublets.[1] The freed Milanese made their way to Borgo Sansepolcro. However, according to Biondo, Piccinino, upon seeing them and mistaking them for enemy troops, abandoned the city and fled to Umbria.

Meanwhile, the Florentine commissioners Bernadetto de' Medici and Neri Capponi, together with the Apostolic legate Mezzarota, attempted – unsuccessfully – to persuade their captains to advance to Borgo Sansepolcro. The mercenary troops refused to comply; instead, around midday, and without authorisation, they went to Arezzo, where they secured the money and goods looted by the Milanese, before returning to Anghiari in the evening.[2]

On the same day, Troilo da Muro and Paolo della Molara, who were in Città di Castello, upon hearing news of the victory, advanced with their men to Borgo Sansepolcro. There, they encountered the released Milanese prisoners and killed some of them.[3]

On 1 July, the army of the League marched to Borgo Sansepolcro, where, just outside the walls, they were met by ambassadors, who handed the city over to the Church.[4]

Subsequently, according to Taglieschi, on 3 July the Florentines, led by Agnolo Taglia and Leale d'Anghiari, advanced on Monterchi, the fief of Madonna Anfrosina da Montedoglio, widow of Carlo Tarlati da Pietramala.

---

1 Capponi, 'Commentari', *Muratori R.I.S.* XVIII col. 1195; Flavio Biondo, *Historie* (Venice: 1547), p.129.

2 Capponi, 'Commentari', 1195; Niccolò Machiavelli, *Istorie Fiorentine* (Milan: Società Anonima Notari or Alpes, 1928), vol. 2, p.93.

3 Biondo, *Historie*, p.129.

4 Capponi, 'Commentari', 1195–1196; Biondo, *Historie*, p.129.

Having sided with the Visconti, this noblewoman was compelled to surrender her lands to the lordship and seek refuge in Mercatello.[5]

On 5 July, it was reported that Piccinino had moved to Gubbio with 3,000 cavalrymen and then on to Perugia. Soon after, however, it emerged that he had changed his plans and, passing through the county of Urbino, had headed for Lombardy.[6]

In response, the allied army resolved to go to Romagna, although tensions soon arose between Neri Capponi and the legate Scarampi, who, in the meantime, had been elevated to the rank of cardinal in recognition of his role in the victory.

Neri headed with 350 cavalrymen under Niccolò da Pisa into the Casentino, the domain of the Count of Poppi. At Rassina, he joined forces with Agnolo Taglia, who had in the meantime taken Bibiena. Within a few days, the entire Casentino fell under Capponi's control, and the city of Poppi was placed under siege. On 29 July, Francesco Guidi, Count of Poppi, was forced to capitulate and abandon his lands, which were annexed by the lordship of Florence.[7] The count took refuge in Bologna with his friend Bentivoglio, where he died around 1447.

Other Florentine rebels also fled Tuscany after the Battle, including Rinaldo degli Albizzi, who first sought refuge in Ancona before continuing towards the Holy Land. He returned in late 1441, but shortly thereafter, on 2 February 1442, died while celebrating the wedding of his daughter Nicoletta.[8]

The League Army advancing into Romagna encountered little resistance, aided by the defection of the Malatesta family, who abandoned the Visconti to realign themselves with Florence and the Papacy.

Under the command of Scarampi, and with Micheletto, Troilo, and Niccolò da Pisa among its leaders, the army rapidly took Portico, Dovadola, Bagnacavallo, and Massa Lombarda. However, they failed to take Forlì, which was strongly defended by Francesco Piccinino.[9]

Meanwhile, in Lombardy, Count Francesco Sforza, commander of the Venetian Army, after securing a victory on Lake Garda, crossed the Oglio River, defeated the Milanese once more and captured Trevi, Caravaggio, Soncino, Orcinuovi, Chiari, along with much of the Brescia countryside. At this point, Duke Filippo Maria opened negotiations for peace and sent ambassadors to Sforza, offering his daughter Bianca Maria in marriage,

5 Lorenzo Taglieschi (Daniele Finzi & Matteo Parreschi eds), *Delle memorie istoriche e annali della terra di Anghiari* (Anghiari: Sansepolcro, 1991), p.176; Capponi, 'Commentari', 1196.

6 Taglieschi, *Delle memorie*, pp.176–177; Anon., 'Diario del Graziani' in *Arch. Stor. Ital.* XVI 1, 1850, p.460.

7 Taglieschi, *Delle memorie*, p.177; Capponi, 'Commentari', 1196–1197.

8 Machiavelli, *Istorie Fiorentine*, vol. 2, pp.93–94.

9 Taglieschi, *Delle memorie*, pp.178–179; Ammirato, *Istorie Fiorentine*, vol. V, p.269.

together with the cities of Cremona and Pontremoli as dowry. Negotiations were held in Ferrara for a few months, but no agreement was reached.[10]

With the onset of winter, hostilities ceased, and the armies withdrew to their respective winter quarters.

In the meantime, Niccolò Piccinino had reorganised his army and, at the beginning of 1441, in the depth of winter, crossed the Adda River and entered the territory of Brescia. There he defeated a force of 2,000 cavalry under Sforza, capturing 800 of them, and proceeded to occupy Chiari, followed by Pontoglio, Palazzolo, and Martinengo. At the same time, Ciarpellone, one of Sforza's most valiant captains, deserted without permission and entered Milanese service.[11]

Francesco Sforza, who was wintering in Venice, upon hearing of the defeat, set out immediately. However, by the time he reached Brescia, Piccinino had already withdrawn to his base. Sforza then requested additional money and men from the Republic of Venice, which in March 1441, engaged Micheletto Attendolo to replace Gattamelata, who had fallen ill.[12]

Also in March, Pope Eugene IV ceded Borgo Sansepolcro to the Florentines in exchange for 25,000 florins.[13]

With the arrival of spring, Piccinino was the first to resume operations, encamping at Soncino. Shortly thereafter, Sforza advanced with a large army and reconquered several territories in the Brescia area. Both armies then moved into the Bergamo area. Piccinino laid siege to the city, while Sforza established himself at Martinengo, from where he intended to support its defence. However, the castle of Martinengo was held by Jacomo Vincese, a valiant Milanese captain, who forced Sforza into a full-scale siege.

Piccinino then encamped at Romano, about a mile to the south, cutting off Sforza's supplies and surrounding him with pits and fortifications equipped with artillery. Within a short time, the Sforza army found itself in a desperate situation, suffering from shortages of food and water and unable to break the encirclement – indeed in greater peril than the besieged defenders of Martinengo.[14]

At this critical moment, however, fortune shifted. Duke Filippo Maria, perhaps weary of the war or offended by Piccinino – who, confident of victory, had presumptuously demanded the city of Piacenza as a reward – sent his *famiglio* Count Guidobono to negotiate peace with Francesco Sforza.

---

10 Capponi, 'Commentari', 1197; Biondo, *Historie*, pp.130–131; M. Sanudo, 'Vite dé duchi di Venezia,' in *Muratori R.I.S.*, XX, col. 1100.

11 Capponi, 'Commentari', 1197; Nicola della Tuccia, *Cronaca di Viterbo* (Firenze: G.P. Vieusseux, 1872), pp.178–179.

12 Capponi, 'Commentari', 1197;

13 Taglieschi, *Delle memorie*, p.181.

14 Capponi, 'Commentari', 1198; Giovan Battista Poggio, *Vita di Niccolò Piccinino* (Perugia: 1619), p.259.

The war ended with a one year truce, and on 24 October 1441, in Cremona, the marriage between Bianca Maria Visconti and Sforza was celebrated, thereby legitimising Sforza's claim to the future succession of the Duchy of Milan.

On 20 November of the same year, the Peace of Cavriana was signed. By its terms, the independence of Genoa was recognised; Florence secured control over Casentino; Venice obtained Ravenna and several territories belonging to the Marquess of Mantua, including Peschiera and Lonato; and Cremona was granted to Sforza as part of the marriage dowry.[15]

15 Capponi, 'Commentari', 1198; Poggio, *Vita di Piccinino*, pp.259–260.

Bibliography

Archive Sources

Archivio di Stato di Roma: *Commissariato delle soldatesche e galere*

Archivio di Stato di Firenze: *Acquisti e Doni*

Archivio di Stato di Firenze: *Dieci di Balìa, Deliberazioni condotte e stanziamenti*

Archivio di Stato di Firenze: *Mediceo avanti il principato*

Archivio di Stato di Siena: Biccherna 261, 1432, *Ruolo della compagnia di Francesco di Niccolò Piccinino*

Archivio di Stato di Venezia, Commemoriali, reg. XII: *Nuove disposizioni del banco degli stipendiari del 1434*

Archivio di Stato di Lucca: *Anziani al tempo della libertà*

Bibliothèque de l'Arsenal, Paris: Basinio da Parma, *'Hesperis'*

Fraternita dei Laici di Arezzo: F. Viviano, *Registri della compagnia di Micheletto Attendolo*

Published Sources, Sixteenth and Seventeenth Century

Baiardo, A., *Libro d'arme e d'amore nomato Philogine* (Venice: 1520)

Biondo, Flavio, *Historie* (Venice: 1547)

Gamurri, F., *Istoria genealogica delle famiglia nobili toscane e umbre* (Florence: 1668)

Poggio, G. Battista, *Vita di Niccolò Piccinino* (Perugia: 1619)

Scardeoni, Bernardini, *De claris civibus Patavinis* (Basilea: 1560)

Thomassini, Jacobus Philippus, *Elogia illustrium virorum iconibus exornata* (Patavii: 1630)

Totti, P., *Ritratti ed elogi di capitani illustri* (Rome: 1635)

Published Sources, Modern

Ammirato, Scipione, *Istorie Fiorentine* (Torino: Cugini Pomba e comp, 1853), vol. V

d'Anghiari, G., *Memorie dall'anno 1437 al 1481* (Bibl. Naz. Firenze)

Balestracci, Duccio, *Le armi, i cavalli, l'oro. Giovanni Acuto e i condottieri nell'Italia del Trecento*, (Roma: Ed. Laterza, 2003)

Boccia, L. G., *Le armature di S. Maria delle Grazie di Curtatone di Mantova e l'armatura lombarda del '400* (Milano: Bramante Editrice, 1982)

Calegari, Giovanni Andrea, *Cronaca di Brisighella e Val d'Amone dalla origine al 1504* (Bologna: Commissione per i testi di lingua, 1980)

Cambin, G., *Le rotelle Milanesi Giornico, 1478* (Farvagny, Vétroz, and Bern: Società Svizzera di Araldica, 1987)

Cappelletti, Giuseppe, *Storia della Repubblica di Venezia*, vol. 11 (Venezia: Antonelli, 1854)

Cardarelli, Romualdo, *Baldaccio d'Anghiari e la Signoria di Piombino nel 1440 e 1441* (Roma: Stabilimento Tipografico Leonardo da Vinci, 1922)

Castiglioni, Arturo, *Il salasso nell'arme gentilizia dei Manfredi, signori di Faenza* (Trieste: Stabilimento Artistico Tipografico G. Paoli, 1930)

Cavalcanti, Giovanni, *Istorie Fiorentine* (Fiorenze: all'insegna di Dante, 1839), vol. II

Cennini, Cennino (Franco Brunello ed.), *Il libro dell'arte* (Vicenza: Neri Pozza, 1982)

Coleschi, Lorenzo, *Storia della città di Sansepolcro* (Atessa: Spalding, 1982)

Colonna, Gustavo Brigante, *Gli Orsini* (Milano: Geschina, 1955)

Comparetti, Domenico, *L'Araldo almanacco nobiliare del napoletano* (Napoli: E. Detken, 1895)

Corio, Bernardino, *Storia di Milano*, vol. II (Torino: Utet, 1978)

Covini, Maria Nadia, *L'esercito del duca: organizzazione militare e istituzioni al tempo degli Sforza: 1450–1480* (Roma: Istituto Storico Italiano per il Medioevo, 1998)

Decembrio, Pier Candido, *Vita di Filippo Maria Visconti* (Milano: Adelphi Edizioni, 1983)

Dei, Benedetto, *La Cronica dal anno 1400 alle anno 1500* (Firenze: Papafava, 1984)

Giulini, Giorgio, *Memorie della città e campagna di Milano*, vol. VI (Milano: Francesco Columbo, 1857)

Goffredo, di Crollalanza, *Gli emblemi dei guelfi e ghibellini. Ricerche e studi* Emblemi (Rocca S. Casciano: Stab. tip. di F. Cappelli, 1878)

Gualtieri, Lorenzo Spirito, *L'Altro Marte* (Venezia: Leonardus Achates, 1489)

Hughes, Graham, *Renaissance Cassoni* (London: Art Books International, 1997)

Laking, Sir Guy Francis, *A Record of European Armour and Arms Through Seven Centuries* (London: G. Bell & Sons, 5 volumes 1920)

Litta, Pompeo, *Famiglie celebri italiane* (Milano: Luciano Basadonna, *c.*1869)

Luchinat, C. Acidini, 'L'immagine Medice' in *Lorenzo il Magnifico e gli spazi dell'arte* (Firenze: Giunti, 1991)

Machiavelli, Niccolò, *Istorie Fiorentine*, vol. 2 (Milan: Società Anonima Notari or Alpes, 1928)

Mallett, Michael, *Signori e mercenari* (Bologna: Il Mulino, 1983)

Mancini, Claudio, *Sipicciano* (Roma: Senza indicazione editoriale, 1994)

Mancini, Girolamo, G., Cortona nel Medio evo (Firenze: G. Carnesecchi e figli, 1897)

Maspoli, Carlo (ed.) *Stemmario Trivulziano* (Milano: Orsini De Marzo, 2001)

Messeri, Antonio, *Faenza nella storia e nella arte* (Faenza: Tipografia Sociale Faentina, 1909)

Osio, Luigi, *Documenti diplomatici tratti dagli archivj milanesi* (Milano: G. Bernardoni di Giovanni, 1872)

Passerini, Luigi, *Le armi dei municipi toscani* (Firenze: Tipografia di Eduardo Ducci, 1864)

Pellegrini, F. Carlo, *Un documento della battaglia di Anghiari* (Livorno: Tipografia di R. Giusti, 1901)

Pezzana, Angelo, *Storia di Parma* (Parma: Dalla Ducale Tipografia, 1842)

Pisetzky, P. Levi, *Storia del costume in Italia* (Milano: Istituto Editoriale Italiano, 1964), vol. II

Rendina, C., *I capitani di ventura* (Roma: Newton & Compton, 1999)

Righi, Bartolomeo, *Annali della città di Faenza*, vol. II (Faenza: Montanari E Marabini, 1840)

Roccasecca, P., *Paolo Uccello e le battaglie* (Milano: Electa, 1997)

Romanin, S. (ed.), *Storia documentata di Venezia*, vol. IV (Venezia: Pietro Noratovich, 1855)

Salvemini, G., *La dignità cavalleresca nel comune di Firenze* (Milano: Feltrinelli editore, 1972)

Savioli, Antonio & Moschini, Carlo (eds), *Faenza nell'età dei Manfredi* (Faenza: Faenza Editrice, 1990)

Scalini, M. (P. Ventrone ed.), *Le temps revient – l tempo si rinuova. Feste e spettacoli nella Firenze di Lorenzo il Magnifico* (Milano: Silvana Editoriale, 1992)

Schubring, Paul, *Cassoni: Truhen und Truhenbilder der italienischen Früh-Renaissance. Ein Beitrag zur profanmalerei im Quattrocento* (Leipzig: K.W. Hiersemann, 1923)

Taglieschi, Lorenzo, (Daniele Finzi & Matteo Parreschi eds), *Delle memorie istoriche e annali della terra di Anghiari* (Anghiari: Sansepolcro, 1991)

Tartaglia, Gaspare Broglio (A. G. Lucani, ed.), *Cronaca Malatestiana del secolo XV* (Rimini: Bruno Ghigi, 1982)

Tonduzzi, Giulio Cesare, *Historie di Faenza* (Bologna: Forni 1967, reprint of 1675 edition)

Treccani degli Alfieri, Giovanni, *Storia di Milano* (Milano: Fondazione Treccani degli Alfieri per la storia di Milano, 1958), XI

Troso, Mario, *Alla ricerca del dardo mistero e fascino di un'antica arma da lancio* (Mariano del Friuli: Edizioni della Laguna, 2014)

Tuccia, Nicola della, *Cronaca di Viterbo* (Firenze: G.P. Vieusseux, 1872)

Zama, Piero, *I Manfredi signori di Faenza* (Faenza: Fratelli Lega, 1954)

Articles and Chapters

Anon, 'Cronaca del Matarazzo' in *Archivio Storico Italiano* 1851, XVI

Anon., 'Corpus Chronicorum Bononiensium' in *Muratori R.I.S.* (Bologna 1922), XVIII, 2 parts

Anon., 'Diario del Graziani' in *Arch. Stor. Ital.* XVI 1, 1850

Anon, 'Militaria, storie, battaglie, armate' in *Araldica* (Mondadori: 2006), vol. 3

Ascani, Angelo, 'La rotta di Niccolò Piccinino' in Ascani, Angelo, *Anghiari dalle origini all'anno 1440* (Città di Castello: Città di Castello, 1973)

Billiis, A. De, 'Historia mediolanensis' in *Muratori R.I.S. 1723–1751*, XIX

Boccia, L. G., 'Le armature di Paolo Uccello' in *L'Arte*, III 1970

Capponi, N., 'Commentari' in *Muratori Rerum Italicarum Scriptores* XVIII

Covini, Maria Nadia, 'Per la storia delle milizie viscontee: I familari armigeri di Filippo Maria Visconti' in L. Chiappa Mauri & P. Mainoni (eds), *Il dominio di Milano fra XIII e XV secolo* (Milano: La Storia, 1993)

Dati, L. di Piero, 'Dal Tropheum anglaricum' in *Giornale Storico della Letteratura Italiana* (Torino: Ermanno Loescher, 1890), vol. XVI

Decembrio, Pier Candido, 'Vita di Niccolò Piccinino' in *Muratori Rerum Italicarum Scriptores* XX

Fabretti, A., 'La Fuga del Capitano' in *Note e documenti da biografie dei Capitani Venturieri dell'Umbria*, vol. Unico (Montepulciano: Angiolo Tumi, 1842)

Fabretti, A., 'Biografie dei Capitani Venturieri dell'Umbria' in *Note e documenti da biografie dei Capitani Venturieri dell'Umbria*, vol. II (Montepulciano: Angiolo Tumi, 1842)

Galli, E., 'Sulle origini araldiche della biscia viscontea' in *Archivio Storico Lombardo*, III 1919

Maetzke, Guglielmo, 'Armi e armature' in *Piero della Francesca* (Milano: Silvana Editoriale, 1998)

Mancini, C., 'I Baglioni della Teverina: una famiglia al servizio dello Stato Pontificio' in *Per una storia delle famiglie delle Tuscia tardomedievale*, XVI Giornata di studio per la storia della Tuscia, Viterbo-Orte, 18–19 dicembre 2009

Masetti-Bencini, I, 'La bataglia di Anghiari' in *Rivista delle biblioteche e degli archivi*, Luglio-Agosto 1907

Minuti, A. (G. Porro Lambertenghi ed.), 'Vita di Muzio Attendolo Sforza' in *Miscellanea di storia Italiana*, VII (Torino: 1869)

Mosto, Andrea da, 'Ordinamenti militari delle soldatesche dello Stato Romano dal 1430 al 1470' in *Quellen und Forschungen aus italienischen Archiven und Bibliotheken*, V 1902

Newbigin, N., 'I Giornali di Ser Giusto Giusti d'Anghiari (1437–1482)' in *Letteratura Italiana Antica*, anno III, 2002

Palmieri, M., 'Annales' in *Muratori Rerum Italicarum Scriptores* (Bologna: Nicola Zanichelli, 1922)

Passerini, L. 'Baldaccio d'Anghiari' in *Arch. Stor. Ital.* IIIs. 1866

Pertici, Petra, 'Condottieri senesi e la rotta di San Romano di Paolo Uccello' in *Arch. Stor. Ital.*, issue 581, 1999

Polcri, F., 'La battaglia di Anghiari dipinta sui pannelli di tre cassoni preleonardeschi' in *Pagine Altotiberine* 13

Predonzani, M., 'La Presa di Pisa' in *Archivum Heraldicum* I 2013

Righini, M., 'L'armatura da 'Homo d'arme' nell'Italia del '400' in *Ars Historiae*, July-September 2006

Rocculi, G., 'Reperti heraldici nella 'chiesa nobile' di Santa Maria del Carmine a Milano' in *Atti della Società Italiana di Studi Heraldici*, 32° Convivio, Torino 11 October 2014

Sanudo, M., 'Vite dé duchi di Venezia' in *Muratori R.I.S.*, XX

Scalini, M., 'Divise e livree, araldica quotidiana' in 'Leoni vermigli e candidi liocorni, Comune di Prato' in *Quaderni* 1, 1992

Simonetae, Johannis, 'Vita Francisci Sfortiae' in *Muratori R.I.S.* XXI

Solmi, E., 'Pagine autografe di Niccolò Machiavelli nel 'Codice Atlantico' di Leonardo da Vinci' in *Giornale storico della letteratura italiana*, vol. 54, 1909

Sora, V., 'I conti di Anguillara' in Arch. della Soc. Rom. di Sto. Patr. XXX 1907

Tomasi, L. Tongiorgi, 'Osservazioni su una tavola poco nota raffigurante 'La presa di Pisa'' in *Antichità pisane*, 1975/2

Treppo, M. Del, 'Gli aspetti organizzativi economici e sociali di una compagnia di ventura Italiana' in *Nuova rivista storica*, 69°, 1985

Treppo, M. Del, 'Sulla struttura della compagnia o condotta militare' in *Condottieri e uomini d'arme nell'Italia del rinascimento*, (Napoli: Liguori, 2001)

Ziggioto, Aldo, 'Le bandiere della cronaca del Sercambi' in *Armi antiche* (Torino: 1980)

On Line Resources

www.archiviodistato.firenze.it , *I blasoni delle famiglia Toscane nella Raccolta Ceramelli Papiani*

About the Author

Massimo Predonzani was born in Slovenia and currently lives in Trieste, Italy. He is an illustrator and researcher, specialising in military heraldry during the Italian and European Renaissance. He is the author of *Anghiari 29 giugno 1440* (2010), *Ceresole 14 aprile 1544* (2012) and *Caravaggio 1448* (2013). Since 2019 he has been collaborating with Helion, with whom he has published a series of six books on the Italian Wars of the Renaissance. He also has a website (www.stemmieimprese.it), where he shares his research and his painted illustrations.

A Time of Knights 400 CE to 1453 CE

The Battle of Adrianople (378 CE) marked the dominance of heavy cavalry over infantry, signalling the decline of the Western Roman Empire and the rise of feudalism. Nobles, in exchange for land, provided knights who became Europe's primary military force, clad in increasingly advanced armour. Beyond Europe, the Mongols relied on disciplined light cavalry, while the Islamic Caliphates combined light and heavy cavalry with trained infantry. China pioneered gunpowder weapons.

Castles and fortified cities shaped siege warfare, leading to increased use of artillery. By the late Medieval period, longbows, pikes, and firearms challenged knights' battlefield dominance, ushering in military innovations that paved the way for the Early Modern era of warfare.

Submissions

The publishers would be pleased to receive submissions for this series. Please email info@helion.co.uk, or write to Helion & Company Limited, Unit 8 Amherst Business Centre, Budbrooke Road, Warwick, CV34 5WE

You may also be interested in:

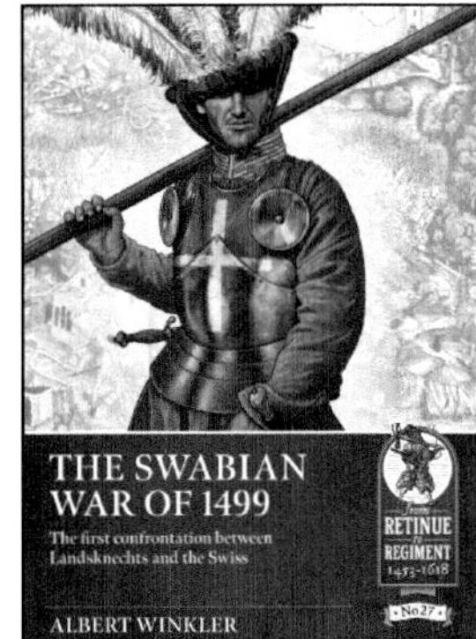